D1527958

Real Options

Evaluating Corporate Investment Opportunities in a Dynamic World

Sydney Howell • Andrew Stark
David Newton • Dean Paxson
Mustafa Cavus • Jose Pereira
and Kanak Patel

FINANCIAL TIMES
Prentice Hall

An imprint of Pearson Education

London · New York · San Francisco · Toronto · Sydney
Tokyo · Singapore · Hong Kong · Cape Town · Madrid
Paris · Milan · Munich · Amsterdam

PEARSON EDUCATION LIMITED

Head Office:
Edinburgh Gate
Harlow CM20 2JE
Tel: +44 (0)1279 623623
Fax: +44 (0)1279 431059

London Office:
128 Long Acre
London WC2E 9AN
Tel: +44 (0)20 7447 2000
Fax: +44 (0)20 7240 5771
Website: www.financialminds.com

First published in Great Britain in 2001

ISBN 0 273 65302 4

British Library Cataloguing in Publication Data
A CIP catalogue record for this book can be obtained from the British Library.

This publication is designed to provide accurate and authoritative information in regard to the subject matter covered. It is sold with the understanding that neither the authors nor the publisher is engaged in ren-
dering legal, investing, or any other professional service. If legal advice or other expert assistance is
required, the service of a competent professional person should be sought.

The publisher and contributors make no representation, express or implied, with regard to the accuracy of
the information contained in this book and cannot accept any responsibility or liability for any errors or
omissions that it may contain.

10 9 8 7 6 5 4 3 2 1

Typeset by Pantek Arts Ltd, Maidstone, Kent
Printed and bound in Great Britain by Biddles Ltd, Guildford and King's Lynn

The Publishers' policy is to use paper manufactured from sustainable forests.

About the authors

Sydney Howell is Senior Lecturer in the Accounting and Finance Group at Manchester Business School (of which he has served as head). A graduate of Cambridge and Manchester, he has industrial experience with Alcan, RHM, Philips and IBM Belgium. He has taught internationally for many companies including IBM, Tesco and C&A, and has served on the scientific committee of the Portuguese Finance Network and on the editorial board of Finance India.

Mustafa Cavus is a senior consultant with Capstone Energy Consulting which is based in Houston, and specializes, among other fields, in options and futures in electricity generation. Mustafa holds Master's degrees from German and British universities, as well as a PhD from Manchester Business School, which he wrote in his third working language, English. Mustafa remains in close contact and collaboration with MBS, which offered him a post-doctoral fellowship on his graduation.

David Newton is Lecturer in Accounting and Finance at Manchester Business School. He began his career as a research chemist, and taught at Cambridge and Warwick Univerities, but later converted to financial teaching and research. He wrote a seminal and widely quoted early paper on the application of options theory to R&D. His research interests include improving the numerical methods for real option valuation, and for this purpose he maintains a close research collaboration with the mathematics department of Manchester University.

Kanak Patel is Lecturer in Property Finance at the Department of Land Economy, University of Cambridge. She received a BSc(Hons) Economics from Queen Mary College, University of London, and a PhD in Economics from the University of Essex. Initially a risk analyst at Lloyd's of London, she taught finance, before Cambridge, at Manchester Business School and at the Management School, Imperial College, University of London. Some of her recent publications on real property options are *Implied Volatility in the UK Commercial Property Market: Empirical evidence based on transaction data* (with T.F. Sing), *Journal of Real Estate Finance and Economics* (January 2000) and *Empirical Analysis of Irreversibility in Property Investment in the UK* (with T.F. Sing) *Quarterly Review of Finance and Economics* (2001).

Dean Paxson is Professor of Finance at Manchester Business School, where he has taught real options to MBAs for several years. He was educated at Amherst College, Oxford and Harvard Business School. Some of his recent (edited) books on 'Real Options' and 'Exotic Options' are *The Blackwell Encyclopedic Dictionary of Finance* (1997), Blackwell Publishers, Oxford, and *Real R&D Options* (2001), Butterworth-Heinemann, Oxford. Some of his recent articles on real options are 'Arbitrage-free Valuation of Exhaustible Resource Firms' (with Milan Lehocky), *Journal of Business Finance and Accounting*, November 1998, 'Real Exotic Options in Eça de Queirós' The Illustrious House of Ramires', *Portuguese Journal of Management Studies*, December 1999, and 'Real Processing American Exchange Options' (with Jongwoo Lee), MBS Working Paper, 2001.

José Antonio de Azevedo-Pereira is a graduate of ISEG (Technical University of Lisbon) and Manchester Business School. He is presently Professor Auxiliar at ISEG, and has previously held a number of Board and Executive positions in Portuguese companies, and continues in several advisory positions to National and Local government in Portugal. He is an active teacher, researcher and consultant in the field of real options, with an interest in applications to real estate decisions.

Andrew Stark is Professor of Accounting at Manchester Business School, and is presently Director of the Manchester MBA programme. A graduate of Cambridge and Manchester, he has taught at among others, Maryland, Yale and Manchester universities. He is a well-known contributor to international conferences on Real Options, and his current research interests include the agency aspects of real options: e.g. how can subordinates be motivated to take option decisions in the superiors' best interests, and what options do superiors and subordinates enjoy against each other?

Contents

Editor's introduction

This book is an enlarged sequel to *Real Options: An introduction for executives*, and it shares much of the introductory material. However, the present book is aimed at practitioners, consultants and MBA (or other) finance students, as well as at general managers. That is to say, it aims to help both numerate and non-numerate readers. The book aims to take a non-numerate reader through from ignorance of any kind of option to a clear understanding of how and why real options methods work, what real options can contribute to business, and what questions to ask of a real options analyst. Such readers should be able to make sense of most of the main text, except for the more formal parts of Chapter 4.

If a numerate reader starts with little or no knowledge of finance or of options, they should be able to gain a strong intuition for the mathematics and the economics by reading the main text. In addition, by studying all the Appendices and the formal parts of Chapter 4, such readers should pick up all the formal knowledge required to build and solve real option models using both continuous time and binomial models, and to appreciate fully what is going on in the case examples of Chapters 5 to 10, and in the more advanced texts and journals. We hope that numerate readers – even if they have no experience of finance – after working carefully through the book should be able to tackle with confidence the fundamental mathematical texts by Dixit and Pindyck and Wilmott, Howison and Dewynne. We have included many references to these excellent texts, and have largely followed the notation of the latter.

This book gives several new intuitive and visual guides to what real options mathematics is doing. In Chapter 2 we introduce a plot of the valuation surface, in both asset price and time $V(S,t)$. This not only gives an intuitively powerful demonstration of diffusion but also correctly reflects how the Black–Scholes equation actually operates mathematically, to define a surface within well-posed boundaries. It also displays the entire set of boundary conditions simultaneously, and it shows how, at a fixed price S, option value declines approximately with the square root of the remaining time to expiry, as does volatility.

In Chapter 10 Jose Pereira and David Newton generalize this type of plot to show the value surface at a given time t for a two-factor model, which we could call $V_t(S_1,S_2)$. An awareness of the time dimension, which is usually omitted from plots of option value, has also helped us in Chapter 2 to give what we hope is a better explanation than usual of the sometimes troublesome concepts of value matching and smooth pasting.

In Chapter 3 we generalize the plot of the valuation surface $V(S,t)$ from a simple call, which has one mode of exercise, in order to value a one-factor (American call) option, which has multiple modes of exercise. To clarify the early exercise decision, we introduce a direct plot of the surface of the time value of the option (this surface is option value minus intrinsic value; the surface $V(S,t) - P(S,T)$ which generalizes to $V(S,t) - P(S,t)$ in the case of a payoff function which is evolving deterministically over time). This plot, which we call a 'shark's fin', shows how the time value is at a maximum if the asset price S ever puts the option 'at the money' for a choice between alternative actions. It also shows how time value tends to fall with the square root of the remaining time to expiry, when the latter is small, reflecting the fact that volatility is doing the same.

Another concept which can be hard to understand intuitively is delta hedging. In Appendix 3 we have given not only a clear explanation of the algebraic motivation of delta hedging but also a visual illustration of how delta, which is the slope of the option's value function V with respect to S, defines the size of the forward or short sale required to hedge a portfolio's value against small movements of S. By varying S around E we can see how delta varies, and this illustrates why delta hedging an option is only a special case of delta hedging any instrument whose value is a function of S. We see how the other special cases can include both S itself and the risk-free asset.

As a completely independent illustration of the way the Black–Scholes mathematics operates, David Newton has given in Appendix 4 the most complete example yet of how heat diffusion relates to option valuation, a topic which almost every book mentions, but few or none explain satisfyingly. In Appendix 5 David has provided intuition on simple, multiple, correlated and mean reverting random walks. Finally, the editor has waged his personal campaign in Chapter 4 for a more economically complete and intuitively useful interpretation of the confusingly named 'risk neutral probabilities'.

The main part of the book contains various extended applied examples by our contributing authors, all of whom have taught and/or completed their PhD degrees at Manchester Business School. We are delighted to welcome Kanak Patel and Jose Pereira as authors. Their examples range in level of difficulty from MBA teaching material to recent PhD results. The actual cases include various problems from real estate (put, call to invest, call to operate, valuation of lease); there is a case from sport management (stadium rental); also from power generation (call options to produce, in both a discrete and a near-continuous process, including the effects of inertia and exchange options) and from finance (two-factor model for valuing a mortgage). These cases are solved by various methods, including analytic Black–Scholes call option and Margrabe exchange option solutions, explicit finite difference and binomial methods. We also briefly describe some of the important work reported by Dixit and Pindyck on decisions for continuous processes. This work bears on decisions to activate and deactivate resources, for example in shipping and mining, and in the hiring, firing and laying-off of staff.

Collections of work by several authors must inevitably be varied in their styles of presentation, and sometimes a paper may be rather terse for an inexperienced practitioner to follow or to replicate. In order to minimize this difficulty we have tried to present in Chapter 4 a unified framework, which should allow the reader to appreciate what is constant and what is changing over a wide variety of potential and actual applications of real options analysis.

The essentials of this framework are:

- the problem as intuitively presented to management;

- the decision to be taken;

- any option-like features of the problem;

- any modifications needed to the Black–Scholes equation;

- the boundary conditions needed;

- the solution method;

- the data sources and the key implications of the solution;

- indications of how the model might be generalized further.

To help the reader to apply this framework to the various extended case examples, the editor has tried at the start of each case to summarize how the above essential features have been handled, listing them in a fairly standardized format. Some over-simplifications have inevitably arisen in these introductions (for which the editor apologizes to the contributors) but hopefully readers will find they have been helped to understand the present book. More importantly, readers should then have much greater confidence in exploring the published literature, and in questioning the structure and the outputs of any given real options analysis.

Our style of presentation departs from convention in several ways. We have tried to make the whole text intuitively understandable, including the Appendices, and have made the latter more equal partners with the main text than is usual. In option payoff diagrams we always omit the option premium. This is because in a perfect market, the premium is an output of the calculation of an option's value, not an input to it – the premium simply eliminates the option's value in order to ensure that the act of purchasing an option has an instantaneous net present value (NPV) of zero (no arbitrage profits from buying or selling options).

Conversely, in an imperfect market (which is the case for many real options) the calculation of an option's value is often a completely separate task from estimating what it might cost to create or to acquire that option. Unlike financial markets, real option markets often offer significant opportunities for arbitrage gains and losses. However, in future we can expect to see increasing trading of real options, both between companies and on markets, which should reduce the opportunities for arbitrage but increase those for hedging.

We also devote unusually little space to the classical analytical solutions of the Black–Scholes equation, or to analytic solutions in general, though the classic Black–Scholes formula for the European call appears in Chapter 5 and in Appendix 1 to Chapter 6. Epoch-making though this solution was, it solves only one exceedingly special case of the general problem of valuing a derivative (including a real option). It is vital that users of real options should understand that the valuation problem in its most general form consists of a Black–Scholes PDE, plus suitable boundary conditions, plus some solution method. In the most demanding real options problems, that solution method has to be a discrete numerical method (as in engineering and physics).

There is one theoretical advantage to an emphasis on numerical methods, namely that in some cases the analytic solution does not model the true behaviour of the option across all the possible states of S and t, but only within boundaries. For example, in the case of a perpetual American call on a dividend-paying asset, if the stock price is ever observed to be above the optimal exercise price S*, the option's value V(S,t) is less than its intrinsic value P(S,T) (and the option should, and could, have been exercised earlier, if trading and value reporting had been truly continuous). However, the analytic solution is of course tangent to P(S,T) at S* (by the smooth pasting condition). In fact, above S* the analytic solution still exists, though it should not be used because it rises above P(S,T). Hence although the analytic solution still exists above S* (the free boundary up to which the solution is defined), it no longer models the value of the option, nor guides decisions. In contrast, a suitably designed numerical method can reflect the fact that the option's time value is declining progressively below zero as S rises above S*. In this example, a numerical solution can be made a more fundamentally and universally 'true' model of an option's behaviour than an analytical solution which is meaningful only within a given domain.

We have striven to avoid a 'worst case' outcome, in which the reader is unable to formulate or to solve a problem in more general ways and is therefore tempted to simplify any actual problem into some unsuitable format, merely because that format happens to have an analytic solution. Of course, even experts can and must use analytical approximate solutions from time to time, in order to gain improved insight, and in order to cross-check a numerical method. For example, a European option valuation sets a lower bound to an American option's value, and a valid numerical solution to the American option should converge to the analytical solution for the European option if the rate of dividend is set to zero; likewise a perpetual option's value sets an upper bound to the value of an option which has a finite time to expiry, and in this case also a necessary but not a sufficient condition for a numerical solution to be valid is that it should converge to the analytical (here perpetual) solution if time to expiry is set large.

The editor is grateful to the authors for all their contributions and for detecting many errors, but the errors that remain are his own, particularly those that arise in the introductions to the work of the rest of the team. I hope to be forgiven for any distortions of their ideas that have been unwittingly introduced.

Sydney Howell
Real Options Group
Manchester Business School

Acknowledgments

I t is impossible for the authors to express all the debts that they owe to their colleagues and students over the years. The authors are united in their respect for the seminal work of Black and Scholes who created this new and fast-growing field, and of the many researchers who are still helping to develop it.

Introduction to real options analysis

1

Real options analysis is one of the most important developments in business decision analysis in the last hundred years. For the first time we have an integrated framework which can address decisions under an extreme form of uncertainty, namely the random walk, which is (approximately) the behaviour seen in financial markets, and which economics tells us we should also see in highly competitive commercial markets. Real options analysis allows us to integrate our decisions on investment, operations and disinvestment, including complete changes of market.

What sorts of business decision can be changed by real options analysis?

- The sequence of stages by which to expand or shrink operating capacity.

- Whether to variabilize costs by buying in instead of making.

- For human resource planning, how to balance new full-time staff against overtime for existing staff and against the use of temporary staff.

- At what price to accept a long-term fixed-price contract for an input or output whose market price is variable (e.g. gas, oil or services).

- How to compare leases or other deals which constrain us in different ways.

- When to cease operating an asset, and when to reactivate it.

- When and how to exit from owning or operating an asset.

- The maximum investment to make in a research project.

- The correct price at which to buy or sell technology or licences.

- The correct price to pay or ask for a brand.

- (For government) how to design policies and incentives that do not cause economically perverse behaviours by businesses.

These are just a few of the applications of real options analysis.

How does real options analysis differ from traditional analysis methods?

In traditional discount cash flow (DCF see Appendix 2) or decision trees, we forecast the future, we treat the forecast as if it were true, and use a high 'risk adjusted' rate of discount (see Appendices 1 and 2). Real options analysis reverses all these: the future is unforecastable, we know only today's market state (plus the rate at which today's state is losing value as a guide to the future) and we use the risk-free rate of discount.

Just what is a real option?

A real option exists if we have the right to take a decision at one or more points in the future (e.g. to invest or not to invest, or to sell out or not to sell out). Between now and the time of decision, market conditions will change unpredictably, making one or other of the available decisions better for us, and we will have the right to take whatever decision will suit us best at the time.

Real options analysis helps to decide: (a) how much money we should spend to acquire an economic opportunity like this; and (b) when (if ever) we should commit ourselves to one of the available decisions.

Some examples of real options

We are designing an electricity generator and want to know whether to invest in flexibility by paying a higher capital cost for a plant capable of burning either oil or gas. The prices of both fuels vary randomly, but in broadly correlated ways. We also have the possibility of 'locking ourselves into' long-term contracts for the supply of either fuel, rather than buying at spot rates.
Examples of decisions for this option: what is the maximum price worth paying for flexibility? How cheap must a single fuel contract be to make flexibility unattractive? See Chapters 4 and 6.

Our scientists think they can develop a textile technology which will make the fabrics in skirts 'swing' with the majesty of a slow-motion advertising film. If we owned such a technology we would of course invest in plants to produce the fabric, provided the fashion for it is strong enough. But market research says that the fashion today is for light, quick-response 'disco' fabrics, so the new fabric would not sell unless there was a return to 'jive' dances and fashions.

An example of a decision about this real option would be: what is it worth spending to create the technology? See Chapter 3.

We own bulk-carrying ships, which we charter for the transport of ore and refined products. A simultaneous economic boom in Japan and the US has created huge demand for such ships, leading to a sharp increase in short-term charter rates.

Examples of decisions about this real option: how high do charter rates have to rise before we bring our older 'mothballed' ships back into use? Should we accept a long-term charter contract at a lower rate than today's spot rate? Even at today's spot rate, it would not be economic to reactivate the smallest of our mothballed ships – how low would the spot charter rate have to go before it would be correct to scrap these smaller, older ships? See Chapter 11.

A best-selling novelist of 30 years ago seems ripe for revival. We could buy the rights to film the stories for TV (for various territories). We could also buy rights to use the author's and characters' names in product spin-offs, and a successful TV film would make commercial spin-offs more likely.

An example of a decision about this real option would be: what should we be willing to offer for each right? See Chapter 3.

We own a scrap metal recycling plant which is unprofitable at today's prices, due to economic recession. However, we are still operating, because if we cease operation the plant itself will deteriorate rapidly, the workforce will be dispersed, and we may have to pay significant costs for a restart. If we close down we could leave a skeleton security staff, or abandon the site entirely.

Examples of decisions about this real option: how low does the scrap price have to fall before we decide to stop producing? How low does the price have to fall before we stop protecting the machinery and abandon it entirely? What is this loss-making operation worth? See Chapter 11.

Some fundamental option terms

See also the Glossary at the end of the book, and the more extended explanations in Chapter 2.

Call option – the right to acquire an asset at some future time for a cost which is known now, however much the asset's market value may change meanwhile. For example, the right to spend $50 million on a factory for a new textile (call option to invest), or the ability to convert a ton of silicon to electronic wafers at a processing cost of $100 million (call option to produce, or spread option).

Put option – the right to sell an asset in future, at a price known now, whatever its market selling price may be at that time. For example, the right to sell off a high-tech factory site at a fixed price as general purpose buildings, even if its product fails.

Exercise price – the known price at which a call (or a put) option allows us to buy (or respectively to sell) a given asset. For example, an exact quoted price at which we could install new production equipment (call) or sell off old machinery for scrap (put).

Also known as *strike price*.

Volatility – the speed at which the market value of the *underlying asset* (the asset which we hold a *real call option* to buy, or a *put option* to sell) tends to diverge randomly away from (and around) today's value as time passes into the future. Higher volatility means a larger expected speed of divergence, giving larger possible variations both upside and downside. This increases option value. For example, if we have a *call option* (to buy at a fixed exercise price), a larger upside increases the size of our largest possible payoff, but the larger downside does not reduce the size of our smallest possible payoff of zero, which we get if our call option expires unexercised.

> **Higher volatility means a larger expected speed of divergence.**

Derivative assets – assets such as (but not restricted to) options, whose value is decided by or 'derived from' the value of some other asset, called the *underlying asset*. The value of a *call option* on a stock is derived from the value of the stock which the call gives the right to buy, and this stock is the underlying asset. The value of a factory is 'derived from' the value of the stream of net revenues which it can generate, and the underlying asset is that revenue stream. Revenue stream changes may be driven by random changes in tastes, competition, etc.

European option – option which gives the right to invest (or to sell out) on only one fixed future date.

American option – option which gives us the right to invest (or to sell) at any time we choose, usually up to some fixed final date.

Perpetual option – option which will never expire (this is most often relevant for decisions on land use, or for exchanges between currencies).

Expiry date – the date when an option to invest (call option) or to sell (put option) expires, e.g. for a real option it may be when a patent or licence expires, or when an endorsing athlete retires, or when competitors are expected to catch up with our technology.

Underlying asset – the asset which a real option gives us the right to buy (call option) or to sell (put option), e.g. a production operation or a revenue stream.

Random factor – a variable whose random walk of value over time will drive the value of some derivative (such as a real option). Sometimes the random factor is the value of the underlying asset, on which the option exists, e.g. for a financial call option, the random factor is the stock or share price. For a real option to build a factory, the random factor may be the value of the resulting expected revenue stream (which evolves randomly with market change). Or an asset's value may be driven indirectly by deeper random factors, such as interest rates, exchange rates, etc.

Random walk – real options analysis assumes that each value-driving factor is subject to an unforecastable random walk. This means that from today's (known) value, an upward move is as likely as a downward move over any future time period (though longer time periods have bigger expected moves). For technical reasons this is actually valid for the logarithm of an asset's price. The optimal (least inefficient) forecast is for the average change, namely zero, i.e. the best forecast is the latest observed value. Random walks can have non-zero trends, but surprisingly, we can ignore a known or unknown trend when valuing the option (see Appendix 3). Random walk analysis is valid under the fiercest type of economic competition – perfect competition.

Exchange option – where at least two values vary randomly, and we have the right to choose whichever value will be the 'best' in the future, e.g. a loan to be repaid in either stocks or bonds, or an option to use either LPG or petroleum as fuel.

More complex types of real options

A simple call option has only one random factor.

A simple call option has only one random factor (the market value of a stock, or the present value of a potential business investment), and we have only two choices – to buy the asset or not, depending on whether it is profitable to do so. We can complicate this by having more than one possible action, and/or by having more than one random factor driving asset values, and/or by having more than one successive option.

We can speak of a multiple or 'multiple choice' option if there are more than two possible actions. For example, instead of a simple decision to invest in one fixed design of factory, we could face a choice between two or more designs of factory. Multiple possible actions can exist even when only one random factor affects values (e.g. there is only one level of demand underlying the market) – see Chapter 3.

We can also have more than one random factor. For example, in retailing, both the quantity and the price at which we can sell may be varying randomly. In an import-export business, both the rate of exchange and the level of local demand may vary independently. In a property business, the rental income can vary with the demand for building space, and interest costs can vary with the interest rate. Both factors vary independently, affecting many decisions – see Chapter 10.

An exchange option involves more than one random factor, e.g. if we are considering whether to scrap a soap factory, we are comparing the value of the revenue stream based on producing soap against a capital value based on (say) the scrap value of the steel in the factory. If both the demand for soap and the demand for scrap are highly volatile, there is no fixed price at which we can 'put' (sell off) the factory in the future, and the decision to move between the operating and the scrapped states is an exchange option rather than a put. Clearly, there could be additional random factors. For example, the real estate values of the site and the buildings, in various uses, can all show random walk evolution – see Chapters 4, 6 and 9.

In a compound option, we have a 'chain' of options in which the payoff of the first option is the value of acquiring the next option in the chain. For example, we may have a real option to pay the cost of an R&D programme. The payoff from exercising this option (i.e. starting the research) is the present value of whatever option we may enjoy to invest profitably at the end of the research: if the research is successful, we will have the real option to invest in a process to exploit the research, but we will invest only if and when this seems profitable – see Chapter 3.

How do real options compare with financial options?

Modern financial option analysis was initiated in 1973 by Black and Scholes. In their model a financial option on (say) the stock of a firm is a 'derivative' asset. This means the option's value is driven by or 'derived from' the firm's value, and decisions about options do not change the firm's value.

But many business decisions have a logical structure similar to a financial option. For example, we can build a factory for a new brand, for a known and stable cost, whereas the demand for the brand itself is varying in a random way. A firm that owns the brand has a call option on whether and when to build a new factory. Unlike financial options, decisions on real options like this can change a company's value.

The study of 'real' options uses many of the tools of financial options. For example, if physical demand varies from 0 per cent to 200 per cent of a factory's capacity, the factory's profit ceiling at 100 per cent capacity resembles the flat-topped payoff function of a 'bull spread' option in finance. Likewise if a football club or a law firm trains performers who are 'too successful', the loss of earnings when they depart resembles an 'up and out' option in finance – see Chapter 5.

The **key difference between a financial option and a real option** is that a decision about a financial option cannot change the value of the firm itself, while a wrong decision about a real option will change the firm's resources and its value. For example, if a firm invests at the 'wrong' time, it throws away part of the value of its real option to invest. This loss of value will be reflected in its share price – see Chapter 8.

In essence, a financial option need not change the activities of the firm at all. It is a bet between two outsiders. If I sell you a financial call option to buy one unit of IBM stock for $140 next month, I am betting that the IBM stock will be worth no more than $140 then, and in effect I offer to pay you the difference if the stock beats $140. IBM itself makes no response to this bet and need not know about it.

In contrast, IBM pays for research to develop potential hardware or software products. Suppose IBM develops a new e-commerce software which it could bring to market for a launch cost of $200 million. The software will not be obsolete for three years. In effect IBM holds a real option 'bet' against the business universe, that within three years the present value of the software revenues will be at least the $200 million which it would cost to enter this market.

How can real option analysis affect business decisions?

Many business decisions are about acquiring or selling real options, and about when to exercise them. For both decisions the firm must allocate 'real' resources (time, money, computing facilities, etc.).

The two key decisions are:

1   how much to pay for a given real option (i.e. 'bet' against the business universe);

2   when if ever to collect on the bet, by exercising the option.

In the last example, IBM paid for research to develop a new e-commerce product. By spending money and time IBM was acquiring a bet (that the market in question would be worth at least $200 million before the bet expired). On or before the expiry of the bet, IBM has to take a decision on whether the current winnings (if any) are worth collecting. The company will have to spend real economic resources (time, money, advertising skills, etc.) if it wants to collect on this bet through spending the $200 million launch cost.

Many other business decisions have one or both of these aspects. For example, decisions to buy or sell rights or brands, as against developing technology in-house, must all involve real resources. Given that its assumptions are met, real options analysis shows which factors to take into account.

Some examples of how real options analysis can lead to unexpected decisions

Real options analysis can contradict traditional economic teaching. For example, traditional economics says we should stop producing if revenue per unit ever falls below variable cost per unit. However, real options analysis shows that it can be optimal to produce in these conditions, for instance if there is a cost to stopping production and a cost to restarting it (see Chapter 11). Likewise it may not be optimal to begin production at the moment that revenue per unit first rises above variable cost.

Similar logic applies to investment and disinvestment; it can be optimal not to invest in fresh capacity even at times when the business is overloaded and highly profitable. Likewise it can be optimal not to scrap a unit of capacity which is presently loss-making (see Chapter 11).

At the strategic level, as we will see in Chapter 3, real options analysis can give highly unexpected results. It may be optimal to start research in a market which is presently unprofitable and is therefore forecast (on a random walk basis) to remain unprofitable, provided that the random element of future market variation (volatility) is sufficiently large. Likewise it can be optimal not to start research in a market which it would be profitable to invest in today (assuming we already had the technology) and which is forecast (on a random walk basis) to remain so.

What drives the valuation of a real option?

The two key decisions about a real option are: (1) how much should we pay for a real option (or equivalently, how much to charge when selling it); and (2) when to exercise the option. The rule for exercising the option controls whatever decision the option gives us, e.g. a decision to invest (call option to invest) or disinvest (put option to scrap), or the decision to operate as opposed to not operating (call option to produce), or the decision to switch resources into new markets (exchange option).

1 For a pricing example, real call options (rights to invest) are the most common type of real option. A call always has some value, however low the market is today, since we lose nothing by keeping the call unexercised, and on a random walk basis there is always some chance (though maybe only a tiny chance if the market today is very poor) that the 'bet' will eventually pay off.

> **A call always has some value, however low the market is today**

In fact, the random walk permits a minute chance of a jump of any possible size. Factors which make a call option more valuable include a longer time to expiry, and a faster rate of unforecastable random change in the underlying asset on which the option exists (higher volatility) – see Chapter 2. It is therefore vital not to overestimate an option's life or its volatility, in order to avoid over-valuing the option – see Chapter 12.

   Other factors which affect a call's value are the cost of the required investment (exercise price) and the rate of interest on risk-free investments (which has different effects on different types of options but can be insensitive in practice). Finally (and obviously) the option's value depends on the state of the market for the underlying asset. An option to invest in mobile telephony is probably worth more today than an option to invest in steam locomotion.

2 The decision rule for exercising an option (e.g. a call option) is simply: exercise as soon as the present value of exercising now (e.g. of investing in a new factory now) equals or exceeds the present value of the unexercised option (which is a chance to invest 'now or later').

How to use this book

If you aren't a mathematician (or a numerate graduate) you have little chance of calculating option values for yourself, except for the binomial method, which is mentioned in Chapter 4, explained more fully in Appendix 4, and exemplified in Chapter 7.

However, Chapters 2 and 3 and Appendices 1, 2, 4 and 5 should give you a feel for what the mathematics is trying to do, and Chapter 12 will give you some awkward questions you can put to your experts or consultants. After reading all this you should also be able to appreciate most of what is coming out of the worked examples in Chapters 5 to 10.

If you are a numerate graduate, especially if you have encountered differential equations before, with analytic and numerical solution methods, this book should enable you to understand the basic mathematics of continuous time finance, and devise your own binomial or finite difference solution methods. You should be able to read the research literature with confidence, and to use the more fundamental mathematical texts such as Dixit and Pindyck and Wilmot, Howison and Dewynne, which we heartily recommend to anyone who wants a complete mastery of the subject.

For numerate readers, first try the intuitive Chapters 2 and 3, then read Appendices 3 and 4, before returning to the main argument of Chapters 4 to 10. You can use Appendices 1 and 2 if you need any refresher on financial basics, and Appendices 4 and 5 cover basic numerical methods and some basic aspects of the random walk.

Summary of the key ideas in this chapter

Real options analysis is altering economics, strategy, psychology and other disciplines – sometimes it overturns common sense, but sometimes the new ideas are closer to intuition than traditional DCF or economics seemed to be.

The two new ideas which real options analysis brings in are that: (1) at least one of the value-determining variables is evolving unforecastably, following a random walk; and (2) we have flexibility (options) in how we respond as that uncertainty unfolds.

The new techniques of real options analysis mean that traditional NPV and decision tree analysis (including dynamic programming) are valid only in special circumstances.

Real option analysis is an extension of the ways in which financial markets value an option on a stock or share. Unlike a financial option on a company's stock, a real option is important to the company's managers because it allows the business to change its economic value.

Real option analysis can assist many types of decisions, for example on investment, and on developing, buying or selling new competences, brands or technologies, and on investments which create flexibility, and on operating decisions and policies.

The main mathematical tool is a type of differential equation. Similar equations apply to physical diffusion processes such as the random diffusion of heat. (In financial models, the 'randomly diffusing' variable is a market variable, such as a share price, or a level of demand.)

It is vital to understand the pitfalls of real options analysis. We can make mistakes in identifying the real options that we have, or in modelling how these options interact, or in setting up and solving the mathematical models, or in estimating the variables that we need as the input. It is especially dangerous to overestimate the option's volatility and its remaining time to expiry.

Essential option concepts **2**

This chapter is a 'non-technical' introduction to both financial options and real options. The central ideas for options are as follows:

- An option gives you the right, in an uncertain future, to pick whatever action will turn out to be 'the best of' two or more actions, as the uncertain future unfolds.

- Real options analysis tries to solve two problems:

    - at what cost should we sell or acquire an option? (For example, how much is it worth spending on research now in order to have the option to invest in a new technology in the future?)

    - When should we actually exercise an option? (For example, how profitable does a market have to be before we go ahead and invest in it?)

There are many new ideas to learn, so we will work in three main stages:

- the basic language of financial options and real options;

- the value of a financial or real option, and the main variables that drive it;

- when to exercise an (American) option.

The basic language of financial options and real options

A **financial option** is an option to buy or sell a financial asset which already exists and is actively *traded* in a financial market in a *standard form* (stocks, shares, bonds, etc.). Buying and selling a financial option on the stocks or shares of a business is a private 'bet' on its market price, between two investors, and this has no effect on the business itself (which need not even know that a financial option on its stock has been created).

In contrast, a **real option** is an option to change the 'real' physical or intellectual activity of a business (e.g. to create or to bring to market a new technology, a new brand, a new factory or an extra unit of output). This means the business has to bring together new, non-standard and non-traded combinations of 'real' resources, such as time and effort by people, wear and tear on machinery, use of consumable supplies, etc.

A real option is effectively a 'deal' between the business itself and the entire outside world, and unlike a financial option it can change the economic value of the business. Therefore the business should actively manage the real option.

The same basic language is used both for financial options and real options, so when we are explaining both types together, we will use italic type to emphasize when an example is a real option (e.g. an *option to invest in a brand,* or an *option to sell an unwanted retail site*). We will use bold type for key terms, e.g. **exercise price** (also see the Glossary).

The basic language for describing an option (financial options and real options)

The most fundamental financial option is the **call option**, which is the right to buy a share at a fixed price. Suppose someone offers you the right (but not the obligation) to **buy** one unit of IBM stock for **$100**, if you wish, on the **last day of next month**. (Incidentally, most work on options uses the standard US term 'stock' instead of 'share', and we follow suit.)

The basic features of this example **call option** are:

- There is a fixed price, here **$100**, at which you can exercise the option, and this price is called the **exercise price**. By spending this sum you are guaranteed – if you choose to exercise the option – to be able to buy a financial asset of one unit of IBM stock. The IBM stock on which your option exists is called the **underlying asset**.

- *In a **real call option**, the **exercise price** is the amount you will have to pay to 'take up your option' to spend money to acquire some real **underlying asset**. As in the case of the financial option, you will make this investment (pay the exercise price) only if market conditions at the time make it profitable to do so.*

Please now read the highlighted examples on the next two pages. You will see that we had a **financial call option** and a **real call option**. The **prices to acquire** these two options were $3 (financial) and $3,000 (real). The **exercise**

The story of one financial option (European call)

A month ago, Jill offered you the right to buy a unit of IBM stock today for $100.

The IBM share was low at the time ($90) and was expected to stay low, so Jill didn't charge you much for the option – only $3.

One week ago you were looking lucky – the IBM stock price had risen to $110.

Today, a shade less luckily, the IBM stock price had fallen back to $105.

Today, just before your option to do so expired, you bought a unit of IBM stock from Jill at the contracted price of $100, and sold it immediately in the market for $105. So you made an immediate **payoff** or profit of $5 today by exercising the option just before it expired.

Allowing for the initial cost of $3 to buy the option (and ignoring for now the interest you might have made by investing your $3 for a month instead of buying the option, your overall profit on the option was $2.

If the stock price had ended higher still, you might have made more profit than $2, and if it had ended lower than $100, you might have made a loss, but you couldn't have lost more money than the $3 you initially paid to Jill, because if the IBM stock price today had been below Jill's price of $100 you simply wouldn't have bought IBM stock from Jill at $100 today.

prices to act on these options were $100 (financial) and $100,000 (real). The **current price** of the **underlying asset** (which is the asset in which you acquired an option to invest – respectively IBM stock and a load of real cap badges) at the start of the deal was $90 (financial) and $90,000 (real), so both options at that time were '**out of the money**'. This means that the market value of the asset concerned was well below the exercise price, at which you had a right to buy the asset, so one month ago you could not have made a profit by exercising your option to buy the asset at the exercise price.

One week ago the market chanced to have improved, and both options were then '**in the money**', meaning that if each had been exercisable, it could have been exercised at a positive payoff, namely $10 (financial) and $10,000 (real). At the moment of exercise, just before both options expired today, both options were still '**in the money**', but by less than last week ($5 for the financial and $5,000 for the real). So both options were exercised, to give an immediate **payoff** ($5 financial and $5,000 real). Net profit, after deducting the initial cost

The story of one real option (European call)

Your company makes electronic cap badges, which display animated logos and slogans, and which you sell to baseball cap manufacturers.

A month ago your marketing staff identified a potential market for the logo of this year's Pan-continental soccer tournament (the logo is valid for this year's tournament only, and will be unsaleable afterwards). Potential business seemed at that time to have a present value or PV (of future variable revenue minus variable cost) of $90,000.

Production and commercial planners told you it would need a set-up investment of $100,000 to create the tools to make this logo, so the set-up wouldn't be justified at that day's expected PV of market income, which was only $90,000. But the expected potential market can rise and fall daily, due to the on-field and off-field exploits of star players, etc.

Technical planners told you at the same time (a month ago) that they could make a design and give you working samples to demonstrate within one month, at a cost of $3,000, thus giving you a chance to show samples for sale today, which is the last possible day for tying up distribution deals. You decided to risk making the samples.

A week ago things were going well: a small-country team with a photogenic striker had played brilliantly, generating many minutes of TV coverage for the contest. In addition, all the biggest teams (with big-spending fans) qualified for the contest. Distributors were so optimistic about sales that they were willing to strike deals with an NPV of $110,000, but not before they saw your samples.

Today you got your logo samples, and visited your distributors. Meanwhile, sales prospects had waned a little: tourist muggings in the host country, and the withdrawal of two famous stars due to injuries, had led the distributors to scale back their plans. The distributors this morning offered you contracts with a PV of $105,000. You took the contracts, and issued orders to spend $100,000 on the set-up and tooling.

So you made an NPV payoff of $5,000 on the logo deals today. This, less your earlier cost of $3,000, gave a net profit of $2,000. But things could have gone much better or much worse. However, the most you stood to lose was the $3,000 you spent making the samples, and this gave you the option of being able to do business today if conditions suited you.

You wonder whether there was any rule for deciding how much to spend on samples. Someone mentioned real options analysis...

of the option, and before allowing for the time delays between buying the option and making the profit, was $2 (financial) and $2,000 (real).

We'll list a comparison of the two options:

In financial markets	*In real asset markets*
Buy from a trader a call option on a stock: i.e. the **right** to buy the stock at a fixed **exercise price**.	*Spend money to buy, or create, the **right** or **power** to acquire some business asset (e.g. buy a licence or a brand, or fund new research). This right lets you acquire a new business asset, provided you make an investment of known cost (**exercise price**).*
(If profitable) pay the exercise price to the trader who sold the option.	*(If expected to be profitable) make the investment needed to acquire 'real' assets, e.g. equipment, advertising, etc.*
Get, in return for paying the exercise price at which you can invest in it, one unit of (IBM) stock, whose current value is actually based on its future stream of expected dividend income.	*Get, in return for paying the exercise price of the required investment, a new business unit, whose current value is based on its future stream of expected net cash flows.*
Only pay the exercise price (only **exercise** your financial option) if the value of the stock in the financial market at the time is at least as high as the exercise price you will have to pay to the option issuer to get the stock.	*Only make the investment (only **exercise** your real option) if the future net cash flows of the new business that you will acquire (discounted at an acceptable rate) are at least as big as the investment cost you will have to pay for the business.*
The value of the stock will follow a **random walk**, whether you exercise or not.	*The expected future net revenue of your potential new business unit will follow a **random walk** (due to changes in competition, technology, taste, etc.) whether you invest or not. So whether you invest or not, leave the expected effects of investing unchanged.[1]*

Our *real option* required two *decisions* (namely: is it worth spending $3,000 to buy the option at the outset, and is it worth spending the exercise price (investment cost) of $100,000 on the day the option expires?).

17

The right to **buy** IBM stock is named a **call** option, since you can 'call for' the stock at a fixed price, whatever the market price does before expiry. The opposite right, the right to **sell**, at a fixed price, is called a **put** option, since you can always 'put away' a unit of stock (for the fixed exercise price) however low its price may fall in the market before expiry. (See the Glossary entry 'put-call parity' for an important link between the prices of puts and calls.)

*In real option analysis, you have a real **call** option if you have the freedom, in future, to spend money to **acquire** assets (or not) in the best way at that time. You have a real **put** option if you have the freedom, in future, to **dispose of** an asset in the best way at that time (e.g. scrap, sell as going concern, etc.). The most extreme **put option** under limited liability is the option to declare insolvency. This guarantees that equity value can fall no lower than zero.*

Our example of a financial call option had a **fixed expiry date**, which was one month after the option was created. Some financial options have no fixed expiry date and so are **perpetual** options, e.g. there is a **perpetual** right to convert one dollar into yen.

*Perpetual options on **real assets** are rare, except for options to develop land: most real investment opportunities are short lived, due to competitor action or general technical change.*

> **US markets traditionally gave the right to exercise at any date up to expiry.**

Our example of a financial call option on the IBM stock could be exercised **only on one date, the expiry date**. This is called a **European option**, because European financial markets traditionally offered only this right. In contrast, US markets traditionally gave the right to exercise **at any date up to expiry**. So an option with this broader right is called an **American option**.

*Real options can resemble **American** or **European** financial options, or a mix of the two. For example, the clinical trials of a drug usually last a fixed time. Only after this (if ever) will it become legal to invest in distribution of the drug (which we will do only if it is profitable). This fixed time delay before exercise looks like a European option, but when the trials end, you probably also have **flexibility to wait for a while** before you decide about distribution. This means that you will hold a late-starting **American option** to invest in distributing the drug.*

*A complication for any drug project is that the drug may suddenly **fail completely** during clinical trials. This is a more serious risk than a normal **random walk** – if a drug fails during trials, the value of the underlying asset (the drug revenues) can suddenly **jump** to exactly zero, without warning, and stay locked there for ever. It is easy to allow for this type of risk, for example by using what is called a **Poisson jump process**. More on this in Chapters 3 and 4.*

The price and the value of a financial or a real option, and the main variables that drive value

How much should we spend to create a technology? How much extra should we invest in a production system to give it greater flexibility? We can answer such questions by valuing the real options that we create (or destroy) by the investment.

Let's look first at the **market price**, **premium** or **cost of acquiring** a financial or real option.

The big difference between a financial option and a real option is that a financial option is sold in a fairly efficient market, so we cannot control its price, and the market price is 'fair' to buyer and seller, so far as anyone knows at the moment the deal is done.

In contrast, if you spend on research to **create a new real option**, you could spend more on the research than the value of the option it creates, because there is no market price for the real option against which to check the cost of the research. Obviously a mistake to avoid.

To sum up the terms we've used so far (with mathematical symbols, as used in Chapter 4 and in the technical Appendices 3 and 4):

Financial option	Real option	Symbol
Stock price (changes continually)	Net present value of the potential investment, if we were to make this investment today (changes continually).	S
Underlying asset of the option (unit of stock)	**Underlying asset of the option** (potential physical or intellectual investment)	
Direction of the right enjoyed by the option holder: To buy (call) or sell (put).	Opportunity to invest (call) or disinvest/sell up (put).	
Continuity of the right enjoyed by option holder: Continuous right exists up to maturity (American)	All these, to plus combinations of them.	
Right only at maturity date (European).		

Financial option	Real option	Symbol
Continuous right for ever (perpetual), etc.		
Exercise price		E
Fixed price at which we can buy (call) or sell (put) a unit of stock.	Fixed price at which we can make a business investment, or sell it up.	
Expiry date		T
Last date of exercise (American) or only date of exercise (European).	Last day for possible investment (American), or only day for possible investment (European).	

In addition to the 'contractual' variables above, we need at least three economic variables about any option:

- **the remaining time before option expiry** (symbol $\tau = T - t$ (where T is the date of expiry and t is the current date);

- **the risk-free interest rate**, i.e. the rate of interest the market is willing to pay on an asset whose payoffs are completely predictable (symbol r);

- the **volatility**, which measures how **hard it will be to predict the underlying asset's price into the future** (symbol σ).

Let's try to value a European call option to buy one unit of stock in the imaginary non-dividend paying corporation ABC, for which the exercise price is $1.

It's simplest to start at the moment when there is no more uncertainty about the option's possible future value because at that moment the option will have no future, namely the moment when the option expires.[2]

The option's possible values at the instant it expires depend on the actual stock price of ABC at that instant, compared to the exercise price of $1.

Our decision rule at this instant is pure common sense: if the market price of the ABC stock is above $1, we should exercise our option to buy the stock at $1 from the option issuer, sell the stock immediately at the market price, and take the difference as riskless profit. In this happy situation we say the option expires **in the money**.

If, in contrast, ABC stock can be bought in the market for less than $1 as our option expires, we clearly should not exercise our option right to buy the stock for $1. Therefore the option expires **unexercised** and is worthless. In this sad situation we say the option ends up **out of the money**. Notice **it doesn't matter how far the option is out of the money**: a stock price on expiry of 99 cents and a stock price of 1 cent would both leave our call option worth nothing.

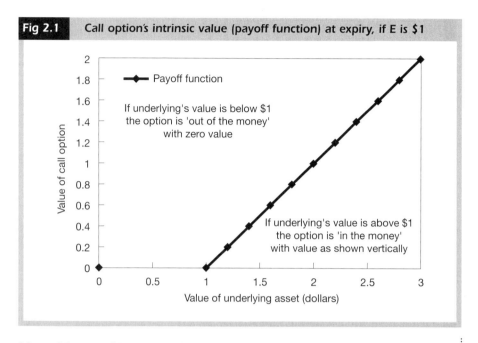

Fig 2.1 Call option's intrinsic value (payoff function) at expiry, if E is $1

It's useful to see this on a graph, as in Figure 2.1. On the horizontal axis we plot the possible prices of the ABC stock on expiry, and on the vertical axis we plot the payoff which the option would give us at each stock price. This is the option's **payoff function** or **intrinsic value**.

Notice (for a limited liability company) that neither the stock price nor the option can ever be worth less than zero. Later we will call zero a **fixed lower boundary** on the option's value. Even if the ABC stock price is as low as 1 cent only one hour before the option expires, there's still a minute chance that the stock price will recover to $1 within that hour, and this gives the unexpired option a very small positive value.

On Figure 2.1, to the left of $1 the stock price on expiry is below the exercise price of $1, so the option expires worthless, and is **out of the money**. To the right of $1 the option expires **in the money** – the higher the closing stock price, the higher the payoff. In technical terms, the payoff function is max(0, S-E) and S-E is the 45 degree line.

At a stock price of exactly $1, which is the exercise price, the set of stock prices that are in the money meets the set of stock prices that are out of the money, at a sharp corner. We can call this stock price **at the money** (at which **underlying asset price** equals **exercise price**). This is the highest stock price, on expiry, at which the option expires worthless, since the holder can just break even (before transaction costs) if they exercise the option, buying at the exercise price of $1 and selling in the market at $1, for a profit of zero. This case of exercising an option at the money, to give a net present value of zero, is important for real options.

Next we must value the option (again depending on the stock price at the time) on a date when the option has not yet expired (say a month before expiry). For simplicity, imagine first that the stock price today chances to be exactly at the money, or at the option's exercise price of $1. At this stock price the option would be worth zero if it were expiring today, but it isn't expiring yet.

The value of the unexpired option when the ABC stock price is at the money or $1 depends on what can possibly happen to the ABC stock price before the option does expire.

The behaviour of the stock price in an efficient market is a **random walk**. This means the ABC stock price is equally likely to rise or to fall between now and any instant in the future (including expiry date). Therefore if the stock price is $1 now, our best forecast for all future times is $1. Our best forecast is always the current value, since a rise is just as likely as a fall over any possible future time period (each is 50 per cent likely).[3]

The behaviour of the stock price in an efficient market is a random walk.

But a rise or fall in the stock price will have different effects on the value of our option. If the stock price happens to be below $1 on the day the option expires (of which there is a 50 per cent chance), our option to buy at $1 will be worth zero. There is also a 50 per cent chance that the ABC stock price will be above its present value of $1 when our option expires.[4] Any such price will give us profit, since we can exercise the call, buy the stock at $1, and sell it at the market price.

The simple average of a 50 per cent chance of zero profit and a 50 per cent chance of 'some' profit is worth more than zero (experts can work out the actual value),[5] so if any option is at the money (stock price equals exercise price) at any time before expiry, it must be worth more than its current **intrinsic value** of zero.

The extra value which an option has because it still has some time to run is called the **time value** of the option. This is over and above the **intrinsic value** of the option, which is its final payoff, as decided by the stock price, at the instant when the option expires. The **longer** the option has to run, the **larger** this **time value**.

What if the ABC stock price today (a month before expiry) happens to be very far above or far below the **exercise price** of $1? In both these cases the potential future price changes of the ABC stock, before our option expires, have relatively little effect on the option's value today (i.e. they add a smaller **time value**). Why?

First suppose that today's ABC stock price happens to be far below the exercise price of $1 (say $0.25), so the option to buy at $1 would be worth zero if it were expiring today. Half of all the possible futures will leave the stock price on expiry below $0.25, and in all these futures the option's value on expiry will still be today's **intrinsic value** of zero.

The other half of the possible futures will leave the stock price above $0.25 when the option expires. But few of these futures will leave the stock price on expiry as high as over $1, which we need in order to make a profit on our exercise price of $1.

Therefore if the ABC stock price today puts our option **far out of the money** (e.g. if it is $0.25), the average of all the likely future payoffs on expiry (mostly being zero) is close to zero. So the option's **time value** is small (and this adds little to today's **intrinsic value** of zero). See Figure 2.2.

Now, in contrast, imagine that the ABC stock price is high today (one month before expiry) at, say, $2, so that the option is '**deep in the money**'. This price would give us an immediate profit of $1 if we were able and willing to exercise the option today (buying at $1 and selling at $2). On a random walk forecast, the expected stock price on expiry will stay at today's price of $2,[6] so the expected payoff from exercising the option on expiry will still be $1.

Now, as before, allow for the possible movements of stock price away from today's value of $2 before the option expires. Half of all possible futures will leave the stock price higher than $2 when the option expires, and the other half will leave it lower than $2. The size of the expected movement away from $2 (either way) is the **volatility** of the stock, and **bigger volatility** means a bigger expected movement during the remaining time before expiry, so a **bigger time value**.

All of the 'below $2' stock prices on expiry will leave us worse off than today's expected payoff of $1. But the most we can lose is all of our currently expected final payoff of $1. Conversely, all the 'above $2' stock prices would leave us with a final payoff above $1, and there is no upper limit to these 'better' outcomes.

So if we average over a 50 per cent chance of an unbounded gain and a 50 per cent chance of a (slightly) bounded loss, the average is slightly in favour of the gain. This means a **deep-in-the-money** option has some **time value**, but not much, and this fact proves important for real options.

To sum up, if a call option before expiry is **far from the money** (in either direction) meaning the stock price is far from the exercise price, the option has a small **time value**. Conversely, if stock price is exactly at the **exercise price**, or **at the money** before expiry, the option's **time value** is at a maximum. This makes sense – waiting before we invest is most valuable when we are in maximum doubt at present whether to exercise (invest) or not.

The result is shown in Figure 2.2. The straight lines are the **payoff** function on expiry, which is the **intrinsic value** of the option, exactly as we saw in Figure 2.1, and the curved line adds in the extra value of the **time value** of the option. The total of the time value and the intrinsic value is the upper line, and

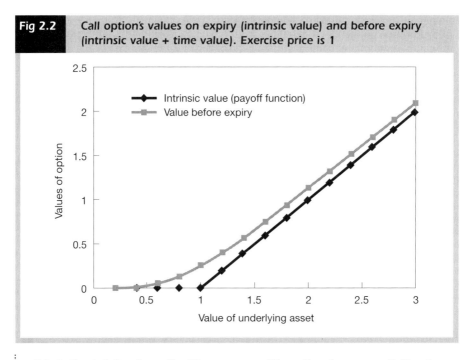

Fig 2.2 Call option's values on expiry (intrinsic value) and before expiry (intrinsic value + time value). Exercise price is 1

this is the **total value of a (European call) option** (on a non-dividend pay-ing stock) at any instant before expiry.

We see in Figure 2.2 that a higher ABC stock price, or higher **underlying asset price**, makes the unexpired call option **more valuable** – whatever its exercise price, and however long the option still has to run. This is because under the **random walk**, today's price is our best forecast for all future prices, including the price on expiry, so a higher price today creates a higher expected or forecast price on any future date, including the expiry date.

How do these financial option valuation ideas apply to real options?[7]

In a **real (call) option** we have the chance to **make an investment** in some business (at a known cost, which corresponds to a financial option's **exercise price**). This investment would give us an **underlying real asset**.

The **underlying real asset**, in which we have an option to invest, has a cur-rently expected **present value** of its future net revenues minus operating costs (this present value is constantly changing, in response to changes in technolo-gy, tastes and competition). **Today's expected present value** of the **under-lying real asset** is the value of the future income stream we could expect to have if we owned that real asset now.

The **net present value** of the **underlying real asset** is the present value of the asset's future income stream (net **revenues less operating costs**), less the **exercise price**, or investment cost, which we must pay to acquire this real asset (this net present value of an investment in the underlying asset, depending on the current market value of that asset's earnings, resembles the payoff function of a financial call option).

If the cost of investing in the real asset (its exercise price) happens to equal the expected net present value of its revenues, the real asset has a net present value of zero. This means we would neither gain wealth (positive NPV) nor lose wealth (negative NPV) if we made this investment – the deal would just break even on our cost of capital, and would leave shareholder value unchanged. This is the only kind of deal which a theoretically efficient financial market ever offers.

Real option values are like financial option values: the **time value** of a real option is **greatest** when the option is **at the money**. This means we get maximum value from being able to delay a real investment if that investment is currently on the borderline between being profitable or not (when it has an expected NPV of zero).

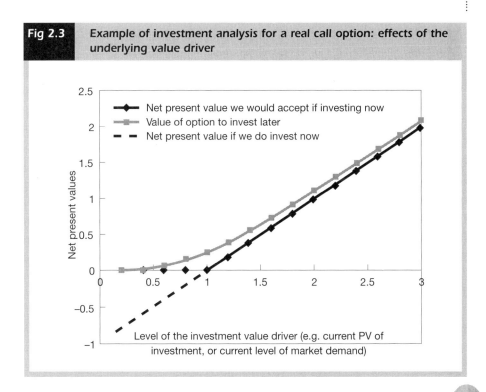

Fig 2.3 Example of investment analysis for a real call option: effects of the underlying value driver

The firms which will gain most from an accurate analysis of what to pay for their real options, and when and how to exercise them, are those which face close competition. Such firms often have to decide whether to make investments whose forecast NPVs are close to zero, and they often have to pay the full fair economic value of any real option they create.

Figure 2.3 shows these features. We have the real option to invest in a project at the end of some window of time. The horizontal axis shows the possible expected present values that the project's net operating revenues (the **underlying asset**) might take on that date (before deducting investment cost). The vertical axis shows the resulting **net present value** of the project (which is the **underlying asset** minus the initial investment cost, or **exercise price**). The sloping dotted line is the net present value of the project. This is zero when the present value of the project's net revenues (underlying asset price) equals the present value of the project's investment cost (exercise price).

The heavy line shows the NPV value we can expect from exercising our option to invest, at its moment of expiry, under various market conditions on expiry. We will invest only if the expected net present value of investing is at least zero. This heavy line is the **intrinsic value** or **payoff function** of our real option to invest.

The uppermost line on Figure 2.3 shows the **total value** of the real option (**intrinsic** plus **time value**) if our real call option has time to run. This is the amount of money it would be worth spending to **buy or create** the real call option given today's forecast (on the horizontal axis) of the present value of the project's revenues. It is also the lowest price at which we should **sell** our rights to invest.

An example of how investment decisions are driven by real option values

Suppose our R&D department has a proposal to **create a real call option** to invest in a facility to produce and distribute a new drug, and the **cost of acquiring/creating** this real option is to pay for research into the drug. Assume our drug has two possible applications, veterinary and human. For veterinary application the research will cost $0.1 million, and for human application the cost will be $0.5 million.

For simplicity we assume that the veterinary and the human drug markets have the same economic size at any moment (identical **underlying asset values** or stock prices, and both are varying randomly through time) and both markets also require the same investment spend to bring the drug to market (identical **exercise prices**). Then the only difference between the markets is the research spend needed to acquire the real option.

Fig 2.4	Effect of market strength on NPV of drug investment, and on value of taking an option to invest

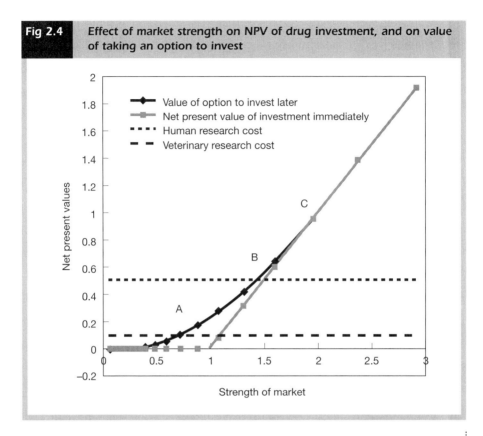

How strong does either the veterinary or the human market have to look before we should commit funds to research in either application (i.e. buy the real call option to invest in that market)?

Figure 2.4 shows the option value and the two possible research costs. For the lower (veterinary) research cost of $0.1 million, the 'cost of research' line meets the 'value of option' line when the current forecast revenue potential is only $0.75 million (point A on the graph). At this revenue forecast the option is **out of the money** (the expected PV of revenue from marketing the veterinary drug is $0.75 million, and this is less than the $1 million **exercise price** or investment needed to bring the drug to market).

This means we wouldn't want to invest in production today, even if the veterinary drug were already available. Yet Figure 2.4 shows that it is worth spending $0.1 million to acquire this real option to invest in exploiting the drug, provided today's market revenue forecast is $0.75 million or above.

This real option value is not just an uncertain possibility, or expectation, it can in principle be made risk free. If we float our drug project as a separate company, we can do forward deals in the stock of our project (**delta hedging**) that will lock in the positive $0.1 million value of our out-of-the-money option, and give us a risk-free return on that value, however good or bad the drug market actually turns out to be.[8]

If we do research into this currently unprofitable market, we are buying a **real option** which is currently **out of the money**, but we are justified if the **cost of the research** is no greater than the **value of the real call option** we acquire.

Now consider the human drug market, where the research costs $0.5 million. On Figure 2.4 the horizontal 'cost of research' line at $0.5 million meets the 'total value of the option' line at a point where the forecast present value of revenues is $1.35 million (point B on the graph).

At this level of expected revenue, the net present value of a $1 million investment in production is already strongly positive, at $0.35 million.[9] So we should begin research on the human application (i.e. we should only 'buy the option' to invest in marketing the human drug) only if the option to produce commercially is already deep in the money by $0.35 million. If, for example, today's expected PV of drug revenues is only $1.2 million, this means that immediate drug production would be highly profitable, but we should not spend $0.5 million to develop the human drug.

So, remarkably, we can get two exactly opposite 'strategic' recommendations for the veterinary drug and the human drug. We should buy a real option to invest in the veterinary drug, even if that market is currently unprofitable (e.g. if today's expected PV of revenue is $0.75 million), but we should not buy a real call option to invest in the human drug market, even if that market is currently profitable (e.g. if today's expected PV of revenue is $1.2 million).[10]

Many biotechnology and dot.com companies look like the animal drug. Their stocks have high prices, even though the companies make losses: these stocks are out of-the-money real call options, to invest far more heavily in the business if and when it becomes profitable, and the option values are high because volatility is high, even though (on a random walk basis) most of these out-of-the-money options will end up out of the money, and worth nothing if unhedged.

To sum up the main drivers of call option value: an **increase** in the **underlying asset price**, or in the **volatility**, or in the **time to expiry** of a call option all **increase the value** of the call (and usually of a put), while an **increase** in **exercise price** will **reduce** its value (and conversely for a put option). There is also a small technical effect of the **risk free rate of interest**, which varies across types of option.

To avoid overvaluing options of any kind, we should in particular never overestimate the remaining **time to expiry** or the **volatility**.

Volatility is the expected fractional change in the stock price per annum, which has a probability equivalent to one standard deviation (about 33 per cent). In other words, if a stock price has a volatility of 0.2, there is a 33 per cent chance that the stock price will change by at least 20 per cent over a year, and a volatility of 0.4 means there is a 33 per cent chance that the price will change by at least 40 per cent over a year.

Volatility increases ever more slowly with lengthening time horizons. Appendix 3 shows how and why volatility varies with the square root of the remaining time to expiry so that option value rises ever more slowly (and falls ever more rapidly) as the remaining time to expiry grows (and falls). See Appendices 3 and 5.

Option values and corners on the payoff graph

An option is about selecting the 'best of' at least two actions in an uncertain future.

In a call's payoff function the values of the two possible actions (invest or don't invest) cut each other at a sharp 'corner'. Consider the European call option on a non-dividend paying share, as in Figures 2. 1 or 2.2. The two possible actions are leaving $100 in the bank or using $100 to buy IBM stock. On the payoff graph the 'sharp corner' between their two payoffs is where they meet at the exercise price of $1.

If the ABC stock price is even a millionth of a cent either side of $1 on expiry, one or other of the two payoffs will be better, and a billion-dollar investor can profit from knowing which payoff is higher.[11]

A fundamental option feature – the incentive to delay a decision whenever payoff value graphs cut at a corner

At any sharp corner on the payoff function, we are at the money (or at a point of indifference) for the choice between two actions, and we can gain value from postponing our decision for an instant to see which action will be better at the end of the next instant. In fact, the value *per second* from waiting actually rises as expiry approaches.[12]

The decision on when to exercise an option – an American call option on a dividend-paying stock

The European options that we have looked at so far can be exercised only on the expiry day, but we can exercise an American option at any time up to expiry – a frequent situation with real options.

The early exercise decision matters if we have an American call option on a dividend-paying stock (though not for an American call option on a non-dividend paying stock – if a stock pays no dividend, all its profit comes from capital appreciation, and even an American option holder should delay exercise until the last technically feasible moment, to maximize volatility during the period before exercise, and hence maximize potential upside appreciation).

If a stock does pay a dividend, there is a disadvantage to postponing exercise – we lose dividend by delaying our ownership of the stock (retaining the unexercised option) since the option pays no dividend. So we must trade off the possible capital gain from delaying the exercise decision (we measure this potential capital gain as the time value of the unexercised option) against the dividend we will lose by delaying exercise (dividend yield of the stock). Dividend itself tends to rise and fall roughly in line with stock price.

It becomes very tempting to exercise the option before expiry if the stock price ever gets far above the option's exercise price (i.e. if the option is **deep in the money**). Why? We know that a deep-in-the-money option has a small **time value**, which means we can't expect much further price (capital) appreciation if we hold onto the unexercised option. Meanwhile, a **higher stock**

> **It becomes very tempting to exercise the option before expiry if the stock price ever gets far above the option's exercise price.**

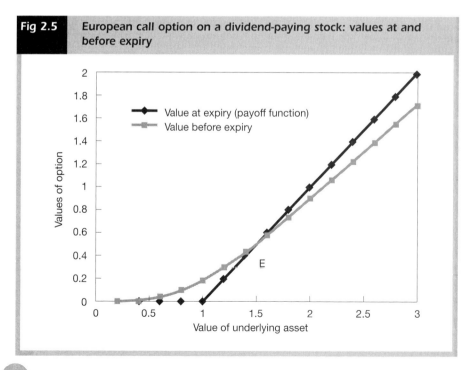

Fig 2.5 European call option on a dividend-paying stock: values at and before expiry

price tends to mean we will **lose out more in dividends** if we delay exercise (i.e. delay buying the stock).

Hence if an option on a dividend-paying stock is deep in the money (stock price far above exercise price), it is unattractive to hold the unexercised option. The market must set a low price on the unexercised option in order to induce investors to hold it.

Figure 2.5 shows how this impacts on a European call option on a dividend-paying stock, before expiry. At some high stock price, marked E,[13] where the option is deep in the money (very profitable to exercise immediately) the market value of the European option falls below the option's intrinsic value (i.e. the market value of the option is lower than the intrinsic payoff we would get if we could exercise the option immediately).

But the hapless owner of a European option can't exercise immediately. He or she must hold the option until expiry date (by which time the option's value will coincide with its intrinsic value).

The value E in Figure 2.5 (the stock price above which it would be more profitable to have exercised the European option than to retain it) tends to fall as the option approaches expiry. This is because volatility (and therefore time value, and the remaining chance of capital profit) falls faster than the remaining chance of dividend as expiry approaches, making it relatively more attractive to exercise.

Now consider an American option on the same dividend-paying stock. The holder can exercise at any time. As the stock price rises, the two value graphs for the unexercised and the exercised European options cross each other, cutting sharply at a 'corner' at E (where the value of the exercised option cuts past the value of the unexercised European option). This is breakeven or at the money for exercising the option early at a profit.

But should the holder of the American option exercise the option as soon as the stock price reaches the corner at E in Figure 2.5?

No. Because at the stock price E, at any time before expiry, the European option would be at the money for profitable early exercise. But we know that when any option is at the money at any instant before expiry, it is always worth waiting one more instant to see whether the price goes 'one side of the corner' (so that early exercise, and purchase of the stock, is best) or the 'other side of the corner' (so that holding onto the unexercised option is still best) at the end of the next instant.

Before an American option expires, the holder has a big supply of extra instants to wait, i.e. American option holders have an option on 'when' to exercise, as well as the option to exercise at all. So the holder of an American option should never be willing to exercise early, unless the value of their 'option' to delay exercise by one more instant has somehow been eliminated. How can this happen?

The answer is that there must be no 'sharp corner' on the value graph at which the value of the **unexercised option** cuts across the value of the **exercised option (intrinsic value)**.

As a result the rule for optimal early exercise of an American option has two logical parts: firstly, there must exist some stock price at which the unexercised and exercised states of the option have the same value (**value matching** of the exercised and unexercised option). Secondly, when the values of the unexercised and the exercised states of the option do meet, they must merge gently rather than crossing at a sharp corner. At the point where their two value graphs meet they must have the same slope, with respect to stock price S. This is called **smooth pasting** between the exercised and unexercised values of the option – see point F on Figure 2.6.[14]

The joint effect of **value matching** and **smooth pasting** destroys any incentive for the option holder to delay exercise after the stock price reaches the level F, at which immediate exercise becomes optimal. How? Suppose the stock price now is at the optimal level for exercise F. Option value (unexercised) equals intrinsic value (exercised), so we are indifferent between exercise and non-exercise at this instant. Over the next instant, both time t and stock price S will change. How will these two changes alter the relative values of the exercised and unexercised states of the option?

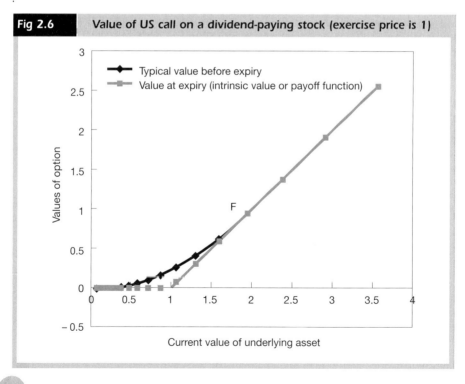

Fig 2.6   **Value of US call on a dividend-paying stock (exercise price is 1)**

The next tiny change in S will be random, so it is unforecastable in direction and size, but it cannot make the unexercised and the exercised option values unequal because they both have the same slope with respect to S, so both will change by identical (random) amounts. Only the next tiny change in time itself can have any effect on their relative values. The passage of the next moment of time reduces the remaining time to expiry, and this must reduce the time value of the unexercised option for any given S. But the intrinsic (exercised) value is constant over time for any given S. So in the next instant, whatever the new value of S, the unexercised option's value is certain to fall below its intrinsic (exercised) value, therefore we should exercise immediately before that happens.[15]

The optimal exercise price signalled by F is higher than E. Intuitively, the holders of an American option use their 'option' to delay exercise a little longer, after the stock price first reaches E, in the hope of even higher price appreciation. Above price F the expectation of yet more price appreciation is too small to justify sacrificing the dividend any longer.

Unsurprisingly, the extra rights of the American option make it worth more than the European option at every possible stock price, as Figure 2.7 shows.

Fig 2.7 Comparative values of American and European options on a dividend-paying stock

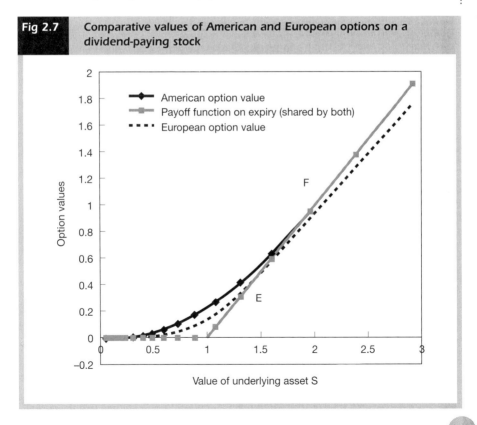

The implication for real options is that if we can safely delay any investment (even a profitable one), we should only ever invest before our option to do so expires if we receive a very strong incentive, i.e. the venture needs to be deep in the money, as at F, to reward us for killing our option by investing early.

The optimal exercise price F, like E, tends to fall as the option approaches expiry, and for the same reasons.[16] The sequence of falling optimal exercise prices over time (values of S above which we should exercise) is called a **free boundary**, between exercising and not exercising. How can we find this free boundary, which gives the decision rule for when to invest before expiry?

The **value matching** and **smooth pasting** conditions on their own are not enough information to decide where the free boundary is (values of S) or what the option is worth along this boundary. We must set extra conditions, in order to 'lock in' the position of the **free boundary** (and indeed every value of the option) at each remaining time to expiry. The extra conditions that we need are called **'fixed' boundary conditions** because each of these conditions fixes exactly where some boundary exists, that limits the option's possible values, and the same condition also 'fixes' what the option is worth everywhere along this boundary.

For example, a call option is worth nothing at any time if the underlying asset is worth nothing, since an option on a worthless asset is worth nothing. This is called the **fixed lower boundary condition** on the call's value (see Figure 2.8).

Likewise the **payoff function** gives the option's value (for each possible stock price) at the instant when the option expires. This is called the **terminal boundary condition**, since it specifies option value on the **time boundary** after which the option no longer exists.

A European option also has a **fixed upper boundary condition**, which fixes the maximum that the option can be worth, at any time, as the stock price S tends towards its own maximum possible value of infinity. As S tends to infinity, the fixed exercise price E becomes negligible, so the payoff S-E tends towards S.

The option's value in between all the boundaries can be thought of as a 3D **valuation surface** – this surface has one height (option value) for every combination of stock price today and remaining time to expiry today – see Figure 2.8.

What decides option value in between the various boundaries? A logical condition called the **Black–Scholes equation** controls how option values can change in response to minute changes of time and/or stock price. For example, the **Black–Scholes equation** says that an unexpired option's value can never change by a sudden step, or by a sharp corner.

The **Black–Scholes equation** works a bit like the rules that govern the shape of a slightly elastic flag (for a different interpretation in heat-flow terms,

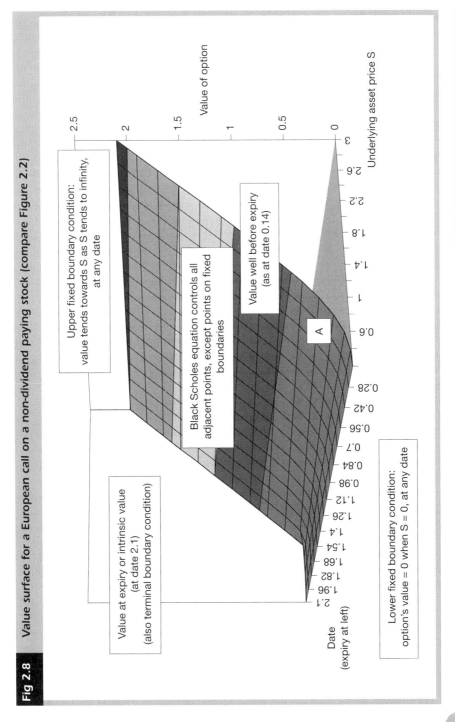

Fig 2.8 Value surface for a European call on a non-dividend paying stock (compare Figure 2.2)

Upper fixed boundary condition: value tends towards S as S tends to infinity, at any date

Black Scholes equation controls all adjacent points, except points on fixed boundaries

Value well before expiry (as at date 0.14)

A

Value at expiry or intrinsic value (at date 2.1) (also terminal boundary condition)

Lower fixed boundary condition: option's value = 0 when S = 0, at any date

Value of option

2.5

2

1.5

1

0.5

0

Underlying asset price S

3 2.6 2.2 1.8 1.4 1 0.6 0.28 0.42 0.56 0.7 0.84 0.98 1.12 1.26 1.4 1.54 1.68 1.82 1.96 2.1

Date (expiry at left)

see Appendix 4). A flag can flap in an infinity of ways, but a flag will not, of its own accord, tear, nor will it fold itself to form a razor-sharp edge. These two limitations are the equivalent, in economic terms, of the rule that an efficient market should not allow arbitrage, i.e. minute changes in economic conditions should not lead to very large leaps in option value, since this would allow options of similar value to be sold at very different prices.

In the case of the European call on a non-dividend paying stock, you can think of the three fixed boundary conditions (the **upper fixed boundary**, the **lower fixed boundary** and the **terminal boundary**) as three fixed edges of an infinite square, along which these edges 'fasten down' the flag of the valuation surface.

The three fixed edges for the flag, plus the Black–Scholes continuity rules, which control the flag's flexing at every point inside the boundaries, give enough information to 'lock in' the position of the flag (i.e. the level of the option's value) at every point that is not on a boundary (see Figure 2.8).[17]

Figure 2.8 sums up the option's value for every possible combination of stock price and time to expiry. For example, Figure 2.2 is simply a slice through Figure 2.8, at one particular time before expiry, and Figure 2.1 is a slice exactly at expiry.

For decisions about real options we usually want to know the height of the valuation surface (the option value) at only one particular point (e.g. option value for today's stock price, and today's remaining time to expiry). In simpler option problems, an exact formula exists for calculating the option's value V(S,t) at any chosen single point on the valuation surface. This is called an **exact** or **analytic** solution. The analytic solution for a European call on a non-dividend paying stock was published by Black and Scholes in 1973 and is quoted in Chapter 5 and in Appendix 1 of Chapter 6.

In more complex cases we have to calculate a huge area of the valuation surface, working out its height for very many combinations of S and t, working backwards from the known future payoff function, at expiry, towards the present time, in order to get the option's value at the one combination of S and t that we are interested in. This much longer (and slightly less accurate) calculation is called a **numerical solution**. Advanced real option problems tend to need them – see Appendix 4.

How does the idea of optimal early exercise apply to a real option?

Many decisions about real assets resemble the above example of an American financial call option on a dividend-paying stock. For example:

- There is a finite window of time during which we will free to invest in some 'real' project (e.g. we may have two years before our competitors catch up with our latest R&D advance). This corresponds to the remaining time to expiry for the financial option.

- We have flexibility to invest (or not) at any stage during this window of time. This corresponds to the American option's continuous right to exercise during the remaining time to expiry of the option.

- We can start to make profits as soon as we invest in our project, at a rate which we know at the moment we make the investment, but after that profit it will vary according to a random walk. This is equivalent to receiving dividends from an underlying asset (stock) as soon as we exercise an American option to invest in the stock. Dividends on the stock also vary unpredictably from the moment we invest in the stock.

There is therefore a trade-off, if we delay investing, between gaining more information (so avoiding any unfavourable market developments before our option to invest expires) and losing profit opportunity by not operating the project while we delay. This resembles the trade-off between making capital gains from holding a financial option, and making dividend gains from holding the stock instead in the case of an American call financial option on a dividend-paying stock.

Real options analysis gives rules for the early investment decision.

Real options analysis gives rules for the early investment decision, and it also tells us how to price any trades in rights or intellectual property which give an option to invest in the future.

Figure 2.6 includes a key finding of financial option analysis, which also applies to real options (in fact we included this feature in our drug development example in Figure 2.4, though we didn't say so at the time – Figure 2.4 assumes that we have some flexibility to delay investing in the drug after successful trials). Optimal exercise is at stock price F, when the option is already deeply in the money. This means that at the (optimal) early exercise price, exercising an American financial option will give a large immediate payoff.

The implication for real options is that if we have the option to delay an investment (even a profitable one) we should only invest early (before our option expires) if we get a very strong incentive, i.e. the venture needs to be deep in the money, as at F, to reward us for killing our option by investing early.

So for a real call option (of American type), we exercise early only if the investment offers a large positive net present value – well above an NPV of zero. In contrast, we should be willing to accept an NPV of zero at the moment of option expiry when we face a 'now or never' investment decision (see Appendices 1 and 2).

In perfectly competitive markets we must expect to take many of our investment decisions at an NPV of zero, after we have allowed for the risk-adjusted cost of capital (see Appendices 1 and 2). This has interesting effects on our possible decisions.

Look at Figure 2.4 and assume that 'strength of market' today is 1.7 (along the horizontal axis). Look upwards from this point. We first hit the horizontal lines for the two research costs, at heights of 0.1 and 0.5. Both of these costs are less than the option's value at this market strength (option value, on the curved line, is higher, at just under 0.7, but we're not looking that high yet).

Since both these options cost us less (in research cost) than their option value, at today's market strength of 1.7, it is worth starting either research project. We next reach the straight line payoff 'NPV of investment immediately', at a height of about 0.6. The positive NPV of investing immediately means it would be strongly profitable to invest in producing either drug today, if we already had the proven drug.

However, still higher than this we reach the value of the unexercised option, at just under 0.7. So the unexercised option (to 'invest now or later') is worth more than the exercised option 'invest now' (its intrinsic value).

This means if today's market strength is 1.6 we should be willing to start research (if it has not already been started), but even if we already had the proven drug we should not actually invest to start producing now, even though it would be highly profitable to do so. To allow for the chance of some downside movement, we should not invest immediately unless 'strength of market' is at least 2 (point C on the graph).

In future, as time passes towards our option's expiry, we will get less choosy. The optimal exercise level, at which we should immediately invest, will fall towards 1, until on expiry day the option's value coincides with the payoff function. On expiry day, if we haven't already invested, we should be willing to invest if we can break even on the cost of money (or anything better). This happens if the 'strength of market' on expiry day is 1, which gives an NPV of zero.

This is a powerful and unexpected finding. Clearly for any investment we need to think very deeply about whether we still have time over which we can safely defer the investment. We may lose value if we fail to defer when it is safe and optimal to do so, but if we overestimate the value of the option to defer, we may lose the opportunity to invest profitably at all.

Luckily it matters far more to get the basic structure right for an option-like decision than to get the detail of the calculations right. This is because early exercise is rather a 'forgiving' calculation – a glance at Figure 2.6 shows that the exercised and unexercised values are pretty close to each other for a long way either side of F (they are also close for a quite long way above F, where the unexercised value is lower, though we don't plot this in Figure 2.6).

This insensitivity means we can get away with fairly large errors in calculating option value, and/or we can exercise at prices rather different from F, without losing too much NPV (see Chapter 11 for an example where accuracy matters more).

A summary of the story so far

We have identified the five variables that define and value a basic financial call option on a non-dividend paying stock, *and we have identified their real option equivalents*, namely the **stock price** or **underlying asset price** (*expected present value of the net revenues which we can gain by making the investment which we have an option to make*), the **exercise price** (*cost of the investment*), **time to expiry**, **volatility** (of the random walk of the underlying asset or investment's value) and the **risk-free interest rate**.

We have seen that among these factors, **higher stock price, higher volatility** and **longer time to maturity** all **raise** the value of a call option, while **higher exercise price** and **higher real interest rate** both **reduce** the value of a call option. The reasons for these effects, and the directions of these effects, are common sense, but the actual value calculations require mathematical and computing skills (see Chapters 4 and 7 and Appendices 3 and 4).

We have seen the difference between a **call** and a **put** option (the right to **buy** at a fixed price and the right to **sell** at a fixed price), and we have looked at both **European** and **American** options (which are respectively rights to exercise on a **single** named expiry day, and rights to exercise at **any time** up to expiry).

The **dividend paying stock** (and its real asset equivalent, the *profit-generating investment*) poses the problem of **optimal early exercise** of an **American** call (or put) option. The (random) **dividend rate** is an extra variable in the valuation, and the calculations get more complex, as we have to compute an early exercise decision.

We have seen examples of a 'free' and a 'fixed' boundary both of which limit the possible values that an unexercised option can take. Early exercise becomes optimal if and when the underlying asset's price rises above a 'free' boundary (it can never cross a fixed boundary).

In simple terms, it can only ever be optimal to exercise an option (early or not) if the option's time value has become zero (no more value from delaying a decision).

A simple real option can be like a single free-standing financial call (or put) option, but many real options form part of a complex chain of interacting options, or **compound options**, where the payoff of one option is the right to acquire the next option (see Chapter 3).

Real options analysis can generate powerful, important and counter-intuitive recommendations whenever the future is unforecastable (in the random walk sense).

Therefore it is vital to beware of the possible ways of biasing a real option analysis (more on this in Chapter 12). It is even more vital to recognize where the random walk itself does not apply at all, or needs to be modified (see Appendix 5 on **mean reverting** random walks, and the example in Chapter 10).

In general, the less 'perfectly competitive' your market is in the economic sense (i.e. if there are only a few, powerful players), the less likely it is that market values will evolve randomly and unaffected by your decisions. In such cases you should use competitive game theory to supplement real options analysis, or even to replace it – see Chapter 11.

Notes

1. This is assumed in the basic mathematics of option pricing. Of course, in some real option situations (and even some financial ones, such as poker games and oligopoly pricing) your decision to invest in the underlying asset or not will be noticed by other players and will itself change the value of that asset. Game theory may be needed in such situations.

2. For technical readers: this intuition of starting at the expiry date exactly reflects how the mathematical solution method itself works. If the value of the underlying asset is modelled as a continuous random walk (Wiener process), the model for valuing a real option on that asset turns out to resemble a backward parabolic diffusion equation. The solution to such an equation must begin at the terminal boundary condition, and the solution diffuses 'backward' from this boundary condition to successively earlier times. In option valuation the terminal boundary condition is the option's payoff function on the expiry date, which is fixed by the option contract (though not explicitly mentioned in the contract). The continuous evolution of value in time can be approximated as a discrete process of numerical solution using binominal or finite difference methods – see Appendix 4.

3. For technical readers: strictly, the random walk assumption is usually applied to the logarithm of the share price rather than to the price itself, since a pure random walk in the raw share price would create the economic absurdity of negative share prices. In the log binominal method of numerical solution, it is explicitly assumed that the log of stock price moves up and down with equal probability over each short time increment, a process that converges, as the time increment tends to zero, to the log normally distributed random walk in continuous time, or Wiener process. See Appendices 4 and 5.

4. In theory there is no chance that the price will remain exactly at $1 if measured to an infinite number of decimal places – see Appendix 5.

5. For technical readers: only a risk-neutral investor would be willing to buy a risky option for its expected value (at least if the risk-neutral discount rate is used). But delta hedging deals, which we discuss in Chapter 4 and in Appendices 3 and 4, allow even a risk-averse investor to price an option at its hedged value on expiry, discounted at the risk-free rate of return.

6. Of course we don't seriously expect the stock price to stay at $2, or anywhere near it: a forecast of $2 is simply the least inaccurate forecast we can make – the unbiased average of all possible futures.

7. We omit italics here since this entire section concentrates on real options.

8. See Appendix 3 and Chapter 4 on delta hedging. Companies may well hedge the values of their new ventures more often in future, floating them off in order to do so (as the British retailer Tesco floated off its internet shopping business). But if you think you can create a drug option at lower cost than its fair value, you should first fund the project privately, and only float it for sale publicly after this arbitrage profit has been made.

9. Strictly speaking, we need an even higher forecast revenue than that to justify starting the research. This complication will be explained in the section below on how to value an American option on a dividend paying stock. In essence, we have an American 'option' as to when (if ever) to start research on either the human or the animal application of our drug. We will learn that two logical conditions must hold for this decision, namely value matching and smooth pasting, and their effect is that the forecast revenue needs to be a little higher than we've so far allowed, before we should start either piece of research. This small refinement doesn't change our basic conclusion, which is that it can be optimal not to pay for research into a presently unprofitable market, but also optimal not to pay for research into a presently profitable market.

10. The human drug is so deep in the money already that its future strategic prospects (time value) are small.

11. So financial markets will one day quote prices as finely as this. And then finer.

12. For an additional insight into the value of waiting, imagine we are in the closing seconds of an option's life. However large we expand the scale of Figure 2.1, as the remaining time to expiry falls, the payoff function has the same shape, and the same incentive to wait. In fact, the incentive to wait actually grows stronger as we shorten time and expand the scale of the graph. This is because the volatility (being proportional to the square root of the time remaining to expiry) is falling faster than the remaining time to expiry. Our expected profit from delaying exercise during the last millionth of a second before expiry, though small, is far bigger than our expected profit from delaying exercise during the preceding millionth of a second.

13. In this diagram E signals a stock price at which the exercised option becomes more attractive than holding the unexercised option. Here E does not mean the exercise price itself which is $1.

14. Of course the unexercised and exercised values could have the same slope and yet be parallel without ever meeting. We need both value matching and smooth pasting conditions to ensure that they both meet and merge.

15. The 'smooth pasting' condition has other names (e.g. 'high contact'). An equivalent and perhaps more intuitively easy condition is that the slope of change of the option's value (as S changes) should always be continuous (no sharp corners when magnified) except of course at the instant of expiry, when the option ceases to exist. You can see on Figure 2.2 that European options (which do not have an early exercise right) already meet this 'smoothness' condition at all points, and American options must also do so.

16. For technical readers: if optimal early exercise takes place at the stock price S^*, this price is a function of the remaining time to maturity t, or $S^*(\tau)$. Tractable analytical solutions for the free boundary $S^*(\tau)$ do not exist except in special cases, but it is usually straightforward to locate $S^*(\tau)$ by numerical methods, which do not require us to pay any conscious attention to the smooth pasting and value matching conditions – see Appendix 4.

17. For an American option on a dividend-paying stock, we need to imagine the valuation surface as a membrane that is supported in a slightly more complex way: it is partly stretched, and partly hanging free, so that a part of the valuation surface (value of the unexercised option) is resting freely on another valuation surface (value of the exercised option) with which it therefore merges (**value matching**) only gradually and without sharp discontinuity (**smooth pasting**). More on this in Chapter 3 and in Appendix 3. The membrane analogy is intuitively helpful, although the Black–Scholes equation is not actually symmetric in time or in space S. See also a physical interpretation in terms of heat flow in Appendix 4.

Applying financial option concepts to real options

Introduction

T o restate the most important points so far: an option is the right to choose the 'best action' out of two or more possible actions in an uncertain future.

The two key questions about any real option are:

- At what price should we acquire or dispose of the real option?

and:

- When, if ever, should we exercise the option?

If we exercise an option we kill its time value, so we should never exercise until the time value is zero.

The reason is that when (if ever) we exercise any option, the only payoff we ever get is the option's intrinsic value at the moment when we exercise. We can never receive the 'time value' of a real option as cash (unless we sell the real option to someone else, thus transferring to them the chance to make more cash by exercising the option at a later date[1]). The actual meaning of an option's **time value** is simply that on average we can expect a **better intrinsic value** if we exercise at a **later date** than the **intrinsic value now**, which we are sure to get if we exercise now. We kill the chance of exercising at a better intrinsic value later if we exercise now.

Therefore if a real call option to invest in a project ever has a high time value, this is an argument *against* investing in the project immediately. Why? Because investing now would destroy the high time value of the option to invest 'now or later'. This point is sometimes misunderstood, even by specialists.

This chapter applies the above ideas to real options. We work in two parts. Part A is a typical example of a compound option in which we have an opportunity to start research which will give us the option to invest in one of two designs of factory. This case contains many of the important types of real option, but it would be rather confusing to force every well-known type of real option into a single case. Therefore part B switches from a problem-centred focus to a technique-centred focus, and in it we list and review many of the better known individual techniques for real options.

A typical case of a compound option

The first stage in our time sequence is the opportunity to start an R&D safety testing project.

The first stage in our time sequence is the opportunity to start an R&D safety testing project (at any time in the next 18 months). If and when the testing project starts it will have a known fixed cost, and a known fixed duration of 18 months.

After completing the tests, the firm will have a proven product (except for some risk of complete product failure during tests – we can easily allow for this in the analysis by using a so-called Poisson jump process (see Chapter 4), but we will omit further discussion of it at this stage). Meanwhile, the market for the product will evolve randomly, and the product may or may not be commercially viable on the day when the tests end (though we are certain at that stage to have a potential product of known characteristics, even if those characteristics are not predictable in detail, and they may include failure).

At this stage the firm will have a further 18-month window, during which the market will continue to evolve randomly. At any time during this further period, depending on how attractive the market turns out to be, the firm will have the option to build either of two designs of factory, a small or a large (American call option to invest).

If the firm does invest in one design of factory, it will subsequently have options for how to operate the factory from day to day, and it will also have options for how to modify the factory's capacity in future, as the uncertain demand and technology unfold. Indeed, if the market turns out to be very bad, the firm will even have options for how best to exit from operating the factory (e.g. scrap, sell as going concern, manage for cash).

For simplicity we will postpone to part B all the operating and reinvestment options that will exist if and when we do ever invest.[2] We will also ignore the risk of total product failure.

The types of option at the successive time stages are as follows:

- The option to start the testing programme is an American option, since we can choose when, if ever, to start testing, up to the point where our option to start testing expires in 18 months (this time limit could, for example, be due to competitors' technical progress). Any delay in starting the tests will produce a corresponding delay in the potential start of profits at the end of the entire process. Therefore we can treat the option to begin testing as akin to an American option on a dividend paying stock – there is an opportunity cost to delaying the tests. The exercise price of exercising this 'option to test' is the cost of the test programme (strictly, the NPV of this programme at the moment of starting to test).

- Once started, the testing programme is a European option, since there is a fixed time duration, during which we will be legally unable to invest in production or to sell any product until the safety tests are over. There is no opportunity lost by not being able to invest in production during this period, so we will treat this option as a European option on a non-dividend paying stock.[3] However, the payoff of this European option is simply the value of the option which it creates, namely the American option to invest in one of two factory designs.

- The American option to invest in one of two factory designs can be called a multiple option because there are more than two potential 'best actions'. Here there are three potential 'best actions' – do nothing, build Factory A, or build Factory B. The payoff function of this option has three segments (rather than the two we have considered so far). This reflects the two potential modes of exercise. Each of them has a different exercise price and a different rate at which payoff varies in response to variations in market demand.

Therefore the shortest possible elapsed time up to actual investment (if we ever invest) is 18 months (assuming we start tests immediately and build a factory immediately after tests are complete). The maximum possible elapsed time before investment, if we hold both the American options to expiry, is 4.5 years.

Two key features of all compound options, including this one, are:

- The payoff function of exercising any one option in the chain is the value of the subsequent option which it creates (less the exercise cost of gaining access to that later option).

  Hence we cannot evaluate any one option until we know the value of the subsequent option. Therefore:

- The correct way to value the entire chain of options is to start from the last possible moment of the last option in the chain, which is its moment of expiry, and to work backwards in time (i.e. towards the present) through all the options in the chain until we value the first moment of the first option in the chain, assuming that this is the present moment of decision.

  This method for valuing a chain of options backwards in time is merely a generalization of the backward method for valuing a single option. The latter also starts at the last possible moment (expiry) and works towards the present.

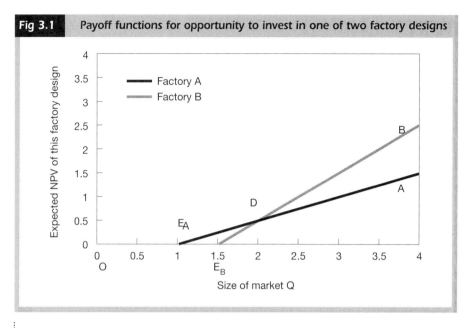

Fig 3.1 Payoff functions for opportunity to invest in one of two factory designs

To implement the backward evaluation of a chain of options, we start with the payoff function of the last option on its expiry date. Then we work backwards in time, towards the present, until we get to the value of the last option on its starting date (in this example, 18 months earlier).

This opening value of the last option, less any cost of accessing the last option, forms the payoff function of the preceding (penultimate) option. Again we work backwards in time towards the present, from the payoff of the penultimate option to the opening value of the penultimate option. This in turn becomes the closing value of the option before that, and so on back towards the present.

In this simple example the last option (in calendar terms) is a real American call option to invest in one of two competing factory designs. To evaluate this option, we begin from the payoff function of the option to build either factory on the day when this option expires.

Figure 3.1 shows the payoff functions of the two individual factories. Factory A is a small, cheap factory, which has low investment cost but high variable costs of production. The larger Factory B has higher investment costs and lower variable costs of production. Clearly one of the two factories will be 'better to own' than the other, depending on how large the future market demand turns out to be.[4] What is the value to us now of having the flexibility to build either of these two designs, or neither, over the unknown conditions of the next 18 months?

For simplicity we will assume that the selling price S is fixed. Hence the random walk factor 'size of market' on the horizontal axis of Figure 3.1 is the physical quantity of product Q that the market will take at the fixed selling price S. (It is easy in principle to model the case where both price S and quantity Q follow random walks, but this needs much more calculation and far more complex diagrams, so it is simpler to postpone the extra complications of this two-factor model; such models are discussed in Chapters 4 and 10 and Appendix 5.)

The cheaper factory A (with lower capital cost and higher variable costs) becomes profitable to build at any physical demand above E_A. This factory has the payoff function OE_AA in Figure 3.1. The more expensive factory B, with higher capital cost and lower variable costs, requires the higher sales volume E_B to justify building it, but after this its lower variable costs give it the more steeply rising payoff function OE_BB in Figure 3.1 if market demand grows.

Note that because the horizontal axis is calibrated in physical quantity, neither E_A nor E_B is an exercise price in money terms. These are simply the levels of physical demand Q at which either factory would have a net present value of zero and hence justify investment.

Which factory, if either, will it be best to build? Clearly if we have to take an immediate 'now or never' building decision, we should build no factory at all if demand Q today is below E_A, we should build the smaller factory if demand is between E_A and D, and we should build the bigger factory if demand is above D.

As with any option, we can get time value from waiting. Suppose, for example, that demand now happens to be exactly at level D. This means that if we have to decide on building a factory today, we are 'indifferent' as to whether to build the small factory or the large one. It also means (since future demand is a random walk) that we are maximally uncertain now as to whether demand in 18 months will be above or below D.

However, suppose we have a costless option to wait 18 months before we decide which factory, if either, to build (for example, while we are forced to wait 18 months during safety tests). Demand during that time is certain to move above or below D (with 50 per cent probability each). The new demand level – whether above or below D – will with 50 per cent probability make one of the two factory designs decisively less profitable than the other. Hence we will on average make money by delaying a decision (since 50 per cent of the time this will make us reverse a decision based on today's Q).

Notice that as usual the **time values are highest** (i.e. the option to defer our decision adds most value) when today's demand puts us at any **'corner' of the payoff function** in Figure 3.1. namely at E_A or D.

Figure 3.2 shows us the value surface for a European option to build either factory, assuming there is no cost to delay, i.e. this figure assumes we are forced to delay the decision on building for exactly 18 months, and we must then take a

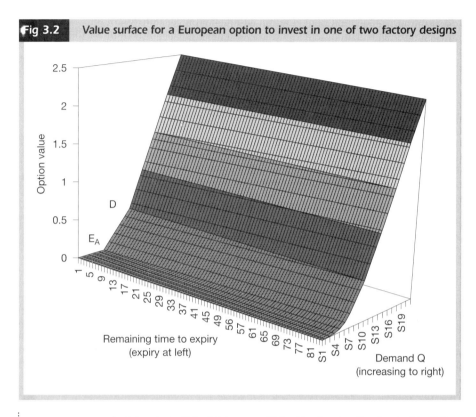

Fig 3.2 Value surface for a European option to invest in one of two factory designs

now or never decision to build whichever will be the 'best action' out of building either factory design or none, as of the day when the tests end. (Note that all the figures in this chapter are produced by numerical methods – see Appendix 4).

But it would be more usual, when tests end, to have an American option to invest: that is, we will have flexibility about how soon, if ever, to invest in either factory. This option resembles an American option on a dividend-paying stock because we will lose profit for every instant that we delay investment after investment has become feasible and looks profitable.

An American call option to build either of two factory designs

For simplicity, and because we are modelling the physical demand quantity Q as the random factor, we will assume that the potential income that we lose if we delay building either factory is driven by a constant percentage of the current level of physical demand Q. (The actual money impact on our income depends of course on the level of the best available payoff, given the current level of demand).

A lower fixed boundary condition is needed for the value of this option, which is simply $V(0,t) = 0$, meaning that when nothing can be sold (i.e. when $Q = 0$), the option to build either factory is worthless at any time (i.e. for all t). The payoff function at time T (terminal boundary condition), namely $V(Q,T)$, is simply the value of the fac-

As is usual for an American option on a dividend-paying asset, we require smooth pasting conditions.

tory that seems best on expiry date $t = T$, given the actual value of demand Q on that date, i.e. $Max(0, P_A(Q), P_B(Q))$ where $P_A(Q)$ for example is the expected present value of Factory A at whatever level of market demand Q will rule as the option to invest expires.

As is usual for an American option on a dividend-paying asset, we require smooth pasting conditions (identical slopes of value for each state of the option, as affected by Q) wherever there is a free choice of when to change between two (or more) states of the option. For example, the value surface of the unexercised option to build either factory now or later eventually meets the value surface of

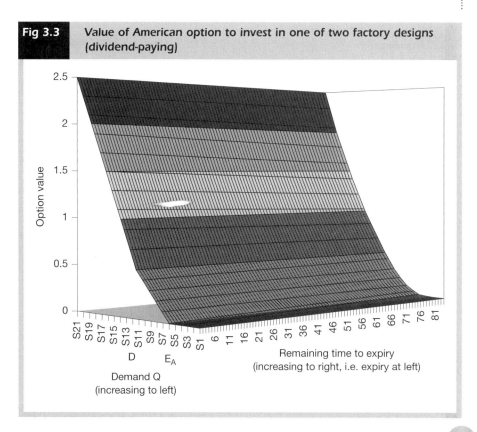

Fig 3.3 Value of American option to invest in one of two factory designs (dividend-paying)

the exercised option to build either factory now (the later surface is simply the payoff function 3.1 which is (P(Q,T) stretched into a flat surface P(Q,t) for all times t, since we get the same potential payoff from a given level of Q at any moment in time). Wherever these unexercised and exercised value surfaces merge, they must have identical slopes with respect to Q.

Figure 3.3 shows the value surface of the American option to build either of the two factories for various levels of market demand Q, and at various remaining times to expiry. This figure looks broadly similar to Figure 3.2 (which is the value of a European option to build one of the two factory designs).

Unfortunately it is hard to pick out by eye on Figure 3.3 where the value surface for the unexercised option merges with the value surface for the exercised option. This is partly because, as a result of the smooth pasting condition, these value surfaces merge imperceptibly with each other, at any level of demand $Q^*(t)$ at which it is currently optimal to exercise at time t. We can use other methods to identify time value more clearly.

Recall that it will become optimal to build one or other factory at a given remaining time to expiry $\tau = T - t$, if market demand Q is such that the option's time value is zero. The 'right' factory to build is the one with the higher NPV as time value reaches zero (unless both have negative NPV). In order to show

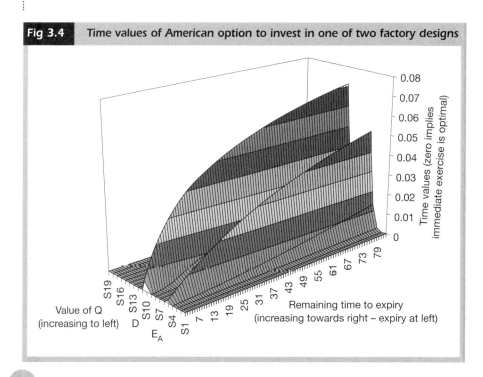

Fig 3.4   Time values of American option to invest in one of two factory designs

more clearly what is happening, Figure 3.4 shows only the time value of the American option to build one of two factory designs (i.e. it shows total option value V(Q,t) less intrinsic value P(Q,t)). Immediate exercise is optimal if we encounter any combination of Q and t at which this time value is zero.

Figure 3.4 concentrates on the times closest to expiry (towards the left of the graph). The range of values plotted for demand Q is from 0 to 4, and the maximum remaining time to expiry, as plotted here, is roughly 1.5 years, a period which the model splits into 83 time steps. The numbers printed beside the axes are simply part of the data housekeeping, to identify rows and columns of data, and have no direct interpretation as values of demand Q or of time t.

There are two 'shark's fins' of high time value in Figure 3.4, which end respectively at the Q values E_A and D, as in Figure 3.1. At these two Q values we are maximally uncertain, respectively, over whether to build either Factory A or no factory at all (when $Q = E_A$), and whether to build either Factory A or Factory B (when $Q = D$).

Hence if Q takes either of these two values before expiry we are 'at a corner' on the payoff function (see Figure 3.1). This means we are maximally uncertain between two 'best actions'. Here it will be valuable to delay a decision, and this is why the time value is above zero on Figure 3.4, which means we should not yet invest.

In common-sense terms, we might expect that if Q happens to stay close to either of these corner values right up to the moment of option expiry, we might remain uncertain whether to invest at all, right up to option expiry. This is exactly what the high shark's fins of time value on Figure 3.4 mean. If the random walk of demand Q happens to remain close to the level E_A throughout the option's life (or to the level D), the time value remains high right up to the moment of expiry, and it never becomes optimal to exercise (build either factory) early, i.e. before the option to do so expires.

It is interesting that this uncertainty even happens around demand level D (the level of demand at which we are uncertain whether to build Factory A or Factory B). If Q happens to be near D very shortly before option expiry, it is almost certain to be very profitable to invest in either factory (since both investments are well in the money, as we can see from Figure 3.1). Yet the high shark's fin, ending at demand D, means that we should delay investing in either factory, right up to expiry, if demand stays close to D. Why?

The reason is that although both factories are profitable to build if the demand level is D, there is a large potential opportunity loss if we build the 'wrong' factory too soon, and this loss is strong enough to dissuade us from building either factory. In fact, this situation is not likely to arise often in practice, since very few random walks will stay within the confines of either shark's fin right up to expiry.

Notice incidentally that the shark's fin falls ever more steeply as the moment of expiry approaches (it falls approximately with the square root of the remaining time to expiry). This reflects the fact that the option's value depends on its volatility over the remaining time to expiry, and volatility falls with the square root of the remaining time to expiry. This fact was mentioned in Chapter 2 and it is shown in simulation in Appendix 5. Appendix 3 explains the theoretical reason for it.

Conversely, if demand strongly favours one of the two factory designs at an early date, we can go ahead and invest in that design quite early. This happens when demand is far from either of the two corner values ($Q = E_A = 1$ or $Q = D = 2$) so that the option's time value lies in one of the zero areas, outside either shark's fin.

For example, we can see in Figure 3.4 that one year before the option expires, if the demand level Q is below 1.2 the time value is small but positive, so we should not (yet) invest (it is in any case unprofitable to invest at all). However, if demand level is between 1.2 and 1.8, the time value is zero compared to the value of building Factory A, and we should immediately buy the smaller Factory A. Next, if demand is between 1.8 and 2.2, the time value is large so we should delay a decision between Factory B and Factory A (with a small chance that it may yet prove correct to buy no factory). Finally, if demand is above 2.2, the time value is also zero above the highest available value of an immediate investment, namely the value of immediately buying the larger Factory B, and this means we should immediately buy Factory B.

If we consider some very long time before expiry, it is possible that we can be so uncertain as to which factory (if either) to build that there exists no level of demand Q at which we would be right to commit to building the smaller Factory A immediately. But there may be some very high level of market demand at which we can justify immediately investing in the larger Factory B.

Within the timescale plotted in Figure 3.4 we do not see such a loss of willingness to build Factory A, but the visual effect on Figure 3.4 if and when it ceased to be optimal to invest in Factory A would be that the flat area of zero time value between the two shark's fins of high time value would start to disappear. In other words, the two fins would start to merge and the flat region between them (over which it is optimal to invest immediately in Factory A) would no longer exist.

It is vital to remember that all the patterns seen in Figure 3.4 are based on one particular set of assumed values for the interest rate, volatility and 'dividend' rate. Changes in all these variables can greatly change the look of Figure 3.4, even if we do not change the payoff function itself for the two factories (i.e. if we keep Figure 3.1 unchanged).

In visual terms, it is the combined values of all the variables that decide the heights of the two shark's fins of time value, and this decides where, if ever, the fins merge during the life of the option. This in turn gives a decision rule for when, if ever, it becomes optimal to build either factory before the option to do so expires.

For simplicity we are not including in this example a random risk of a complete and permanent failure of the product. It is not hard to add this risk into the calculation, in the form of a Poisson jump risk. We do so by raising the interest rate that we use in the valuation calculation during any time period affected by the risk (see Chapter 4). Of course, the existence of a risk of failure can change both the value of the option itself and the optimal decision rule for exercising the option (i.e. an increased risk that the product will fail might reduce the maximum amount of money which it is worth spending on research to 'create' this real option, and it can also change the decision rule for actually investing in a factory).

This completes our analysis of the American option to build one of two factory designs at any time of our choosing during an 18-month window. However, we can only acquire this option if we first start and complete a fixed 18-month programme of tests. This makes the option to build either factory a delayed American option, and since the final decision on investment is delayed by a further 18 months (as compared to Figure

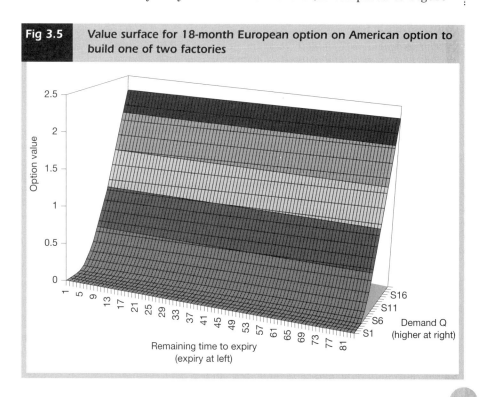

Fig 3.5 **Value surface for 18-month European option on American option to build one of two factories**

3.4), this makes the option to build a factory more valuable than we have so far calculated at the moment in time when the tests begin.

Figure 3.5 shows the effect of this fixed time delay. The earliest calendar time value of the option to build a factory, as shown in Figure 3.3 (at the right-hand end), becomes the terminal value, or the payoff function, of the option created by starting to test as shown in Figure 3.5 (whose earliest value in this figure, also at the right-hand end, is higher still). This valuation assumes that we suffer no opportunity loss from not being able to produce during the testing period. This means we can value the 18-month time delay, during the completion of the testing, as if it gave us a European option on a non-dividend paying stock. (Our assumption is that every other potential player will also need to test for 18 months, and therefore the capital value of all profits after 18 months will be encapsulated in the capital value of the project at the end of the 18 months; if so, and if the test programme is economically justified, the option's value at the end of tests will in expectation fully compensate any player for the fact that there is no income during the testing delay.)

For reasons of space we will not show a separate plot of the time value of the option whose total value is shown in Figure 3.5. This is because the time value of a European option on a non-dividend paying stock is rather simple: we know from Chapter 2 that its time value is always rising with increasing time to maturity. One effect of this is that the two shark's fins merge immediately, since there can be no region of zero time value. This means that on starting the tests, it is neither necessary nor possible to predict which factory, if either, we will eventually build.

In Figure 3.5 we have not yet allowed for the cost of doing the testing, but clearly the value of the option created by testing, as shown in Figure 3.5, will not exist unless we pay for the testing programme that creates the option. Hence the net value of the act of starting the research (at the moment in 18 months' time when our option to start research expires) is the greater of zero and the option's value as shown in Figure 3.5, less the NPV of the cost (as at that time) of doing the tests.[5] Clearly we would not start testing unless the value of the option equalled or exceeded the cost of the tests. This gives the curved payoff function seen at the left-hand end of Figure 3.6, which is max(0, value of the option created by testing immediately – cost of testing immediately).

But we do not have to start testing immediately. We have an American call option on when, if at all, we start testing at any time during the next 18 months. Therefore the terminal value of this American option to start tests is the value of starting to test immediately at that time. Hence, as noted, the American option to start testing has a curved segment of payoff function, after a straight segment of value zero, over which the value of the option to produce (created by the tests) does not repay the cost of the tests.

We have already noticed that any delay in starting the research must delay the

Fig 3.6   **Value of American option to start research**

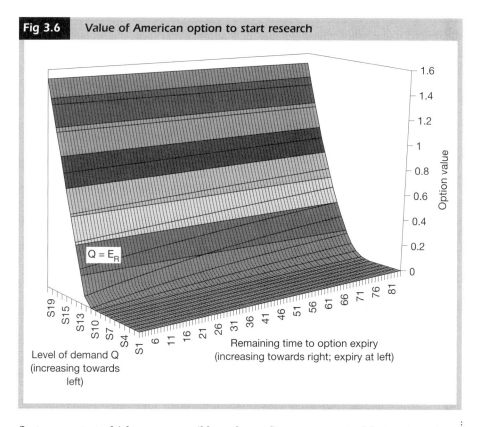

first moment at which we can possibly make profit on any eventual factory invest-ment, so we treat the American option to start testing (or, intuitively, the option to delay starting such tests) as an American option on a dividend-paying stock.

Figure 3.6 shows the resulting value surface (note the curved payoff func-tion). As with Figure 3.4, it is hard to see from Figure 3.6 exactly where the time value becomes zero, so Figure 3.7 shows the time value alone of this option to start testing. As always, exercise becomes optimal (in this case, start-ing the tests becomes optimal) if and when the level of demand Q at any par-ticular remaining time to expiry is sufficiently high that the time value of the option to start testing now or later falls to zero, i.e. we should exercise our option to invest in testing if and when the combination of demand Q and remaining time to expiry gives us a zero height on the time value surface shown in Figure 3.7.

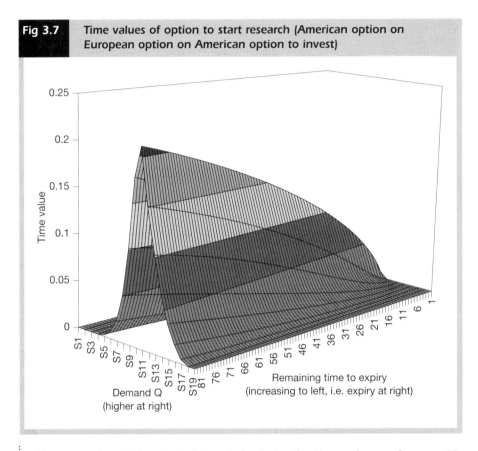

Fig 3.7 Time values of option to start research (American option on European option on American option to invest)

To summarize, at the start of the whole chain of options, when we have an 18-month window in which to start the tests, we should be cautious and start the tests only if the market demand Q today is at least 3.2 units. Some 18 months later, when our option to start tests is expiring, we are less cautious and willing to start tests if demand is at least 2.

At the end of the test programme, we should be willing to build Factory B immediately only if demand is at least 2.2, and we should be willing to build the small Factory A only if demand is between 1.2 and 1.8. A further 18 months after that, our option to build either of the factories is about to expire and we become less cautious: if we have not already done so, we should be willing to build the large factory if demand is at or above 2, and the small factory if demand is anywhere between 1 and 2.

When our option to start tests is expiring, we are less cautious.

For the numbers assumed in this example (in which the research is assumed to cost nearly as much as the cheaper Factory A), the analysis does not recommend us to make a deep strategic gamble on the new technology – at the moment when our option to test expires, the decision rule to start our test programme is: test only if market demand is at least 2. For comparison, a market demand of 2 (if this remained unchanged at the end of the test programme) would be enough to leave us a positive net present value after the costs of an immediate investment of 1 in Factory A, plus the 0.8 cost of the test programme (both numbers are assumed in the data underlying the example, though neither appears on the plots as shown). However, there is downside potential for Q over the two years of tests, and in fact we are only willing to undertake the testing programme at all if the initial demand level is 2, because this downside is partly offset by the large upside potential of the option to build the more efficient Factory B if demand proves strong enough. We would be more reluctant to invest in testing at a demand level of 2 if this upside option on Factory B did not exist.

What if we could build more than two possible designs of facility?

A possible **payoff function** for an option to build one of three different factories is shown in Figure 3.8. We have added a third factory, C, which has intermediate investment cost and intermediate variable costs between the other two, giving the payoff function OE_C C.

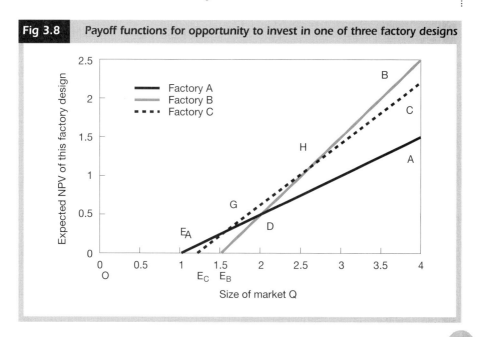

Fig 3.8 Payoff functions for opportunity to invest in one of three factory designs

The option's payoff function is now the maximum over zero and the three indi-vidual payoff functions, which is max(0, $P_A(Q)$, $P_B(Q)$, $P_C(Q)$).

Comparing Figures 3.1 and 3.8, each of the original factories now has a smaller range of demand over which it is 'best factory of all' (the small Factory A is now best from E_A to G, where G is lower than the former 'cut point' D, and the large Factory B is now only best factory of all above H, where H is higher than the former 'cut point' D).

This trend would continue if we could add further intermediate designs of factory. Each successive intermediate design would add some value (provided it was not totally dominated by, or inferior to, any existing design). The new design would tend to 'flatten out' some corner of the existing payoff function, just as Factory C destroys the corner that we previously saw at D when we only had a choice between Factories A and B.

Each successive new intermediate design, like C, would tend to be 'best of all' over an ever smaller interval. It would also tend to reduce the range of demand over which the two existing designs, on either side of it, would now be 'best of all'. Also, the difference in payoff between the 'best' and 'next best' design at each side of a new corner like G and H would be smaller than on each side of the old corner D that has disappeared. Hence each extra design would tend to add less extra value in total.

This fact has at least two implications. When we design real options in a live business, we may get most of the available value by designing only a few alter-natives, which span the exercise area of interest. Creating extra possibilities, at any one stage of a compound option, may not add much extra value. Likewise there will eventually be diminishing returns to subdividing into a larger num-ber of stages within the same overall time duration.

A related effect is that whenever we have to analyze a real-world option decision which is in reality highly complex, we may well often get much the same decision, and much the same final economic value, if we base our analy-sis on a simplified approximation to the vastly more complex real situation.

Options for operating a facility once we have built it

We will consider operating options in the next section. Note that after suitable relabelling of the axes, Figure 3.1 could represent the operating economics within a production system, which we own because we have previously exer-cised some option to invest, i.e. instead of the profits of two factory designs, Figure 3.1 might represent the relative payoffs of operating a large and a small photocopier, or of two different labour payment systems (small staff working high overtime, or larger staff working low overtime).

A summary of some real option techniques as they are conventionally named in the literature

Option to defer investment

The 'option to defer investment' is simply what we have so far called the value of waiting, or the time value of a call option to invest. We should defer exercising any option as long as its time value is above zero.

The actual time value of an 'option to defer investment' depends on what type the call option is (see Chapter 2). For example, if the option is a European or an American call option, on a non-dividend paying asset, the 'option to defer' can be treated as a direct 'instruction to defer' because deferral is always advantageous, given that a call option's time value is positive up to expiry for a non-dividend paying asset.

Likewise a European option on a dividend-paying asset is, by contract, an instruction to defer the investment decision, but this can be disadvantageous since its time value can fall below zero before expiry (but we have no chance to exercise early), although this time value will rise back to zero at expiry.

Hence European options to defer real investment are not very interesting. Real options to defer investment become more interesting if they are American options on dividend-paying (profit-making) assets, and there is therefore a decision on how long to delay, and a balance to be struck between the costs and benefits of delay.

The decision for this type of option is simple: defer exercise until the time value becomes zero. Hence the 'value of the option to defer' is simply the remaining time value (if any) of the option.

Most real call options are of this last type. Hence the title 'option to defer' needs no new economic ideas beyond the theory of American options on dividend-paying assets. However, it is often intuitively appealing to speak of an 'option to defer' (rather than an 'option to invest') even though the two are economically equivalent, since in the social reality of management we often first consider a specific investment in principle and then consider whether we can or should defer our decision on it.

Option to discontinue construction

In a similar way, this piece of real option terminology also reflects the psychological situation that managers find themselves in, even though the decisions it requires exist in financial market theory under different names.

The underlying idea applies when we have a construction project in a form such that we can discontinue or branch the project after each of many stages. For example, typical stages might be: (a) prepare land (or sell green site), (b) lay foundations, (c) build phase 1 (or sell brown site), (d) build either phase 2A or phase 2B (or sell part-completed development), etc.

In essence this construction sequence is a compound option, consisting of a chain of call options, some or all of which may also have an alternative put option. Before each construction stage we should look at the current market value of that stage (including all the option values that it would create at any subsequent stages) before we take a decision on whether to invest in that stage. Alternatively, we could sell (put) the project without investing further, or we could delay a decision.

Of course, construction is not unique as an example of such a compound chain of real options – we have already looked at a compound call option, which consisted of R&D tests followed by production investment, followed by operating decisions. We could of course break an R&D project itself into phases, making it into a compound chain of call options (including put or exchange options if licences or technology can be sold at intermediate stages).

At any point in such a chain of investments it can be optimal to exercise our option to invest in the next stage in the chain, even if that next stage looks unprofitable or out of the money in itself, provided that this spend opens sufficiently valuable future options. Of course, this effect is not unique to chains of call options – even a single call option has some value, and can be worth buying, when it is out of the money.

Therefore it might be argued that the option to 'discontinue construction' requires only those economic decisions that are already present in any compound chain of call options. A decision to discontinue construction is in effect a decision not to exercise the next call option to invest in construction. This decision may or may not be followed by the exercise of a put (sale) option.

However, as in the case of the phrase 'option to defer', the phrase 'option to discontinue construction' does express something close to the intuitive reality of managers. Psychologically (or even legally) a manager may feel committed to continuing with all the future phases of a project. In such a case discontinuing construction would be an active decision, whereas continuing to invest would be tantamount to no intervention. This distinction is psychological rather than economic, but the phrase 'option to discontinue construction' does at least remind us that we can add value to any project by designing option-like flexibility into it, for example if we increase our scope to defer or to omit later stages, or even to exit the project.

For example, at various points we may be able to sell or lease some or all of our green land, brown land, building shells, or fitted-out buildings. These options to sell or disinvest may be treated as **put** options, or options to sell at a fixed price (we do this if the disposal values, such as brown field land values or scrap steel values, are far less volatile over time than the values in use), or we can treat these options to exit as **exchange options**, namely to exchange between value on disposal and value in use (exchange options become relevant if the values on disposal are undergoing random walks which are about as volatile as those of the values in use).

If such exit options exist, we should take their value into account before deciding whether to exercise any of the calls within the chain, just as we should take into account the value of all the call options that we would destroy later in the chain, before we decide to exit the entire chain by exercising one of the puts (see Chapter 11). Valuable puts make us more willing to invest in the first place, while valuable calls make us less likely to exit after investing.

Options to expand or contract capacity

Starting from today's capacity (assuming we have already exercised a call option to invest), we usually have further call options to invest in extending today's capacity. Similarly, we often have a put option to reduce today's capacity. The put exit option will in some cases give us an actual cash inflow if we disinvest (e.g. proceeds from the sale of redundant land or buildings, or from scrapped machinery). In other cases we may have to make a costly payment in order to exit (e.g. we may have to pay employee severance or environmental clean-up costs). This payment may be justified if it allows us to terminate existing operating losses.

A word of caution is needed here because traditional 'plain vanilla' financial options contain too few variables to be efficient as models of operating capacity in all circumstances, and are therefore not adequate to guide decisions in all circumstances.

To be economically realistic, a model to guide operating decisions may need to include some or all of the following variables: a variable rate of physical output, a constraint on the maximum rate of physical output, a variable revenue per unit of output, a variable cost per unit of output, a fixed cost per period, and the operation's capital value, as well as a model of market potential, in the form of a demand curve for the level of physical output required at various price levels.

Unfortunately a 'plain vanilla' financial option contains far fewer variables than this. There is therefore a risk that we may seriously oversimplify the effect of a capacity change if we try to model it as a simple call or put option.

For example, it is common to treat production capacity as a series of European call options to produce, one in each future period of the asset's life (see Chapter 6). This means that in each future time period (e.g. day) the factory gives us a real European call option to purchase a single unit of output on that day. In each future period we are free to pay a fixed exercise price (e.g. the avoidable cost of production for that day) and if we do so we will obtain one unit of output, for sale at the market price of that day (assuming no storage is permitted).

We will exercise our option to produce if the market price on any day exceeds avoidable cost. We own one (European) call option of this type for every future time period of the factory's life.

Unfortunately this model cannot handle decisions about using or investing in various fractions of our present capacity. For example, if we buy a large number of identical production units, each is an identical bundle of European calls. In theory we will always run all the units or none, depending on whether market selling price is above or below our avoidable production cost per unit.

Likewise if the market price ever justifies paying the capital cost of one extra production unit (thus buying us a new bundle of European calls to produce) it will be profitable to buy an infinite number of such production units.

Therefore when applying any real option model to a capacity problem, it is vital to check that the assumptions of the real option model adequately reflect the particular decision to be taken.

Options to shut down and reopen, and the frictional cost of starting and stopping production

If we own a continuous process (e.g. electricity generation) we have the option to switch it on at any instant, for example whenever the selling price of output rises above our avoidable cost of producing. This gives an infinitely large bundle of call options to produce or not, in infinitely many future instants of time. Unfortunately, this may in theory require us to 'switch the system on and off' infinitely often, which is physically or economically infeasible.

The reason is that the random walk of the selling price for output may frequently cross the avoidable cost of producing the output (exercise price). Since this is our decision point for whether to produce or not, we may frequently reverse our decision as to whether to produce.

Under the mathematical assumptions of the continuous random walk (Appendices 3 and 5), the price makes infinitely many jumps within any short time interval, and although these jumps tend on average to be small, each of them has in principle no limit to its size. So if the output selling price happens to be close to the exercise price (avoidable cost of production), there is no limit to the total number of times that selling price might cross avoidable cost during any finite interval.

As an example, consider an electricity generating plant (see Chapter 6). If the plant's avoidable cost of production is \$X per unit of electricity, ideally we will produce only when the market price is above \$X.

In theory the market price is changing continuously, which may require us to switch on and off infinitely often. Real market conditions are not quite continuously variable, but they are trending that way. Of course, in practice there is a cost and a time delay for powering a generating plant up or down. Therefore if the plant is running, we have a motive to leave it running, even if the selling price dips slightly

Real market conditions are not quite continuously variable, but they are trending that way.

below avoidable cost (since there is a 50 per cent chance that the random walk will next rise, and nearly a 50 per cent chance that this rise will be big enough to take us back into profit before we incur the cost of powering down).

Similarly, we should not power up an idle plant at the first instant that selling price rises slightly above avoidable cost. We should let the price go a little higher than avoidable cost before we start production in order to minimize the risk that we will soon be producing at a loss.

Many other industries face this sort of decision, and more detail is given in Chapters 6 and 11.

Options to abandon

The option to abandon a venture is an extreme case of either a put or an exchange option. If we start from a position where production today is not profitable, we have a hierarchy of put options beyond merely ceasing to produce output: (a) make the asset inactive (mothball it); (b) scrap or sell the asset; (c) liquidate the company.

The decision rule for taking any of these options is that we should abandon (by one specific way) when the net present value of 'abandon now' (by that specific way) is greater than the net present value of any alternative combination of active assets plus the associated options to abandon (now or later) plus any associated options to reinvest (now or later). The existence of a valuable option to abandon should make us more willing to invest, just as the existence of a valuable option to reinvest should make us less willing to abandon. Hence the option to abandon has an economic effect on decisions and cannot usually be valued in isolation.

Care is needed when valuing a company's options to abandon. A 'naked' put option (such as might be available to an investor who had no equity stake in a company or project) has a payoff function which rises steadily as the market value of the asset falls. In contrast, the type of put available to a project's own-ers often takes the form of a constant 'floor' to the project's value based on its scrap or disposal price (see Chapter 7). This floor price does not rise as the pro-ject's value falls. Moreover, if any project has been valued simply as a call (either to invest or produce), this value already has a constant floor of zero, irre-spective of market conditions. There may therefore be a risk of double counting the benefits of various different 'floors to value', since these options have over-lapping exercise areas and/or benefits (see next section). In particular it can be incorrect to add the payoff of a put (as enjoyed by an outsider) to a valuation which already takes into account one or more existing floors to value as enjoyed by insiders. The literature has not always stressed this risk.

Interactions between options, and the value of flexibility

We saw in Figure 3.8 that the value of a set of multiple options whose exercise areas overlap can be less than the sum of the values that each of the individual options would have in isolation, if we only had that option. For example, in an elec-tricity generator, if we have the flexibility to burn either gas or oil, we can burn 'the better of' the two fuels, whatever the market price of each. But the value of being able to burn both fuels is less than the sum of the independent values of being able to burn either fuel alone. In a single-fuel plant (say gas), our option to burn gas as fuel is more valuable, since gas always offers us our only chance to produce elec-tricity at all. In a multi-fuel plant, at least one fuel is not being burnt at any moment, so our ability to use that fuel is earning us nothing at that moment.

The value of flexibility

We can use real option methods to assess how much it would be worth investing to create flexibility, for example to add the ability to burn oil to a gas generator. We can treat our gas generator as a bundle of simple call options to produce electrici-ty or not from gas in future time periods (more strictly, since both gas prices and electricity prices are evolving randomly, we have a bundle of spread options, which we will exercise if the difference or spread between electricity and gas prices is wide enough to justify operating the plant). In contrast, we can treat a flexible dual-fuel plant as a bundle of three-way spread options to produce electricity (or not) from the cheaper of oil or gas (one such option in each future time period).

We can compare the values of the two bundles of options. The higher total value of the bundle of three-way spread options is due to the increase in value produced by fuel flexibility. We should invest to create fuel flexibility only if the cost of our investment to create flexibility is less than the increase in option value that the flexibility will create. This information is useful for generator marketing.

Options to switch uses (inputs or outputs)/options with multiple random walk factors

The previous example was a real option to switch between inputs, namely to switch between oil and gas fuels. Similarly, we have real options to switch between outputs, and these allow us to switch either the product itself or the market into which we sell it, always selling to the 'best of' the competing outputs, under future uncertainty.

Such problems usually involve more than one random walk factor (though we can sometimes get away with modelling the ratio of two costs as a single random factor – see the discussion of Margrabe exchange options in Chapters 4, 5 and 9, plus the Dixit and Pindyck formulation of a similar problem mentioned in Chapter 11). Often the payoff functions are curvilinear, but there is no problem in handling such payoffs by numerical methods (see Figure 3.6 as an example; numerical methods are discussed in general in Appendix 4).

For these and many other topics consult Trigeorgis (1996).

Discrete versus continuous decision variables

So far we have discussed problems in which the random factor and/or the internal decision variable are continuous (e.g. the price of oil, or the price of an IBM share, can vary continuously in principle, though not quite in practice). In contrast there are some real options which have a very small and countable number of possible outcome states (e.g. a drug either works or it doesn't; or a law suit against us by our competitors will either break our patent or not).

The most basic method for discrete situations is the binomial method. This method, which is also a powerful and convenient way to approximate a continuous problem, is introduced theoretically in Chapter 4, exemplified in Chapter 7 (for an alternative approach see Chapter 8) and explained further in Appendix 4.

Notes

1. It may also be possible to lock in today's time value until the end of the option's life, by a series of hedging deals called delta hedges (see Appendix 3 and Chapter 4). Delta hedges require forward sales of shares in the project, or of the project's outputs, or of any equivalent asset. But even delta hedging requires someone to hold the option until its time value is zero.

2. Though strictly speaking the existence and the value of all these options should affect how willing we are to invest in the first place.

3. We further assume that any player trying to enter this market will face the same testing duration. This ensures that there is no opportunity cost for any player from lost income opportunity during the testing period, since the necessary capital returns on developing the product will be encapsulated for any player in the capital value of the project at the end of testing.

4. Similar payoffs can exist in a service industry. For example, Figure 3.1 could show payoffs of operating two sizes of airliner, such as where A is a Lear jet and B is a Jumbo (ignoring the maximum utilization limit on either aircraft).

5. Perhaps we can create options to branch or terminate the research itself during the 18 months. If so, these options can add significant value, and we should therefore (a) design in an efficient chain of sub-options and (b) add these options to the total chain for analysis.

Some modelling techniques for tackling and solving real options problems

Introduction

I n this chapter we outline a range of mathematical tools for formulating and solving real options problems. Later chapters will describe various case problems by different authors, and an editor's introduction will briefly relate each case to the general framework of this chapter.

It would probably be a vain goal to give an example of every type of real option in the literature (indeed we have not attempted this), but in any event a reader may well encounter a problem which has not previously been tackled in the literature. We hope that the general framework of this chapter will help readers to understand both existing and future applications.

This chapter falls into two main parts. The first is fairly technical, and deals with the Black–Scholes model in continuous time. It is likely to be fully meaningful only to numerate readers who have worked through Chapters 1 to 3 and Appendices 3 and 4 (plus the basic introductions in Appendices 1 and 2 if needed). The second part of the chapter is a little less technical, and it includes both some elementary introduction and some theory for the binomial model (see also Appendix 4 for further details).

In the first part of this chapter we describe a range of ways to vary the continuous time model, firstly by varying the Black–Scholes equation, and secondly by varying its boundary conditions. Then we discuss how to solve the resulting continuous time problem. We note that analytical solutions are available only in special cases, but that the explicit finite difference method is a very general fall-back, which can often be fast and convenient. It is important to realize that (a) adjusting the Black–Scholes equation, (b) adjusting its boundary conditions, and (c) implementing a solution for the problem that results from both these sets of adjustments are three quite different tasks.

The second part of the chapter deals with the binomial tree method. We give a fairly basic and intuitive explanation of both the model and its mathematics. In practice the binomial tree is almost always used (either directly or indirectly) as an approximation to the continuous (Black–Scholes) case. It is therefore essential to explain the binomial tree in its own right, as a discrete model, and also to introduce how it can be set up to act as an approximation to the continuous case.

The binomial method is able to bypass many of the complications which the continuous time model imposes – if data arise in discrete time, the binomial tree allows us to model them directly in discrete time without first transforming them into a Black–Scholes partial differential equation (PDE) and defining all its boundary conditions.

A further reason for introducing the binomial method at this point is that although the method is easy to use, some of the explanations in the literature are intuitively confusing.

Ways to formulate a problem in continuous time

By varying the Black–Scholes equation

The basic Black–Scholes equation is derived in Appendix 3, namely

$$rV = r(\partial V/\partial S)S + \partial V/\partial t + 0.5\, S^2\sigma^2\, (\partial^2 V/\partial S^2)$$

where S is a single underlying asset which the option gives us the right to buy (call) or to sell (put). More generally, S can be any other random factor whose movements drive the value V of some asset 'derivative' from S (including a real option); r is the risk-free rate of return, and V is the value of that asset whose value is derived only from the value of S. The basic equation above assumes that S itself can give value to its owner solely through its capital or price appreciation (for example, S can be a non-dividend paying stock or a zero-coupon bond).

We need to add extra elements to this basic equation when modelling certain types of real options. Most important is the case of a call option when the underlying asset S pays a dividend or (equivalently) in which there is some other disadvantage (opportunity cost) to delaying the exercise of the call option. If there is a loss of opportunity due to delaying exercise, and if this loss is proportional to the current value of S, then we can model S as a 'dividend-paying' asset, as described in Appendix 3.

A simple assumption is that the rate of dividend lost by the option holder is the fraction δ per unit of time of the underlying asset's current value S. Appendix 3 explains how we can derive this modified equation.

$$(r - \delta)(\partial V/\partial S)S + \partial V/\partial t + 0.5\, S^2\sigma^2\, (\partial^2 V/\partial S^2) = rV$$

The 'dividend fraction' δ can represent a wide variety of flows of benefit to the holder of S, which are proportional to the current value of S but which are not enjoyed by the holder of an unexercised option to buy S. Such benefits can include dividends, profit, rent payments avoided (if, for example, S is a house), convenience yield (if, for example, S is a raw material), etc. There might arise a special case in which this 'dividend yield' to the owner of S is negative. If so we can reverse the sign of δ in the Black–Scholes equation (for example, if S is gold, the holder of asset S may need to pay insurance charges proportional to the value of S, which the holder of an option to buy S need not pay).

Conversely, the holder of an unexercised option may in some cases receive a flow of benefit which will be terminated by exercise of the option (i.e. the option itself is 'income paying'). Income-paying options are rare in financial options, but in real options a common example is the option to develop agricultural land: if the land is presently being farmed, it may be earning a fixed contractual rate of rent per unit of time, until the holder exercises the option to invest in developing the land. Conversely, in some problems the sign of this 'flow' might be reversed so that the holder of an unexercised option may have to pay a fixed sum per time period in order to retain tenure of the option (e.g. a recurring fee for an exploration licence, or a maintenance fee for a land site – see Chapter 7).

It is straightforward to model such terms since, as Appendix 3 shows, the modified equation has been divided throughout by dt, and hence it is a model of events over the time interval dt. In general, a fixed flow of M units of money per unit of time to the option holder, sustained over the time increment dt, gives rise to a term Mdt, so the equivalent term to add to the LHS of the modified equation above is simply M (this gives the option a higher value at any moment but a slower rate of appreciation from moment to moment). We would need a negative M in order to model a case where there is a fixed flow of M units of money per unit of time that must be paid by the holder of the unexercised option (e.g. licence fees, payments for rights, the cost of keeping a technical or marketing team in being until used, etc.). See the example in Chapter 7.

Many real options allow exchanges between the values of two (or more) assets, each of whose values are randomly changing (e.g. the future value of a construction site if it is completed as a hotel, and its value if completed as a cinema, are both evolving randomly, and this affects the decision as to whether and when to commit the site to either use; likewise the value of a dual-fuel generator when it is burning gas, and its value when burning oil, will both vary over time, and this affects the decision as to which fuel to burn; similarly, the value of a factory in use, and its value as a redevelopment site, will both change unpredictably).

As we explain in Appendix 3, if one of the two values that can be exchanged is effectively constant, we can value the right to exchange for that value (and we can derive decision rules for exercising that right) by using variants of simple or plain vanilla calls or puts, in which we set appropriate boundary conditions to reflect the fact that the exchange is possible at a fixed price (see an example in Chapter 7; more generally, the boundary condition itself could be a deterministic function of time, which is particularly easy to include in a binomial model). But if both of the two values to be exchanged are showing material amounts of random variation, we may need to include both of them as random factors explicitly in the model (see Chapter 10). A choice between two randomly evolving values is often called an exchange option or a spread option, where a spread option involves paying some fixed exercise price in addition to making the actual exchange between two randomly evolving values.

> **A choice between two randomly evolving values is often called an exchange option or a spread option.**

When there are two or more random factors, we need to specify the variance σ^2_i of each factor, plus all their pair wise correlations ρ_{ij}. Hence the more general form of the Black–Scholes equation replaces the single second order term $S^2\sigma^2 \, (\partial^2 V/\partial S^2)$ with the summed term $S^2 \Sigma \rho_{ij}\sigma_i\sigma_j(\partial^2 V/\partial S_i\partial S_j)$ where the summation is over all i and j. Correlation ρ_{ij} between the random walks i and j might reflect the fact that certain joint movements of the two factors are more likely than others. For example, in Chapter 10 we see the effect of two random factors (interest rates and house prices) on the value of a mortgage. These two random walks may be negatively correlated because we are unlikely to see house prices rising when mortgage interest rates are rising.

We also need to include the first order terms for each asset i, and each of these may have its own convenience yield or dividend yield, which means that we have a first-order term $(r - \delta_i)(\partial V/\partial S_i)S_i$ for each i and we must sum all these (the boundary conditions for an exchange option are discussed below and also in Chapter 11).

The exchange option model of Margrabe (see Chapters 5 and 6) simplifies this problem by building a model of the ratio between the two randomly evolving values (simply the difference between their logarithms) and deriving its random walk as a single variable. This transformation of the variables also causes a transformation of the boundary conditions. Under various assumptions there is a range of analytical solutions – see Chapters 6, 9 and 11.

We can often vary the modelling of a real option problem by selecting how many random factors to include. For example, we may choose to define random variation as happening in price only, or in quantity only (see Chapter 3), or in price and quantity simultaneously (this produces a two-factor model, which could be used to describe a randomly evolving demand curve – compare Chapter 10 and Appendix 5) or in some ratio between prices and/or quantities (as in Margrabe's and other versions of the exchange model – see Chapters 5, 6, 9 and 11). Similarly, in a property development problem we might choose to model property rental prices separately from property construction costs (using a two-factor model), or we could specify a single variable as the randomly evolving ratio of the two (see Chapter 9). Any of these variations in the choice of which random factors to use will require variations in the boundary conditions, and it will have powerful implications for the economic meaning of the model.

Poisson jump processes

The risk of ruin (or the risk of any other unpredictable and large change in value, such as the total or partial loss of an asset) can be modelled as a Poisson jump process. If the probability of a discrete loss (or the probability of any other violent change) is a constant probability λ per unit of time, the risk over the interval dt is λdt. If so the option can be valued by normal methods, but we must use λ to modify the risk-free interest rate r in some way when evaluating the option. The exact modification that we need depends on what the rare event in question does to the value of S, but in the special case where the rare event wipes out S, we simply add λ to the risk-adjusted discount rate r, then evaluate the option in the normal way. Useful information is given by Dixit and Pindyck (1994). In more extreme modelling problems, if the risk event has complex consequences that are 'hard to model', one can always treat the state of the risk event (either on or off) as an additional random (two-state) variable.

The converse treatment would apply in the very rare event that the jump 'risk' is a small chance of a large and irreversible *upward* jump in the underlying asset's value (in effect participation in a lottery, perhaps to achieve some major technical breakthrough). Clearly, in this case we may need to subtract λ from the risk-free interest rate r before we apply standard methods to evaluate the option.

Path-dependent options (and many other complex problems) can in principle be modelled by defining an additional 'state variable'. This variable records the state of any variable which cannot be recovered simply by observing the present state of the random walk variable S. As an example, suppose that a real option model must allow for the likelihood of an engine breakdown, and suppose that in this model S represents the instantaneous (randomly evolving) rate at which we are rotating the engine. For some types of technology we might need to know the peak level that S has achieved in the past, for example if such over-revving will increase the risk of unforeseeable catastrophic failure. Alternatively, the main risk might simply be that the machine will wear out through sheer old age, and if so the integral of S over time (total number of revolutions during the engine's life) might be useful as an index of cumulative wear and tear. Neither of these variables (peak revolutions or integral of revolutions) is 'remembered by' or recoverable from the current value of S, so it is potentially useful to add either variable to the model as an additional state variable. An intermediate form of model might integrate the level of S only over some 'forbidden' range (e.g. total number of revs performed at more than 6,000 revs per minute) and many variations can be devised.

Useful approaches to the mathematics of such state space models are given in Wilmott, Howison and Dewynne (1995) under the topic of 'path dependent' options. Monte Carlo methods (simulation of a large number of random outcomes) can also be used to value such options (see Appendix 5).

Mean reverting random walks

The values of some economic variables are believed to follow a 'mean reverting' random walk, which means that in addition to pure random walk variation there is a drift towards some long-term mean (which may itself be evolving). The economic reason for this is that although prices follow random shocks in the short term, very high prices will eventually call forth additional supply, thus eliminating the high prices, and conversely very low prices may trigger exits from the industry. The equivalent term in an additive random walk model would be

$$dX = \eta(\underline{X} - X)dt + \sigma dz$$

where $\underline{X}$ is the mean of X. Here the random drift of X is towards its central or mean value $\underline{X}$, since if X is above $\underline{X}$ the term $\underline{X} - X$ will be negative, and vice versa. The coefficient η measures the speed of this drift (zero if there is no reversion towards the mean). Notice that mean reversion gets stronger as X wanders away from $\underline{X}$, but the slope of this mean reversion, which is $\eta(\underline{X} - X)dt$, tends to revert to zero as X approaches $\underline{X}$. This is unlike the effect of a gravitational attraction between X and $\underline{X}$ which would grow with proximity. This is called an Ornstein Uhlenbeck process. We could use the resulting increment dX either as an addition to S or as a multiplier for S, as in the standard geometric Brownian motion random walk (see Chapter 10 and Appendix 3).

Setting boundary conditions

Mathematically speaking, most of the features that make one option different from another actually take the form of differences between boundary conditions rather than of differences in the B-S equation itself. For example, the major identifying feature of most options is the payoff function on expiry $P(S,T)$ which is, mathematically speaking, the terminal boundary condition. This sets out how the option's value will be defined (as a function of S) at the option's moment of expiry $t = T$.

The most fundamental (upward sloping) payoff function is that of the basic call seen in Chapter 2. The downward slope (as S rises) of the basic put on S is shown in Figure 4.1. The payoff function for a factory site which can be either invested in at a cost of 100 or disposed of for scrap at a known fixed price of 20 is shown in Figure 4.2 (see also Chapter 7). We saw examples in Chapter 3 of the payoff function for a multiple option, where there was only one random factor Q, but two or more modes of exercise.

The latter and many other real options problems give rise to payoff functions which have more than two line segments. For example, there are payoff functions which have a flat maximum, resembling an 'S curve', and others which have a sharp peak at one particular value of S. Many such unusual payoff functions exist, or can be synthesized, in financial markets. They can often be

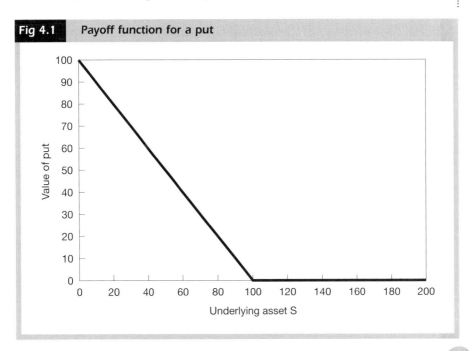

Fig 4.1 Payoff function for a put

(x-axis: Underlying asset S; y-axis: Value of put)

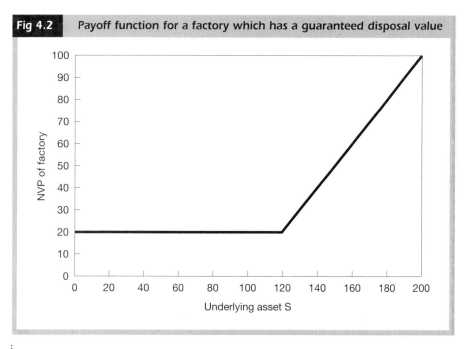

Fig 4.2 Payoff function for a factory which has a guaranteed disposal value

valued analytically by combining the values of various plain vanilla options which have appropriately chosen exercise prices, and many standard solutions exist in the finance literature (see, for example, Wilmott, 1998).

One interesting class of asset is a wasting asset (e.g. a lease, a mortgage or a physical asset). Its terminal boundary condition (or payoff function) at expiry time T is uniformly zero, because at that time the asset legally or physically wears out. An example is in Chapter 7.

In a plain vanilla call (or put) option to buy (or sell) one unit of S, the random factor is identical to the underlying asset S. This means that the slope of any segment of the payoff function, as a function of S, is always either 0 degrees (no payoff) or 45 degrees (payoff varying directly with S). In more general cases, as for example where an option has multiple modes of exercise, and/or where the random factor which drives value is not identical to the asset being bought, no segment need exactly be at 0 degrees, or at 45 degrees, or even straight (curved payoffs can arise if, for example, the random factor is an interest rate, or a gross national product level). An exchange option will have at least two intersecting payoff functions, one for each individual asset, and in general cases both can be curved. This can pose problems for analytical methods, but numerical methods can handle such cases without difficulty.

Other boundary conditions are needed in addition to the terminal condition. The simplest are fixed boundary conditions. For example, a call option has a fixed lower boundary condition at all times t if S ever takes the value S = 0, which means that the option's value is V(0,t) = 0 for all t. A logarithmic (or geometric) random walk process which begins above zero can only ever change by a non-zero multiplication, so it can never reach the 'trapping value' at which S and V remain permanently at zero, but a Poisson jump process can. Conversely, a put option may have a lower fixed boundary V = 0 at S = infinity.

The upper fixed boundary condition of a European call option on a dividend-paying stock is given in Appendix 3. The call's value C(S,t) tends to $Se^{-\delta(T-t)}$ as S tends to infinity, since in the limit owning the option becomes equivalent, in capital value terms, to owning the present capital value of the asset itself, but without enjoying the dividend income of the asset over the remaining time to expiry T – t.

Where there are more random factors than one, each factor may have its own fixed boundaries, and these boundaries show how the option's value will behave when that factor takes its most extreme values. Careful thought may be needed to define suitable conditions at the meeting points of two or more such boundaries (i.e. jointly extreme values of two or more random factors).

In certain problems some of the fixed boundary conditions may not be constants but may themselves be functions of time (e.g. the fixed upper boundary at infinity for a European option on a dividend paying share, as above). For a path-dependent option, the payoff function itself is randomly evolving over time, and Wilmott, Howison and Dewynne (1995) suggest ways of dealing with this.

The most subtle boundary conditions are those that hold along a 'free boundary'. This defines the market conditions under which the exercised and unexercised states of an option meet, and along which it becomes optimal for the option holder to move from one state to the other (e.g. by exercising the option). The 'value matching' and 'smooth pasting' conditions must hold at all points where the exercised and unexercised states of the option meet, as explained in Chapter 2 and Appendix 3.

As equivalent conditions, option values must be continuous and must have continuous differentials with respect to S everywhere 'except on fixed boundaries'. Everywhere else, the Black–Scholes PDE applies. The exceptional minority of points to which the Black–Scholes PDE does not apply includes the points along any fixed boundary – for example, the Black–Scholes equation does not in general hold along an option's terminal boundary or payoff function which is not usually a solution of the Black–Scholes equation. However, the Black–Scholes equation must apply at all other points, including all points along 'free boundaries'. (In fact this is one intuitive interpretation of the term 'free': such a boundary exists through the free operation of the Black–Scholes equation itself, which operates undisturbed at all points along the free boundary; the only 'constraint' on the Black–Scholes equation in such a case is that it is forced to create some such boundary at all – but at a position decided by the equation's own free operation.)

A further type of boundary arises if fixed cash payments arise at known (or computable) moments in the life of the derivative asset. For example, fixed coupon payments may be made during the life of a bond, or rent payments during the life of a lease.

The instants of these payments can be treated as 'fixed boundaries' in time, even if the actual timing of a payment, and even the size of the payment, are both randomly set. The Black–Scholes equation itself does not hold instantaneously at such boundaries in time, but so-called 'jump continuity conditions' must be set so that the holder of a derivative cannot make a risk-free profit at the instant of such a payment (i.e. the value of the derivative must fall at the instant when the holder of the derivative receives a payment, so that the value of the derivative just after the holder has received/paid a payment must equal the value of the derivative just before the payment, minus/plus the value of the payment itself). The Black–Scholes equation holds on either side of these points of discontinuity, and additional continuity conditions may apply, which constrain the behaviour of the Black–Scholes solution as it approaches and departs from the jump (see Chapter 10 and Wilmott, Howison and Dewynne, 1995).

Compound options

As mentioned in Chapter 3, if the payoff of one option is the right to acquire some later option (maybe after paying some entry cost), the opening value of the later option must be used as the payoff function of the first (more strictly, the payoff of the first option is the maximum of zero, and the opening value of the second option, less the payment needed to access the second option). As usual the valuation proceeds from the last possible moment of the last option's life, moving earlier in calendar time until we reach the earliest required moment in the life of the earliest option in the chain.

Solving a problem in continuous time (analytical and finite difference methods)

Having formulated a problem in continuous time (by setting a partial differential equation and its boundary conditions), the problem of solving it numerically is discussed in Appendix 4. Analytical methods typically exist only for European options on non-dividend-paying assets, and for perpetual American options. Otherwise we normally have to use numerical methods or approximation formulae.

To implement numerical methods for solving the Black–Scholes diffusion equation (with given boundary conditions) essentially we must linearize the Black–Scholes diffusion equation using Taylor's theorem (this means approximating the curved true problem as a linear problem). We then evaluate this linear equation over short discrete increments of asset price and time. It is often recommended in the literature to transform the variables (and hence to transform the equation and the boundary conditions) before solving the equation.

Transformation of variables can sometimes make a numerical (or analytical) solution more stable (and/or more tractable) but at the cost of requiring a change to the boundary conditions. Alternatively, at the cost of doing a little more algebra if we apply Taylor's theorem to the untransformed Black–Scholes equation, it is often possible to avoid a lot of housekeeping effort on transforming the variables, the equation and the boundary conditions. The calculations for the untransformed Black–Scholes equation may be slightly slower (not usually an issue in real option applications) and also less numerically stable under extreme values of the inputs (e.g. large S and large $\tau = T - t$, since the Black–Scholes equation contains terms in S^2), but the untransformed equation retains the original, intuitively meaningful boundary conditions, which can be far easier to interpret and to 'reality check'.

Given a suitable linearization of the Black–Scholes equation (whether or not we have transformed the variables, the equation and the boundary conditions before linearizing) the solution method begins from the solution at time T as given by the terminal boundary condition (based on the payoff function P(S,T) at expiry time T), and we then operate the linearized diffusion equation as a difference equation, with the direction of time reversed, so as to derive the solutions for progressively earlier times. The main solution methods are discussed in Appendix 4. Explicit finite difference is usually the fastest and easiest method and it is often adequate (although stability considerations must be watched – see Appendix 4).

Binomial trees (see the next section) are built up from the outset as models in discrete time. This is especially convenient when the problem data are specified in a discrete form (e.g. annual payments). It avoids the loop of taking the discrete data, devising a continuous model of them (in a form of the Black–Scholes equation, with appropriate boundary conditions), and then returning to the discrete form by linearizing the Black–Scholes equation using Taylor's theorem and evaluating it over finite increments of t and S. The trinomial tree (in which there is an explicit probability of no change, as well as of an upward change and a downward change) can be formally identical to linearized Black–Scholes models.

Binomial trees are built up from the outset as models in discrete time.

There is some debate in the literature over which of the various numerical solution methods is best, under which circumstances. Under certain circumstances almost every numerical method has been accused of inaccuracy or instability. For example, errors have sometimes been detected in the main valuation V and/or in the associated estimates of the so-called 'greeks'. In Appendix 3 we explain the basic 'greek' which is delta (Δ) in delta hedging (delta defines the way in which the option's value responds to small changes in S). Other greeks include rho (ρ) (the way in which option value responds to small changes in the risk-free interest rate) and vega (the way in which option value responds to small changes in volatility). Such sensitivities should always be explored when evaluating real options by numerical methods.

In financial markets it is common to hedge not only by using Δ (so as to protect against changes in S). If the investor wishes also to protect against incorrect estimates of the values (or against actual changes in the values) of the assumed parameters such as the risk-free interest rate r and/or of the volatility σ, the investor can also hedge against changes in these parameters using the other greeks: rho and vega (see any standard financial option text).

Certain advanced valuation models assume a stochastic (random walk) behaviour for volatility and/or for interest rates. Such models express these variables as explicit random factors, which are continuously evolving within the model, rather than as fixed parameters, which will only occasionally be disturbed from outside the model. Such topics have been little discussed for real options.

Formulating a problem in discrete time (binomial)

The simplest case is when there are just two possible future states (binomial) at one time step into the future, and we wish to hedge away the resulting uncertainty so that we will get an identical payment under either future state.

Notice that if we do succeed in hedging, so that we get identical payments under each of the two possible states, we will be indifferent towards the actual probabilities of the two states. We only need to know what these possible future states are. The same will be true of the mathematical model for hedging a binomial risk: the actual probability of either future state will not enter the model.

To use a concrete example, suppose we are considering buying a factory to produce a new kind of surgical dressing, for which we already have the know-how (so we have a real call option to invest). The currently expected present value of all the future net operating revenues (sales minus operating cost) from operating such a factory, assuming we already own the factory, is $100 million, but it would cost us $120 million to set up the factory, and therefore the investment is not justified at present (time t = 0). However, the government is testing our product for possible adaptation by the military, with a decision expected at time t = 1.

How will the military decision, one period ahead, affect the value at that time of our call option to invest? If the military reject our product at time t = 1, some of our existing customers will lose faith in us, and the present value of the factory's future revenues is expected to fall from its present $100 million to $66.7 million. This clearly would not justify spending $120 million to build the factory, so in this particular 'possible' future state, our technical ability to build for $120 million will have no value. However, if the military do accept our product, they will buy from us and that will attract extra customers, so the present value of the factory's revenues will rise to $150 million. In this possible future we would choose to secure these revenues by investing $120 million to build the factory, making a net present value (wealth) gain of 150 − 120 = $30 million. News of these two decisions (by the military and by ourselves) would therefore raise the market value of our company by $30 million, if and when they occur.

To sum up the possibilities, defining S_t as the value of the underlying asset (the operating revenues) at time t, and E as the exercise price of $120 million.

$t = 0$	$t = 1$	
Market value	Market value	Payoff from option
S_0	S_1	$max(0, S_1 - E)$
	150	30
90		
	67	0

Notice that S_1 will be either uS_0 or $(i/u)S_0$, where u is 1.5, but we do not need to know which of these two possible jumps (if either) is more likely.

Suppose we now, at time t = 0, receive an offer from a competitor to buy the technology needed to build a factory. What value should we place at time t = 0 on our option to build a factory at time t = 1 for $120 million, assuming that we have no idea how likely the military are to accept our product at that time?

A possible tactic is to hedge away all the uncertainty about the military's decision. One method for this is to 'sell ahead' an asset which is also affected by the military's decision, selling this asset at some version of today's price (t = 0), but waiting until after the military's decision before we deliver against the sale, which we will do by buying the required asset in the market at its future new market price (at time t = 1).

That way, if the military's decision is favourable, the asset S will rise in price to 150, and we will gain from our option to invest, since we will invest 120 to build the factory, and will gain a positive NPV of 30, but we will also lose on our forward sale of S because we will have sold at today's price (100) but will have to cover the sale by buying at the new higher price of 150.

We can implement a forward deal of this type for S in several ways (e.g. sell for cash now, then bank the cash until time 1, or take no cash now but take a contractually fixed payment of $e^{r\delta t}S_0$ at time 1 where δt is the length of the time increment in years, and r is the annual interest rate and S_0 is the price of S at time 0). None of the possible ways of implementing the forward deal requires us to spend any cash at time 0, and none of them can give us any instantaneous increase or decrease in our wealth at time 0, which is the moment when we make the forward deal. In market theory, the value of a forward sale at the instant of its creation must always be zero, and the same must be true of a short sale.

In symbols, in whatever way we implement the forward deal, the cash proceeds at time 1 from one unit of S sold forward at time 0 will be $e^{r\delta t}S_0$. Hence if the military decision at time 1 turns out favourable, our 'profit' on the forward sale will be the forward sale proceeds at time 1 (namely $e^{r\delta t}S_0$) less the cost of meeting the forward sale in the market at time 1, which is uS_0 so our net loss will be $uS_0 - e^{r\delta t}S_0$.

Hence under state $S_1 = uS_0$ we would lose money from the forward sale (since $uS_0 > e^{r\delta t}S_0$ in our example). More generally, it will not always be possible to define the higher and lower future states of S_t as inverse multiples of S_0. In that case we can replace uS_0 by U and replace $(1/u)S_0$ by the more general expression D where $U > S_0 > D$. Clearly under state $S_1 = U$ we will at the same time gain a payoff of U – E from exercising our option.

Conversely, if the military's decision at time 1 is adverse, our ability to invest in the factory will be unused and worthless, but we will make money from having sold S forward at today's price of 100, when its future price will be 67. Our profit at time 1 on one unit of S sold forward, if the down state D of S occurs, will be $e^{r\delta t}S_0$ – D. Hence under state D our option would be worth zero, but we would make a gain on our forward sale.

Clearly the direction of the military decision has opposite effects on the value of our option and on the value of our forward sale. There exists a certain number h of units of S which we can sell forward, so that these opposite effects cancel each other. If we hold a portfolio at time 0 containing the option plus a forward sale of h units of S, we will be indifferent at time 1 between a favourable and an unfavourable decision by the military, since our payout at time 1 will be the same under both cases, and therefore risk free.

If such a hedge is possible, the future payment at time 1 will be fixed, and the value of our option now, at time zero, is simply the value of the right to collect that fixed and risk-free future payout at time 1, discounted back to the present day at the risk-free rate.

To value the option now we can first work out the hedging ratio h, and then work out what the fixed final payout will be. Let us first find h. If we define the upper possible state of S (150) as U and we define the down value of S (66.7) as D, then we require

$$\text{portfolio value if state U occurs} \quad = \quad \text{portfolio value if state D occurs} \quad (1)$$

$$\text{option + forward sale value if U} \quad = \quad \text{option + forward sale value if D} \quad (2)$$

Rewriting this in symbols:

$$\max(0, U - E) + h(e^{r\delta t}S - U) \quad = \quad \max(0, D - E) + h(e^{r\delta t}S - D) \quad (3)$$

The solution for h is straightforward. We give it in some detail here because it is not customary in the literature to include the value of the cash asset of the forward sale, nor to derive the option's value in the light of it, as we do here. As Howell (2000) points out, it has also been customary to ignore the cash proceeds of the forward (or short) sale when valuing the delta hedged portfolio in the continuous case. This omission does not prevent the correct derivation of the valuation equation (in either the discrete or the continuous case), but it can lead to pedagogical and conceptual confusion in interpreting the valuation equation and the delta hedged portfolio.

It is convenient first to reverse the signs inside the bracket in the second expression on the LHS

$$\max(0, U - E) - h(-e^{r\delta t}S + U) \quad = \quad \max(0, D - E) + h(e^{r\delta t}S - D) \quad (4)$$

collecting terms in h, the terms in $he^{r\delta t}S$ cancel each other (which is why the traditional derivation, which ignores these terms, leads to the correct valuation equation) and we get

$$h(U - D) \quad = \quad \max(0, U - E) - \max(0, D - E) \quad (5)$$

so that

$$h \quad = \quad \frac{\max(0, U - E) - \max(0, D - E)}{(U - D)} \quad (6)$$

or returning to words:

$$h \quad = \quad \frac{\text{difference between possible option payoffs}}{\text{difference between possible asset values}} \quad (7)$$

Notice that h for the binomial problem above is identical in form to the delta hedging ratio which we use in the continuous case (Appendix 3). In fact, we can make the binomial case formally identical to the continuous case by letting the time increment δt tend towards zero, for a suitably specified binomial model, as we discuss below. Notice that the above hedging equation also applies to the risky asset itself (for which the hedge ratio is of course 1), and it also applies formally to the risk-free asset (whose value is not varied by the unforeseeable change of S at all, so that the formally required hedging sale is zero units of S).

Knowing h we can work out the closing value of the hedged payoff at time 1 by substituting the value of h, as given in (6), into either the RHS or the LHS of equation (3) (repeated):

$$\max(0, U - E) + h(e^{r\delta t}S - U) \quad = \quad \max(0, D - E) + h(e^{r\delta t}S - D)$$

Since these payoffs are identical, the time 1 outcome is risk free, and the value of the option now (at time zero) is simply its time 1 value discounted over one time period. For example, if we substitute for h in the LHS to compute the value V_0 of the option at time t:

$$V_0 = e^{-r\delta t} [\max(0, U - E) + h(e^{r\delta t}S_0 - U)] \tag{8}$$

In order to generalize the type of binomial model used here to the continuous case (see Appendix 4 for alternative methods) it will be convenient to express the two possible states of S_1 (up and down jump) in the more specialized forms $S_0 u$ and $(1/u)S_0$ and let $d = 1/u$. It will also be convenient to generalize the two possible payoffs of the option after these jumps, in order to be able to represent (for example) the payoffs of puts as well as calls, and to do this we use the more general terms f_u and f_d to represent the option's payoffs after up and down movements of S respectively (we are here using the notation of Dixit and Pindyck).

We therefore substitute $S_0 = S$; $U = uS$; $D = (1/u) S = dS$; $f_u = \max (0, U - E)$; $f_d = \max (0, D = E)$ and this gives $h = (f_u - f_d) / S(u - d)$. Making these substitutions in the LHS of (3) gives the hedged value at time 1 as:

$$f_u + \frac{f_u - f_d}{S(u - d)} (e^{r\delta t} - u)S \tag{9}$$

Cancelling S gives:

$$f_u + \frac{(f_u - f_d)(e^{r\delta t} - u)}{(u - d)} \tag{10}$$

and using a common denominator gives:

$$\frac{f_u (u - d) + (f_u - f_d)(e^{r\delta t} - u)}{(u - d)} \tag{11}$$

Multiplying out and grouping like terms gives:

$$f_u \frac{(e^{r\delta t} - d)}{(u - d)} + f_d \frac{(u - e^{r\delta t})}{(u - d)} \tag{12}$$

But we note that:

$$1 - \frac{(e^{r\delta t} - d)}{(u - d)} = \frac{u - e^{r\delta t}}{(u - d)}$$

Hence if we define w as:

$$w = \frac{(e^{r\delta t} - d)}{(u - d)} \tag{13}$$

then the fixed future value of the hedged portfolio at time 1 is $wf_u + (1 - w) f_d$ and its present value at time 0 is:

$$V_0 = e^{-r\delta t}(w f_u + (1 - w) f_d). \tag{14}$$

Equations (13) and (14) have long been known in the literature, but it has not previously been realized that the bracketed term on the RHS of (14) actually defines the risk-free closing value of the portfolio that has been delta hedged (and which a risk-averse option holder can choose to create).

Because the hedged and discounted payout (14) is risk free, the resulting option value (14) is independent of the objective probabilities of the states $U = S_0 u$ and $D = (1/u)S_0$. (Indeed the reader will have noticed that during our derivation of (13) and (14) we did not use, or even define, the probabilities that states U and D would arise.) We will argue that because the literature has been unaware of this simple meaning of (14) (believing instead that the delta-hedged portfolio is a negative quantity – see the example in Dixit and Pindyck, 1994, starting on page 30), it has attempted to interpret (14) in other ways, and these can be pedagogically and even theoretically unhelpful. (In plainer terms, we suggest that the literature's attempt to explain w and $(1 - w)$ as being 'risk-neutral probabilities' is at best unnecessary, and at worst difficult to understand or even misleading.)

Before attempting to set out the literature's more complex interpretation of (14) it will be useful to show an example of how this arithmetic actually works for a binomial tree with two successive branchings (four end states). Consider the tree below for the possible values of an underlying asset S, where after each node the possible outcomes U and D (with unspecified probabilities) will multiply or divide S by 1.5.

S_0	S_1	S_2
		225
	150	
100		100
	67	
		44

We will assume a risk-free interest rate of 10 per cent and that u = 1.5 and d = 1/u = 1/1.5, so by (13) w = $(e^{r\delta t} - d)/(u - d)$ = (1.1 − 0.667)/(1.5 − 0.667) = 0.520.

Next, we will define a call option to invest in S, expiring at time 2, with exercise price E = 80. We add in bold the final payoffs for each outcome at time 2. These are the option's possible values at time 2, namely V_2 = V(S,t) = V(S,2) = max(S_2 − E, 0):

S_0	S_1	S_2
		225
		145
	150	
100		100
		20
	67	
		44
		0

Now, for each pair of adjacent nodes at time 2, as just defined, we define the upper outcome payoff as f_u and the lower outcome payoff as f_d. We apply the weightings w and (1 − w) to these possible outcomes, to give a hedged (fixed and risk-free) outcome to whichever single node at time 1 leads to these two nodes at time 2. We discount the hedged (fixed) outcome of these two final nodes at the risk-free rate as in (14). This gives the value of the previous node (at time 1) as $e^{-r\delta t}(wf_u + (1 - w)f_d)$. Repeating this for the other time 1 node, we have both of the option's possible values at time 1. Reiterating this process to calculate the option's value at time 0, we apply the risk-eliminating weightings w and (1 − w) to the two possible outcomes (just calculated) at time 1, to give the hedged and risk-free value at time 1. This discounts to 40.65 at time 0 as below.

		225
		145
	150	
	77.3	
100		100
40.65		**20**
	66.7	
	9.45	
		44
		0

The above set of valuations is standard in the literature, but what has not been recognized in most of the literature is that these values given by (14) are identical to the risk-free values which result from delta hedging the future values of the option at each time step. This is proved formally by our derivation of (14) from (8), but it is worth exemplifying it arithmetically, and we will do so first for a single time step, and then for two successive steps. Consider the time 1 node at which S = 150. The hedge ratio h is given by (6) as 125/125 = 1.

For this hedge ratio, we take the option value of 77.3 as calculated by (14) and use (3) to show the effect of delta hedging this (3) (repeated):

$$\max(0, U - E) + h(e^{r\delta t}S - U) \qquad = \qquad \max(0, D - E) + h(e^{r\delta t}S - D)$$

The LHS (value of hedged portfolio at time 2, when S_2 is 225) = is 145 + $(1.1 \times 150 - 225)$ = 85. The RHS (value of hedged portfolio when S_2 is 100) = 20 + (1.1*150 - 100) = 85. Hence the value is risk-free, as it was constructed to be. This value discounts at the risk-free rate (factor 1/1.1) to give the option its value (when S = 150 at time 1) of 77.3 as shown. Hence the value calculated by (14) can indeed be delta hedged, and the risk-free payment at the end of the step is indeed $wf_u + (1 - w)f_d$.

We can, if necessary, repeat this process for the preceding time step, confirming that the option's value at time 0 of 40.65 can be delta hedged in the same way.

It is perhaps more interesting to illustrate the effect of extended delta hedging over several time steps, since this generates a more complex cumulative portfolio, due to the reinvestment of the profits, or compounding of the losses, on intermediate hedging deals. Consider a portfolio which initially consists at time 0 only of the option itself, whose value V_0 = 40.65. If it is possible to delta hedge this value, without risk and without additional equity investment, over both of the successive time steps, the closing value of the total portfolio at time 2 should identically be the option's opening value of 40.65, as compounded forward at the risk-free rate over two periods, namely $40.65 \times 1.1^2 = 49.2$. This should be true for all of the four possible paths through the tree.

We will exemplify the calculation for one of the four possible paths, namely the path which consists of two successive downward movements of S. We will replicate each step of this path, using the explicit hedge calculation (3) on the option values that were derived above from the equivalent (and much simpler) process of weighting the outcomes by w and (1 − w) before discounting.

The hedge ratio at time 0 by (6) is h = (77.3 − 9.45)/(150 − 66.7) = 0.814. We sell h = 0.814 units of S forward, which at time 0 costs us no cash (and makes no realized profit or loss) so the equity value of the hedged portfolio at time 0 is simply the option's value V_0 = 40.65.

Given a downward movement of S at time 1, the option's value will fall to 9.45, but there is a gain to be made on the forward sale of h = 0.814 units of S (which was struck at time 0 at a price of 100). The gain on this sale, if S falls from 100 at time 0 to 66.7 at time 1, is $0.814*(1.1 \times 100 - 66.7) = 35.24$.

Hence the value of the hedged portfolio at time 1, if a down movement of S occurs, consists of the option, now valued at 9.45, plus the profit on the forward sale. These total to 9.45 + 35.24 = 44.69. This (hedged) value at time 1 does of course represent risk-free growth on the option's value of 40.65 at time 0 (since that was how the option's value was defined).

Now consider the subsequent time step from time 1 to time 2, in this case where there has already been a downward jump of S at time 1. The new opening portfolio at time 1 consists of the option itself, which is now worth 9.45, plus the cash proceeds of 35.24, which were realized on the hedging sale which we just closed out at time 1. We invest the cash at the risk-free rate (this will yield 38.8 at time 2) and we make a fresh forward sale to hedge the time 1 value of the option, a deal which costs us no cash immediately at time 1. The hedge ratio h required is (20/(100 – 44) = 0.357. What are the possible outcomes of this time 1 portfolio, one step later at time 2?

Clearly both an upward jump and a downward jump by S at time 2 should yield an identical hedged value for the total portfolio at time 2, being risk-free growth in the option's value from time 0. We will exemplify this for the case where there is a second downward jump in S. The portfolio's value at time 2, after a second downward jump of S, is the closing value of the option in the case where S = 44, plus the profit made at time 2 from closing the forward sale made at time 1 (after which S has fallen from 66.7 to 44) plus the compounded profits retained from the earlier hedging sale that was made at time 0 and closed at time 1.

The final value of the option itself is zero since it expires unexercised. The profit made at time 2 on the forward sale of h = 0.357 units of S made at time 1 is $0.357*(1.1*66.7 - 44.4) = 10.34$. The profits of the time 0 hedging sale which we closed at time 1 are 38.8 when compounded to time 2. Therefore the final time 2 value of the continuously hedged portfolio is 0 + 10.34 + 38.8 = 49.1. This sum is equal to a risk-free compounding over two periods of the option's initial value of 40.65 at time 0.

Identical portfolio values at time 1 and time 2 (subject to numerical accuracy) will arise along every one of the four possible paths through the network (recall that the actual probabilities of any of these four possible paths are irrelevant, since they have no effect on the hedged payoffs). Paths which begin with an upward jump of S give identical hedged values at times 1 and 2 to the paths which begin with a downward jump of S, but the portfolio's value is then made up in a different way. The reason is that after an upward jump of S the option has made a profit (gain in value) but this profit has not yet been realized in cash because the option has not yet been exercised. However, a cash loss (debt) has been incurred on the forward sale that was struck at time 0.

There is no cash available yet to meet this debt, since the portfolio began at time 0 simply as an option, plus zero cash, plus a forward sale, which was worth at that time zero. Therefore this cash debt must be borrowed, and compounded forward at the risk-free rate until cash becomes available to pay some or all of it. Cash will become available in only two cases: either some later downward movement of S produces a cash profit on a hedging sale, or (if there never is a downward movement of S) cash proceeds are finally received from the exercise of the option at a profit, to offset the cumulative and compounded losses on hedging sales.

How should we interpret w and $(1 - w)$? They are *weightings* on the two *possible outcomes* which define a *risk-free* outcome value, irrespective of the probabilities of the two outcomes, and irrespective of the degree of (positive) risk aversion of the investor. Notice that investors must have some degree of risk aversion, or they would not be interested in hedging at all. However, once the option has been hedged, its value is identical for every risk-averse investor, whatever their exact degree of risk aversion, and irrespective of the actual probabilities of the outcomes (hence all investors are free to disagree both about the probabilities and about the 'correct' degree of risk aversion).

It may seem startlingly simple that w and $(1 - w)$, the risk-eliminating weightings, are linear multipliers which sum to unity. This fact might seem to call for a deeper explanation (an explanation which the literature has sought in terms of probability). However, this fact is predicted by basic economic arguments, which have nothing to do with the probabilities of the two outcomes.

The initial arguments are that the option's hedged value must include a linear weighting of its two possible outcomes, and that there can be no constant term within this weighting. The second of these arguments must be true because an investment of zero in the option must produce a return of zero (since then there can be zero probability of either outcome payoff) and this means there must be no constant term. Also, if any finite investment in the option is multiplied by k it must produce k times the return. These arguments ensure that the hedged value is a linear weighting of the two possible payoffs, and without a constant term, but they do not ensure that the two weightings sum to unity.

An argument that the two weightings must sum to unity can be based on the limiting case where the two possible payoff outcomes f_u and f_d converge towards a single value (i.e. the option itself is tending towards being a risk-free asset). We need to treat the risk-free asset as a limiting case, because h is formally zero (and economically correctly so) in the case of a pure risk-free asset, for which $f_u = f_d$. Since the hedged 'risk-free' value is in general a linear weighting of the two possible payoffs, these two weightings must tend to sum to unity as the two payoffs

f_u and f_d tend to coincide. Otherwise the weighted sum of two values, as these two values coincide to an identical value, cannot tend to the identical value itself. But as given by (13), w and $(1 - w)$ are identical for all pairs of payoffs f_u and f_d, since w is a function of u and d but not of f_u and f_d. Hence w and $(1 - w)$ sum to unity for all possible values of f_u and f_d and irrespective of their relative probabilities.

The fact that the weightings w and $(1 - w)$ are constant across all the nodes in the network, because u and d are also constant across all nodes, is true by construction, and alternatives to this assumption can be used (see Appendix 4 and Wilmott, Howison and Dewynne (1995)).

The literature has long known that the value of the option is $e^{-r\delta t}(wf_u + (1 - w) f_d)$ as in (14). However, the literature has not previously recognized that this value is identically the discounted value of the hedged portfolio itself. As Howell (2000) has pointed out for the continuous case, the literature's consistent error has been to ignore the cash proceeds of the uncovered forward or short sale when valuing the hedged portfolio. The omission of this positive term makes the final value of the hedged portfolio seem to be a negative quantity, and neither the sign nor the magnitude of this quantity are visibly related to the option's value, which is the positive quantity $wf_u + (1 - w) f_d$.

It is probably because the literature has lacked an accurate economic intuition for the meaning of the weightings w and $(1 - w)$ that it has pursued alternative economic intuitions by attempting to define them as probabilities, which is unnecessary, and potentially confusing to the beginner.

To repeat our own argument so far, w and $(1 - w)$ are weightings on two possible outcomes, and they define a fixed outcome value which can be guaranteed by delta hedging whatever the actual probabilities of the two outcomes. These weightings will be used by all risk-averse investors, and since they eliminate risk, they are independent of the individual investors' varying attitudes to risk. The fact that these two weightings sum to unity is predicted by fundamental economic arguments which have nothing to do with probability.

In contrast, the literature has found it 'natural' to try to treat w and $(1 - w)$ as probabilities, on the simple grounds that they sum to unity (which, as we have seen, they do for reasons completely unrelated to probability, and for reasons which apply to investors of any positive degree of risk aversion).

The two alternative interpretations of w and $(1 - w)$ (namely our interpretation as weightings that predict risk-free value, or the conventional interpretation as 'risk-neutral probabilities') are easy to identify from a diagram of a binomial tree with six nodes. Essentially we must treat the network below as being a generalization either of the 'left-facing arrow' BAC (the diagram consists of three such arrows) or the 'right-facing arrow' BEC (the diagram contains one complete version of this arrow, plus three incomplete versions).

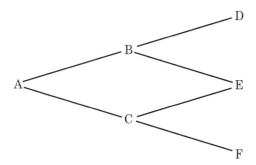

We know that the value of each node is defined as $wf_u + (1 - w)f_d$, and this is true even within an isolated binomial branching (e.g. the nodes ABC). Although value A is determined from the values B and C to its right, it is an event (hedging) at the left (earlier time) node A which makes this possible. However, in trees as large as ABCDEF and larger, there is also at least one node such as E where we can note that the value at node E has 'been passed' on to influence values at two different earlier nodes, namely B and C, and that these weightings sum to unity.

This is formally equivalent to a diffusion process for the value at E, and since the two previous nodes B and C are mutually exclusive events, whose likelihood of preceding E is set by chance, and whose value is not fully defined by the three values observed at E, B and C, we must interpret this diffusion process as risky and probabilistic. Formally, the probabilities of the assumed diffusion process are the weightings w for the downward diffusion EC and $(1 - w)$ for the upward diffusion EB. The literature has sought to explain w and $(1 - w)$ as probabilities in a risky diffusion process, in which the value C is determined randomly by the values diffusing from E and F, even though the resulting 'expected value' must be valued as if it were risk-free (because the value at C is in fact a hedged and riskless value).

Clearly if we do try to interpret w and $(1 - w)$ as probabilities, the only investors who would treat probabilistic outcomes as though they were risk-free would be risk-neutral investors. But the risk-eliminating weightings w and $(1 - w)$ were defined without any use of probabilities, and they are valid under every conceivable set of observed probabilities. Hence it is only by rare coincidence that w and $(1 - w)$ will coincide with the observed probabilities of the high and low asset outcomes Su and Sd in any situation.

There is a catch here: risk-neutral investors would be happy to use the observed probabilities for valuation (they never choose to hedge). Therefore if we want to interpret w and $(1 - w)$ as probabilities, we have to cheat in two ways: firstly, we have to assume risk-neutral investors, even though none exist, and even though, if we assume away risk aversion, we assume away half of the subject matter of finance.[1] Secondly, we have to assume the valuation answer that we require (i.e. the one given by the risk-eliminating weightings of (14)) and then we must invent a set of imaginary probabilities, which coincide with the risk-eliminating weightings of the possibilities but which therefore do not agree with the probabilities actually observed.

The literature takes care to make clear that if we do interpret w and $(1 - w)$ as 'risk-neutral probabilities' these 'probabilities' will in general have no relationship to the actual probabilities of upward and downward movements of S in the problem at hand. They are simply the probabilities that f_u and f_d 'would have to have' if we want risk-neutral investors (who do not hedge, but act on probabilities) to reach the same valuations as risk-averse investors (who do hedge, but ignore probabilities). This in turn requires us to set invented 'probabilities' on the possible multipliers u and d for S (which we need in order to produce the required probabilities w and $(1 - w)$ for the possible values f_u and f_d of the option). These invented probabilities for the multipliers u and d for S must in turn be completely unrelated to the observed probabilities of the multipliers u and d for S in the real world. (These observed probabilities do exist, even though hedging investors can ignore them, but we must have our risk-neutral investors ignore them also if they are to reach the same values as hedging investors, despite the fact that in practice risk-neutral investors would always act on observed probabilities.)

The simple conclusion of all this is that it might be better to replace the term 'risk-neutral probabilities' with 'risk-eliminating weightings', and to stop talking about risk-neutral investors or risk-neutral probabilities, since despite their great elegance, the explanations in terms of risk-neutral investors do not justify the values we give to options and tell us nothing about the risk-averse investors we actually live among, whose behaviour defines option values.

> **The explanations in terms of risk-neutral investors do not justify the values we give to options.**

However, the term 'risk-neutral probabilities' is well entrenched. When studying a specific application, therefore, users must simply look up or calculate the so-called 'risk-neutral probabilities' and use them to weight the two possible option payoffs from each node, before discounting as in (14) – see the examples in Chapter 7 and Appendix 4. Beyond this, students should expect to find any explanation of 'risk-neutral probabilities' highly confusing, and of little use deriving or interpreting option values (14). Beginners should realize that 'risk-neutral probabilities' are not related to any objective (frequency) probabilities and we do not value options by assuming that investors are risk neutral. So-called binomial 'risk-neutral probabilities' aren't probabilities at all: they simply define the value that risk-averse investors are guaranteed to get if they hedge away all risk under any probability distribution.

Using a recombining binomial tree to model a continuous process

It can be useful to build a 'tree' of successive binomial decisions in order to act as a model of a continuous time random walk (e.g. of the multiplicative Wiener process, also called geometric Brownian motion, as described in Appendix 3). The advantages of the binomial approximation are ease of computation and the fact that the binomial problem can be formulated directly in discrete terms or 'difference' terms, without first devising a continuous form of it in Black–Scholes form, then 'discretizing' it by Taylor's theorem.

If we need to use the binomial as a model of the continuous time random walk of S, there are three key features of the geometric random walk that we have to model.

Firstly, the random walk must have a multiplicative and symmetric effect on the current value of the underlying asset S in the same way as in the continuous model. In the continuous model there is a symmetric random walk in the log of S, in the sense that a randomly chosen increment dz_t over the time period t to t + dt produces $\log S_{t+dt} = \log S_t + \log dz_t$ which means that $S_{t+dt} = S_t \exp(dz_t)$. Conversely, the equally likely increment in the opposite direction $- dz_t$ produces $\log S_{t+dt} = \log S_t - \log dz_t$ so that $S_{t+dt} = S_t / \exp(dz_t)$. Hence the random outcomes of the two (equally likely) random jumps by a normal deviate of size dz (but of opposite sign) cause either multiplication or division of S by an identical quantity. This effect must be imitated by 'equally likely' jumps of the binomial process.

Secondly and equivalently, the random walk must be approximately normally distributed in the logarithm of S. Thirdly, as in the continuous time random walk, variance must be linear in time. We see in Appendix 3 that the reason for this is that successive increments of time must produce independent variations in S. (In the continuous case, this means that variance is linear in time, so the square root of variance, the standard deviation, must be proportional to the square root of time, and hence the standard deviation of the standardized random increment dz that takes place over the time interval dt is √dt.)

We can achieve the first effect by making the jump at each node of the tree a multiplication by either an 'up' number or a 'down' number, which are reciprocals of each other. Hence the four-jump sequence up, up, down, down returns S to its opening value unchanged, as does the sequence down, down, up, up, as does the sequence down, up, down, up, and so on. This is called a recombining tree (see Appendix 4) and it means that (except after an unbroken series of up or down jumps) the present node in the tree preserves no record of the particular sequence of upward and downward jumps by which that node has been reached.

We achieve the second and third effects by making the size of the variance over the time interval dt (which measures possible change) have the same variance as the continuous distribution over the same time increment. Hence if the variance of the continuous time random walk (in the log of S) over the interval dt is $\sigma^2 dt$, the standard deviation of its increment over the interval dt is $\sigma\sqrt{dt}$. To model this we make the standard deviation of the binomial step over the finite time interval δt equal to $\sigma\sqrt{\delta t}$.

How can we ensure that a discrete binomial distribution, which has only two points, will have the same mean and variance as a chosen normal distribution, which has mean μ and variance, for example, σ^2? This proves to be simple. If the required variance is σ^2 we simply need one point at $\mu + \sigma$ and one at $\mu - \sigma$. The mean of these two points is clearly μ, as required. As for their variance, each of the two points deviates from μ by σ, so each of their squared deviations from μ is σ^2 and this is also the mean of their squared deviations, which is the variance of the two points, as required. In practice, care is needed to deal with the difference between the logarithmic nature of the continuous random walk and the discrete nature of the binomial process (see, for example, Wilmott, Howison and Dewynne, 1995) but the basic idea is as here.

In the logarithmic binomial case, where the log of S has two possibilities at the end of each time interval δt, the two possibilities are to add or subtract $\sigma\sqrt{\delta t}$. Whatever the current value of S, the next value will be either $S \exp(\sigma\sqrt{\delta t})$ or $S/\exp(\sigma\sqrt{\delta t})$.

Notice that for hedging purposes we will not need to specify the probabilities of the upward and downward jumps – only their sizes. If their probabilities are equal, S has a drift-free geometric random walk in discrete time, but if the probabilities of the upward and downward jumps are unequal, S also has a constant deterministic drift (of exponential growth or decay) in discrete time, in addition to its random walk. The size of this random drift is set by the market, and it is determined by two factors – a 'risk-free' element, which reflects the market's rate of time preference, and a 'risky' element, which reflects the market's degree of aversion to risk (i.e. this element of the drift is a function of the volatility σ – see Appendix 2).

It is well known that in the case of the additive (as opposed to the multiplicative) binomial process, as δt tends to zero, the approximation to the normal distribution approaches perfection. This is when the number of steps N and the number of end points N + 1 in the binomial distribution both tend to infinity. As a crude rule of thumb, the approximation to the continuous distribution begins to grow progressively more acceptable as N rises above 30, though with diminishing returns to larger N.

But why should we make the variance of the binomial model imitate the variance of the continuous random walk at all? The reason for doing so in the binomial model is not that we want to predict the probabilities of the possible end states at time t + k as such. In the world of delta hedging we become indifferent to the relative probabilities of the two possible outcomes after any binomial step because the hedged portfolio's value at the end of the step can be fixed.

The reason why we imitate the variance of the continuous distribution is partly simply to see how wide a range of 'likely' end states it is worth including in our model after some time interval k = Nδt, and partly in order to get a fine enough subdivision of the possible value differences within this range. In effect, the only use we actually make within the binomial model of the variance which we have imitated from the continuous model is to decide the size (not the probabilities) of the possible up and down movements of S (viewed as multiplications of S). In the micro steps of delta hedging we can and do become indifferent to the probabilities that S will show either an upward or a downward movement at each step. Hence we are indifferent to drift or trend.

Strictly speaking this is also true of the Black–Scholes equation for the continuous time random walk: the valuations that we get are the result of delta hedging over infinitesimal periods of time, over which the next outcome has an unbounded set of possibilities, but in the continuous case, delta hedging has eliminated all risk and all trends over the likely range of these possibilities. (See Appendix 3 for how both the drift and random components of the Wiener process dz are eliminated by hedging – only the volatility, in the form sigma squared, remains in the hedged model, because this does not disappear in expectation.)

Hence if we try to interpret the Black–Scholes equation as a 'diffusion' equation, by analogy with the diffusion process for the stock price, we find that the value of a hedged option – as modelled by the Black–Scholes equation – does not have the same diffusion parameters as the objective distribution of the stock price. Just as in the binomial model, the Black–Scholes equation in effect includes the volatility σ only as an index of the possible (and hedgeable) diversity of the value of S after a short time period dt, but the objective probabilities that S will take any of these states can be ignored because of hedging. As shown in Appendix 3 if we try to interpret the Black–Scholes equation as a diffusion equation, its trend term is the risk-free rate r (or for a dividend paying stock r − δ) rather than the stock's objective drift of m. As Appendix 2 shows, m is (μ − δ) where μ > r.

Binomial methods are illustrated in Chapter 7, while Chapter 8 gives an alternative approach to binomial valuation. This values a node by replicating its risk with identically risky market assets, rather than by eliminating its risk by making delta hedging trades in assets of exactly opposite risk.

Notes

1. The other half is time preference (i.e. the risk-free interest rate). Of course the hedge ratio (6) is also defined for a real interest rate of zero, and this allows a risk-free return to an investor who is risk averse but indifferent to the passage of time. Hence by a simple extrapolation of current usage it would be consistent to call w and $(1 - w)$ the 'risk-neutral and time-neutral weightings', and we would have assumed away the whole subject matter of conventional financial economics, while still allowing delta hedging by an investor who was averse to risk but indifferent to the passage of time.

Real football options in Manchester[1]

5

by Dean Paxson

Editor's introduction:

Here Dean identifies some real option-like decisions that confront a football club, and shows how particular forms of these problems might be solved. He also shows the effect of varying the parameter values assumed in the models. Dean has selected some aspects of the following options to look at in slightly more detail, using the limited information that is publicly available.

1. How to price concessions to use the club logo

The decision: *how to price the concession, and what form of deal to offer (e.g. fixed flat fee, totally variable fee as a percentage of all sales, intermediate mix of some flat element and some variable element, i.e. a percentage of all sales over some minimum).*

Option-like features: *call option to enjoy the 'best of' flat fee element or percentage of sales element.*

Solution method: *standard Black–Scholes.*

Implications: *the choice of which contract is best (at a given price) is implicitly a bet about the future volatility of concession sales.*

Limitations and possible extensions: *may be hard to hedge; other forms of deal may be possible.*

2. Youth club player arrangements

The decision: *whether to hire youth players from school; when to fire them; when to promote them to second team and full team.*

Option-like features: *the average youth player hired at 16 is an out of the money call option to bring that player into the youth team; a player who is better than average at 18, but not of star quality, may be worth less* to the club than the option of hiring an untried player of 16 (who on average will turn out to be a worse player than the good 18-year-old but has a small chance of being far better). Hence there is an 'up or out' promotion policy at age 18. A similar policy exists at the later levels of advancement from youth team to reserves to full team. Options to promote a player into the next level resemble American exchange options or spread options in finance. A player who is 'too successful' leaves the club, and his crowd-pulling ability is lost (or it must be bought back at full market value). This resembles an 'up and out' call option in finance.

Random walk variable: *player quality.*

Equations: *values of the same person as youth player, as reserve player and as first-team player may need to be modelled as all evolving randomly, having different volatilities and some correlation between the player's performance at different levels in the same club.*

Boundary conditions: *payoff to the 'up and out' call option rises steeply then falls to zero; American exchange options need value matching and smooth pasting conditions.*

Solution method: *standard analytic solutions for 'up and out' option: numerical solutions for American exchange options on 'dividend-paying' players.*

Implications: *have an 'up or out' promotion policy.*

Possible extensions: *model the compound option to award two successive promotions, to reserves and to first team; add concept of 'dividend loss' if a promising player is promoted too late.*

3. Stadium expansion planning, and option-like deals for financing it

The decision*: when to invest in new capacity, and how to price the fixed and variable revenue.*

Option-like features: *American call option to invest in new capacity, which is a 'dividend-paying' underlying asset (i.e. the club may suffer lost ticket sales until an extension is built). Manchester City's position has been more volatile than Manchester United's, so City's options probably have higher time value. Funding methods can be either pure equity or pure debt, or derivatives that mix the characteristics of both. Manchester City has a stadium financing deal which shares variable seat revenue with the stadium owner, and should be valued by real option methods.*

Random walk variable: *the potential seat sales of the club, perhaps itself depending on the club's random walk position in the league.*

Equations: standard Black–Scholes for a dividend-paying asset (seat revenues).

Boundary conditions: when there is an upper limit on stadium size (before or after extension) this represents an option held by nature against the club, i.e. the club will get the 'worse of' selling all the seats that it has available (if demand exceeds capacity) and selling all the seats that fans want to buy (if capacity exceeds demand). The terminal and fixed upper boundary conditions resemble those of a 'bull spread' option in finance.

Introduction

Manchester United PLC is one of the most successful sports management/ entertainment companies in the world. Manchester City FC, on the other hand, is one of the more volatile football clubs, having been in Divisions 1 and 2 and the Premier League over the past three years. It is questionable whether traditional investment evaluation and financial management methods are appropriate for football clubs. These methods involve forecasting future net cash flows, and discounting those forecasts at risk-adjusted rates. Investments are accepted based on positive net present values. However, football clubs face: (1) designing and evaluating media and merchandising outsourcing contracts, where there may be substantial upside and limited downside exposure; (2) stadium expansion planning, where the option to defer investment or to share excess revenues may involve capacity usage diffusion processes; (3) season ticket (equivalent to take-or-pay contracts) pricing and sales; and (4) many other elements in sports management, where real options prevail.

Real football club options

Manchester United holds a number of records, including finishing either first or second in the FA Premier League since the 1992–1993 season. In comparison with this persistence of performance, Manchester City is a volatile club, having been in Divisions 1 and 2 and the Premier League over the past three years. The importance of this contrast appears in the valuation of contingent claim contracts, where volatility benefits the holder of any option, and is not beneficial for any issuer or writer of real option contracts.

For the year 1999–2000, around 32 per cent of ManUtd's turnover was from gate receipts and programme sales, 26 per cent from television, 20 per cent from merchandise and other, 16 per cent from sponsorship and 6 per cent from conference and catering, with an increasing percentage from TV (doubled over the past five years). Some of these revenue sources are directly tied to performance,[2] and some might be indirectly tied to performance through revenue-sharing arrangements.

The strategy for increasing turnover and profits is to increase: (a) gate receipts, (b) TV and other media, (c) merchandising revenue, all of which are dependent presumably on increasing the intangible brand image (partly reinforced by player success), while (d) not spending all of the revenue on increased player compensation and transfer fees or on cost of sales and other administrative costs.

Gate receipts

Gate revenues depend on stadium size and facilities, as well as performance. There is a trade-off between encouraging supporters to attend matches (especially in less than 100 per cent load stadiums) by reduced ticket prices, and the increased revenue from 'inside gate expenditures'. There is another trade-off between TV rights, including pay-to-view, and stadium attendance. Since ManUtd experiences excess demand for seats, and has a limited (if large) capacity, gate receipts would be increased by increased ticket prices.[3]

The security of advanced season ticket sales is an appropriate revenue stream for securitization.

The security of advanced season ticket sales is an appropriate revenue stream for securitization, since such ticket sales are essentially 'take-or-pay contracts', similar to contracts in natural gas (see Thompson, 1995). Other clubs have used stadium revenue securitizations to finance stadium and player expansions. With a near 100 per cent usage, Newcastle United sold in 1999 a £55 million bond tied to ticket and hospitality income.

An alternative securitization directly tied to club performance is the 'Sampdoria Performance Bond'. The four-year bond has a guaranteed 2.5 per cent minimum annual interest coupon; should the club be promoted from the Serie B to the Serie A division at the end of the season, the coupon will increase to 7 per cent. If Sampdoria stays in Serie A, the annual coupon will be 5 per cent, but this could rise to as much as 14 per cent if the club finishes as one of the top four teams in Serie A. This is a bond with embedded financial options, which is a real option, dependent on Poisson processes (or possibly extreme value distributions).

TV and other media

With the arrival of British Sky Broadcasting (BSkyB), football TV viewing in the UK has partly shifted from free-to-view TV to pay-to-view TV. There are questions regarding the team contract arrangements for pay-to-view, which could involve a fixed annual fee or alternatively a reduced minimum annual fee plus a percentage of revenue from actual TV viewers, especially in the future.[4] Among the issues for ManUtd in the takeover bid by BSkyB was whether in the future there would be pay-to-view contracts for the entire Premier League coverage, or per dominant team. There was also the question of whether pay-to-view operators should own dominant clubs, and thereby obtain a 'toehold' in negotiating league contracts. One of the fall-back options for BSkyB was that instead of the Premier League contract being a 'must have', it might acquire 'retail' rights only, or alternatively acquire only ManUtd games.

TV rights are similar to sponsorship and advertising contracts since the actual/potential audience is not accurately measurable (unlike sales of merchandise). However, potential contractual arrangements may be similar to revenue-sharing out-sourced merchandise deals.

Merchandising revenue

Merchandise sales developed for ManUtd in 1999–2000 with the opening of the Megastore in Old Trafford, and flagship stores in Singapore and Dublin. In 2001 these were extended to Kuala Lumpur and Capetown.[5] The strategy is globally developing the brand 'through key strategic business partners around the world',[6] including the New York Yankees. Contract sales agreements, which involve combinations of fixed fee and sales or profit sharing, are modelled in the next section.

Other options

There are several characteristic football player options, which range from the simple spread over what ManUtd earns from marketing players less players' pay, including amortized transfer fees and training costs, to the 'farm' system, where players are more or less considered up-or-out call options.[7]

A number of outstanding ManUtd players arise from the youth and junior sponsored clubs.[8] Each summer the club signs a number of 16-year-old boys into the Manchester United Academy. The boys earn a nominal sum during a two-year apprenticeship. Some are then promoted to the Youth club, and then to the Reserves. A few eventually make it to the first team. Essentially ManUtd holds options on players who are promoted through the youth system, where the equivalent option premium is the expense of supporting and training the potential player until the option is exercised or extinguished.

On all players, ManUtd eventually earns the spread between the player revenue (in terms of a mixture of gate receipts, merchandise profits, and TV and sponsorship) and player wages. It is impossible to attribute specific revenue to specific players, perhaps in contrast to other professional service firms (such as lawyers, accountants, consultants and academics), and there are problematic time delays in both player revenues and wages.

The player spread option is essentially like a Margrabe exchange option value, with the player as the 'asset' exchanged for the revenue (see Margrabe, 1978). Even if there is a high correlation between the player compensation and the revenue generated, the spread option is worth more than the simple difference of player compensation and revenue, unless that 'option' is exercised when compensation continuously exceeds revenue generated.

Now that detailed historical statistics are available on each valuable player, player values can be updated after each match throughout the year (see Bateman *et al.*, 1999) and compared with the compensation (and estimated revenue generated). Interactive fantasy games and spread betting will also offer 'shadow' market prices for players.

Outsourcing contract options

There are several possible types of outsourcing contract arrangements for merchandising, TV and other media, conference and catering, and Internet sales and advertising, ranging from a flat annual fee to a fee plus a percentage of revenue over a minimum, to profit sharing, to own manufacturing and distribution.[9] The fixed annual fee is like an annually renewable bond. A reduced annual fee plus a percentage of excess sales is like a call option held by the club, where the difference between the full fee and the reduced fee amounts to the club paying a call premium in return for a percentage of sales over the minimum amount. A straight percentage of sales contract is like a long forward commodity position.

Here are some illustrations of the possible trade-offs in contract arrangements. Suppose that the full flat fee is a fair arrangement. Suppose the club accepts an arrangement where it receives initially a reduced fee in return for a percentage of the sales over a minimum. We calculate the value of a call option on 100 per cent of the sales over the minimum (which is equivalent to the exercise price). We use the analytic solution of Black and Scholes.

The call option W(P) on 100 per cent of sales over the minimum for a T year arrangement and where the sales revenue is a normally distributed value is:

$$W(P) = P \, N \, (d_1) - e^{-rT} \, M \, N \, (d_2) \tag{1}$$

where P is the present value of the current expected revenue, M is the minimum specified revenue, N( ) is the cumulative normal distribution function:

$$d_1 = \frac{ln\left(\dfrac{P}{M}\right) + (r + .5\ \sigma^2)T}{\sigma\sqrt{T}} \tag{2}$$

$$d_2 = d_1 - \sigma\sqrt{T} \tag{3}$$

where r = risk-free rate, T = time to contract renegotiation, σ = expected sales volatility.

Then several different types of fair alternative arrangements can be calculated which are equivalent to the full fee. The minimum sales level could be held constant and the percentage of upside varied. Or the percentage of upside could be held constant and the minimum sales level held constant.

Figures 5.1, 5.2 and 5.3 illustrate 'generic' possible outsourcing arrangement trade-offs. It is assumed (unless otherwise specified) that the expected present value (as at the beginning of the year) of sales is £100 million, sales volatility is 50 per cent, the contract time arrangement is one year, the riskless rate is 6 per cent, and the fair straight fixed annual fee is £70 million. The minimum sales level is set at £100 million (as at the end of the year).

Fig 5.1	**Real football club outsource contract alternatives**

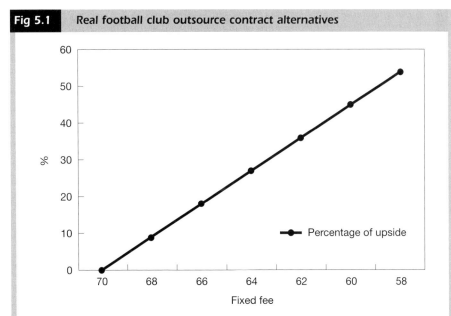

The 'fair trade-off' between a fixed annual outsource contract fee and an option on 50 per cent of sales over the minimum of 100. Assumes expected sales = 100, interest rate is 6 per cent, expected sales volatility is 50 per cent per annum, T = one year. If the alternative sole fixed fee is 70, then an alternative fee of 58 and an option of 54 per cent of sales over 100 is fair.

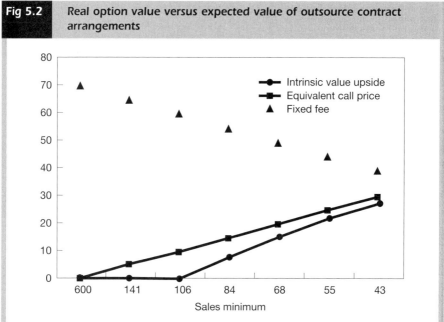

Fig 5.2 Real option value versus expected value of outsource contract arrangements

The 'fair trade-off' between a fixed annual contract fee and an option on 50 per cent sales over the minimum sales. Assumes expected sales = 100, interest rate is 6 per cent, expected sales volatility is 50 per cent per annum, and the time horizon is one year. Contract arrangements are based on total sales over one year. If the alternative sole fixed fee is 70, then an alternative fee of 40 and an option on 50 per cent of sales over 42.9 is fair. Instrinsic value = Higher of {% Sales times [Expected sales − Minimum sales], or nil}.

In Figure 5.1 first the 'full call price' for 100 per cent of sales over the minimum level is calculated; then the 'equivalent call price' is the 'full call price' times [percentage of upside]. The percentage is 'derived' as that which equates the (reduced) fixed fee plus the equivalent call to £70 million. So if the (reduced) fixed fee is £60 million, a call price on 45 per cent upside is worth £22.21 million times 0.45 or £10 million. Naturally there is the implicit constraint that the (reduced) fixed fee will not be below a figure which results in the percentage of upside in excess of 100 per cent.

Figure 5.2 illustrates the difference between the 'expected' value and the real option value of such arrangements, with the trade-off between the alternative fixed fees and the (various) minimum sales levels, at 50 per cent of the excess sales. With the minimum sales level of £106 million, there is no 'intrinsic value', since the expected sales is less than the minimum sales level. If sales had no volatility, the option would be worthless. With a volatility of 50 per cent, the option on 50 per cent of excess sales is worth £10 million, so an alternative fixed fee of £60 million and 50 per cent of the sales over £106 million would be fair. At a very low minimum sales level, the option value will approach the intrinsic value.

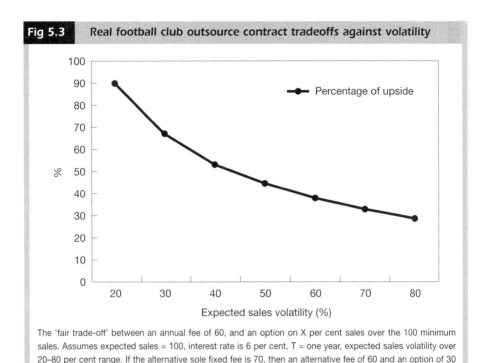

Fig 5.3 Real football club outsource contract tradeoffs against volatility

%

Expected sales volatility (%)

Percentage of upside

The 'fair trade-off' between an annual fee of 60, and an option on X per cent sales over the 100 minimum sales. Assumes expected sales = 100, interest rate is 6 per cent, T = one year, expected sales volatility over 20–80 per cent range. If the alternative sole fixed fee is 70, then an alternative fee of 60 and an option of 30 per cent of sales (if volatility is 80 per cent) is fair.

Figure 5.3 shows the outsource contract alternatives (with £60 million fixed fee) for X per cent of sales over the minimum level of £100 million, for different levels of expected sales volatility. Then the 'equivalent call price' is the 'full call price' times [percentage of upside]. So if the fixed fee is £60 million and volatility is 50 per cent, a call price on 45 per cent upside is worth £22.21 million times 0.45 or £10 million, the same as noted for Figure 5.1. However, Figure 5.3 shows that the warranted fair percentage upside is a convex function of the expected sales volatility, so that high expected volatility (such as 80 per cent) would result in a low percentage (30 per cent) of excess sales. This illustrates the importance of focusing on expected sales volatility if a football club enters into a contingent claim type of arrangement for merchandise or other outsourcing. Both the expected sales and the expected volatility of sales over the contract period must be forecast. Of course, both figures will be dependent on the success of the club relative to past years, or possibly on the supporters and media interest in the club based on the competitive levels of similar clubs throughout the year.

Other more complex merchandise and other contractual arrangements may also be appropriately modelled as real options.

Real stadium 'gate receipt' sharing arrangements

The Maine Road stadium, used by Manchester City, has a current capacity of around 34,000 seats (although some of these are temporary), which is slightly more than the usual attendance, except for critical games.

With the stadium approaching near 100 per cent usage for some home matches, the directors of the club and the Manchester City Council have entered into a (convenient) arrangement regarding a new stadium, the City of Manchester stadium, built for the Commonwealth Games 2002. We consider first a template for modelling football club stadium usage.

The maximum stadium capacity (current carrying capacity = N*) is considered fixed in the short term, and the actual attendance is modelled as a logistic diffusion process.[10] The logistic growth is:

$$N = N^*[1 + \left(\frac{N^*}{N_0} - 1\right)e^{-at]-1}$$ (4)

where N = attendance at time t, N* is the carrying capacity, N_0 is the initial attendance, and a is assumed to be a constant growth (or decline) coefficient. This

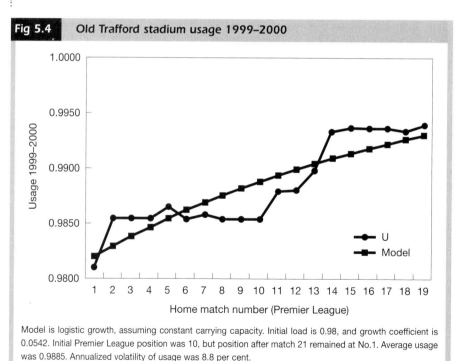

Fig 5.4 Old Trafford stadium usage 1999–2000

Model is logistic growth, assuming constant carrying capacity. Initial load is 0.98, and growth coefficient is 0.0542. Initial Premier League position was 10, but position after match 21 remained at No.1. Average usage was 0.9885. Annualized volatility of usage was 8.8 per cent.

implies that the specific growth rate of the actual attendance is in direct proportion to the usage U = [N/N*].

The Old Trafford stadium occupied by ManUtd is the largest club stadium in England, and has for sev-

As with most UK football attendance records, there is a tendency for the usage to increase over the season.

eral years been more or less filled to capacity. Figure 5.4 shows the logistic growth model applied to the actual attendance for League games in 1999–2000 (from August 1999 to May 2000).[11] As with most UK football attendance records, there is a tendency for the usage to increase over the season, especially in this case as ManUtd rose to the top of the Premier League. The initial load or usage (actual attendance divided by stadium capacity) is very high (98 per cent), and the growth coefficient is around 5 per cent. The annualized volatility of actual attendances is around 8.8 per cent. While this is not an exciting model of stadium usage, it provides perhaps a paradigm against which one might view ManCity in its current and future stadium.

The Maine Road stadium in M14 (just south of the university) has four stands, with a current capacity of 32,760 seats, along with two uncovered sections with an additional capacity of 2,236, or a total stadium capacity of 34,996.[12]

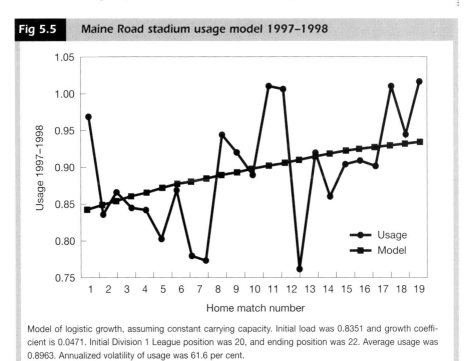

Fig 5.5 — Maine Road stadium usage model 1997–1998

Model of logistic growth, assuming constant carrying capacity. Initial load was 0.8351 and growth coefficient is 0.0471. Initial Division 1 League position was 20, and ending position was 22. Average usage was 0.8963. Annualized volatility of usage was 61.6 per cent.

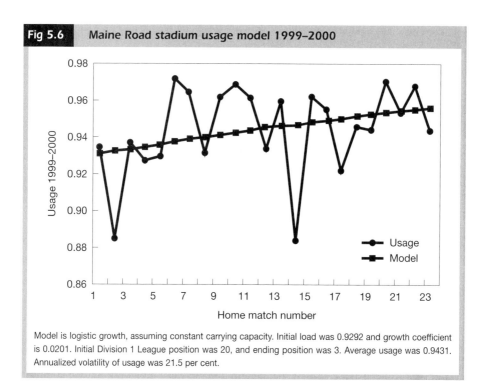

Fig 5.6   **Maine Road stadium usage model 1999–2000**

Model is logistic growth, assuming constant carrying capacity. Initial load was 0.9292 and growth coefficient is 0.0201. Initial Division 1 League position was 20, and ending position was 3. Average usage was 0.9431. Annualized volatility of usage was 21.5 per cent.

Figure 5.5 shows the logistic growth model applied to actual ManCity attendance at home games in 1997–1998. This simple model is not satisfactory on several accounts. First of all, the best fitting parameters show an initial attendance lower than the average attendance, although the first game of the season was nearly sold out. The growth coefficient a is small. Even though ManCity started and finished at nearly the bottom of Division 1, attendance was quite high in the last few games. The attendance is considered to be time (or match number) dependent, but the model ignores the particular visiting team played or the success (or failure) of ManCity throughout the year. The volatility of attendance is around 61 per cent, which is hardly altered by adjusting the actual attendance by the growth coefficient for the season.

Figure 5.6 shows the logistic growth model applied to actual attendance at home games in 1999–2000. The first game of the season was at a medium 'load factor', as eventually City rose to nearly the top of Division 1. Even so, the growth coefficient a is small, and the attendance volatility was around 21.5 per cent. (Note that the scale of Figure 5.5 is 0.75 to 1.05, while the scale of Figure 5.6 is 0.86 to 0.98.)

While it is difficult to forecast attendance volatility, considering the past attendance records is at least a first step in modelling the future attendance and rental options in the new stadium. Thus we assume as the 'base case' an initial growth of average attendance of 3 per cent, and an attendance volatility of 40 per cent (both slightly less than mid-way between the parameters derived for fitting 1997–1998 and 1999–2000 usage). Of course, both the actual future growth coefficient and the volatility may be altered by having a new stadium exceeding the capacity of Maine Road, but attendance will surely also reflect the future performance of ManCity.

The City of Manchester stadium is part of Sportcity, a multi-million-pound project for the redevelopment of East Manchester. Manchester City Council, the Lawn Tennis Association and Sport England are funding the facilities. The stadium was originally expected to cost £90 million.[13] This is on a 146-acre former industrial site in Eastlands, 1.5km east of central Manchester (Piccadilly train station), adjacent to Ashton New Road and Alan Turing Way (M11). The stadium will have limited on-site car parking, but will be served by a planned Metrolink line. The planned capacity is 48,000, with a bowl design so that 'every spectator will be within 100 metres of the centre spot'.[14] Designed by Arup Architects and built by Laing, the arena will be almost circular, with high and low elevations providing a 'saddle shape' skyline landmark. After the Commonwealth Games, the stadium will be the home of ManCity as well as hosting other multi-spectator events.

| Fig 5.7 | 'Payoff diagram' for ManCity and council gate receipt sharing arrangement |

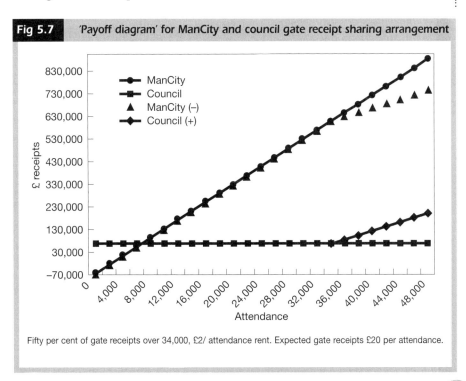

Fifty per cent of gate receipts over 34,000, £2/ attendance rent. Expected gate receipts £20 per attendance.

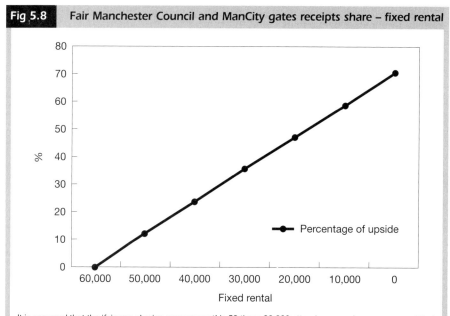

Fig 5.8 **Fair Manchester Council and ManCity gates receipts share – fixed rental**

It is assumed that the 'fair non-sharing arrangement' is £2 times 30,000 attendance per home game, and that the expected attendance is 33,000, or around the current capacity of the Maine Road stadium. The volatility of Maine Road stadium attendance has been around 10–60 per cent p.a., but this is a factor of the visiting teams and the status of Manchester City (Premier, First, Second Division) in each year and the League position order for each game. Assumes volatility of 40 per cent, and gate profits of £20.

We assume that the 'rental agreement' between Manchester City Council and Manchester City FC is equivalent to a nominal fixed amount (maintenance expenses and the value of Maine Road), with a sharing agreement for attendances over 32,500. As an illustration, suppose that a 'fair straight fixed rental' per game is 30,000 times £2 or a total of £60,000 (times a season average of 23 games equals £1,380,000 or a yield of 1.5 per cent on a (hypothetical) construction cost of £90 million or £1,875 per seat capacity). Such a 'fair rent' would amount to a yield of 10.6 per cent on the council's contribution to the construction costs (assuming that the lottery grant is a donation towards the Commonwealth Games 2002). Suppose in addition that there is a sharing agreement that the council receives an additional 50 per cent of the gate receipts over 32,500 and that the average gate receipt is £20 per attendance.[15]

The 'payoff diagram' for such an arrangement is shown in Figure 5.7. In a non-sharing arrangement, the ManCity 'ascending line' represents a fixed rental agreement, with City losing £68,000 in the unlikely event that a game is played without any spectators to a maximum of £892,000 for a sold-out game.[16] The council 'horizontal line' shows a fixed rental receipt of £68,000 regardless of attendance.

The sharing arrangement is equivalent to ManCity writing a call option to the council at an exercise price of 34,000 attendance, and buying a call option (cap) from the council at an exercise price of 48,000 attendance. The council ends up with a simple call option 'bull spread' or a collar with an exercise price of 34,000 and a cap (maximum payout) of 48,000 (times the sharing percentage times the gate receipt average). In this case the lower payout is the fixed rental. In a strategic context, perhaps one would consider the option premium paid by the council as any shortfall in the 'full rental' with no upside sharing arrangement compared to any full fixed rental.[17] The sharing payout is reflected in the Man-City (–) line, which shows the club receiving reduced gate revenue, below the continuously ascending straight line, and the Council (+) line shows the council receiving larger gate revenue above the horizontal line (assuming a 50 per cent gate sharing arrangement for attendances above 34,000), so that in such a sharing arrangement the council could receive as much as £208,000 for a sold-out match, while City's revenue for the match would be reduced to £752,000.

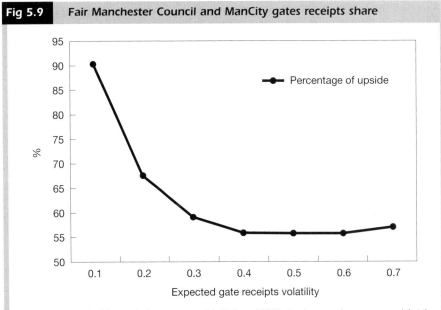

Fig 5.9   **Fair Manchester Council and ManCity gates receipts share**

It is assumed that the 'fair non-sharing arrangement' is £2 times 30,000 attendance per home game, and that the expected attendance is 33,000, around the current capacity of the Maine Road stadium. The volatility of Maine Road stadium attendance has been 20–60 per cent p.a., but this is a factor of the visiting teams (location and status), and the status of Manchester City (Premier, First, Second Division) in each year, as well as the League position order. If a fair straight fixed rental is 60,000, an alternative rent of 10,000 and a share of 57 per cent of gate receipts over 32,500 is fair, if attendance volatility is forecast to be 70 per cent. An increasing range of volatilities is shown.

The valuation of such a revenue sharing arrangement is shown in Figure 5.8. It is assumed that the 'fair rental' is £60,000, that the expected average attendance is 33,000, that the attendance volatility is 40 per cent per annum, and that the attendance pattern is expected to follow a lognormal random walk. The equivalent one-year call price is #6326 (tickets), so that an alternative rent of nil and a share of 72 per cent of the gate receipts over 32,500 would be equivalent to £60,000 = {6326 − 2170}*20*0.7221. The call option cap held by ManCity at an exercise price of 48,000 is valued at #2170. An iteration algorithm is used to determine the fair sharing arrangements for different levels of combinations of fixed rent and sharing. (Since there is a cap on the maximum attendance of 48,000, at nil rent the cap sharing fair arrangement is 72.2 per cent, compared with 47.43 per cent if the stadium capacity was unlimited.)

The valuation of such a revenue-sharing arrangement is shown in Figure 5.9, with different assumed attendance volatility assumptions. It is also assumed that the 'fair rental' is £60,000, that the expected average attendance is 33,000, the attendance pattern is expected to follow a lognormal random walk, and the alternative rent is £10,000. At an assumed attendance volatility of 70 per cent, the equivalent call price is #9948 less #5609 for the cap, so a share of around 57 per cent of the gate receipts over 33,000 would be equivalent to £50,000 = (9948 − 5609)*20*0.5761. At such a high volatility, the cap has a value equivalent to around 56 per cent of the original call option. (The capped sharing fair arrangement is 57.61 per cent percentage of upside, compared to 25.13 per cent if the stadium capacity was unlimited.)

Thus the framework of real option pricing illustrates that the rate payers of Manchester and the shareholders of ManCity will want to have carefully considered the expected volatility of future attendances at the new City of Manchester stadium, in order to decide the appropriate rental terms.[18]

Stadium funding revenue-sharing arrangements, in connection with the Commonwealth Games 2002, are not necessarily unique in the UK[19] and are likely to be repeated elsewhere (for instance, Portugal for Euro 2004).[20]

Conclusion

Essentially a football commercial enterprise is an exchange option, where the players' compensation and other expenses are exchanged for revenue, including gate receipts, sponsorship, media and merchandise, in common with other professional service firms.

Initially we outline some of the possible real options that are likely to be important for some football clubs. Then we provide a simple template for evaluating the possible trade-offs between fixed fees and combination of reduced fixed fees and a share of the possible revenues. A similar approach is then applied to the ticket profit sharing arrangement

These and other real options are likely to be appropriate methodologies for related sports businesses.

between ManCity and Manchester City Council in the prospective relocation of the club from Maine Road to Eastlands. Important considerations in evaluating such arrangements are the expected level of attendances and ticket profits, the specification of the specified minimum attendance which triggers any sharing of profits, and the expected volatility of future attendances.

Although attendance in a (state-of-the-art) stadium exceeding the capacity of the current facilities is difficult to forecast, the template can be used to alter expectations and valuations as and when the club moves.

These and other real options are likely to be appropriate methodologies for related sports businesses where the future cash flows are highly uncertain, and where club management has several choices regarding contract arrangements covering marketing, player and capacity strategies.

Notes

1. Thanks to Dominic Broadhurst, the MBS class students Davis *et al.* (1999), students in real option classes in Braga, and to the participants in the BDP Instituto Mercado de Capitais seminar on real football options in Lisbon, September 1999, for helpful comments.

2. Premier League domestic TV revenue is distributed in a sharing formula. In 1998/99, 25 per cent was divided among the clubs on merit based on end positions in the League, and 25 per cent was divided as facility fees among the clubs whose matches were broadcast (see MMC, 1999, page 131).

3. However, ticket prices increased only 6–14 per cent in the five years to 1998, comparable to average match-day tickets for the other Premier League clubs (MMC, 1999, pages 70 and 126).

4. See MMC, 1999, regarding possible 'individual selling rights' or revised dominant club collective arrangements.

5. MMC, 1999 noted (page 67) that ManUtd sells and licenses the right to sell replica player strips and a range of other items that carry the ManUtd emblem, and planned to expand merchandising operations overseas with 150 shops, either under direct ownership or in joint ventures with third parties.

6. ManUtd, *Annual Report 2000*, page 2.

7. See Malos and Campion (1995) on career up-or-out options, as applied to other professional service firms.

8. 'I have always considered that the player you produce is better than the one you buy', Alex Ferguson, *Manchester United Illustrated Encyclopedia* (1998), page 39. Among the great players who have graduated to the first team from the Youth team are: G. Best, B. Charlton, R. Giggs, M. Hughes and G. and P. Neville.

9. An example is a 'media deal' which BSkyB arranged with ManCity. According to David Conn, 'UK: Football-Manchester City Hit Lottery Jackpot', *Independent*, 11 November 1999, page 31, BSkyB will pay £5.5 million for 9.9 per cent of City (or around 99 pence per share) 'and a further £2 million potentially rising to £5.5 million for the right to act as City's exclusive "media agents". Sky would be paid 30 per cent of any *extra* revenue they earn for the club'.

10. See Banks, 1994.

11. Attendance statistics from Rollin and Rollin (1999, 2001).

12. This is somewhat greater than the model capacity in 1997–1998, due to the additional seats and uncovered sections added over the past four years. The day ticket prices for these uncovered sections are around 70–75 per cent of the price for a prime main stand block.

13. According to David Conn, *Independent*, 11 November 1999. page 31, '£77 million is provided by the lottery and £13 million from the council'. The club is given a 250-year lease on the stadium in exchange for the Maine Road stadium, and is responsible for the new stadium's upkeep but no rent. After an attendance of 32,500, 'the council will take a share of the profit on each ticket'.

14. Some facts are available on *www.mcfc.co.uk* and *www.manchester.gov.uk / leisure / leisurematters / stadium.htm*.

15. The expected average attendance assumption is based on the 1999–2000 average attendance times a 3 per cent growth factor. The average gate receipt (or more precisely ticket profit) is based on an estimated average ticket price of £15, increased by one third to reflect ticket inflation by 2002–2003 and better seating for all fans. Ticket sales price is assumed to equal ticket profit since 'additional revenue from ticket sales was pure profit' (SUAM), MMC (1999), page 43.

16. The inputs are slightly altered in this illustration for convenience of graphing: minimum rent 'barrier' is 34,000, the minimum rent is £2 times that amount.

17. The actual arrangement is more complex than this simplification.

18. Perhaps to hedge such uncertainties, the council has also entered into two share option arrangements with ManCity. The first option is to subscribe for a 2.5 per cent stake for £1.875 million, if the market value of ManCity is greater than £75 million, and the team is not in the Premiership, exercised within six months from entry into the lease on Eastlands. The second option is to subscribe for 5 per cent of ManCity's shares for £5 million, whether or not the club is in the Premiership, any time up to July 2009 (with a limit if both options are exercised of 5 per cent). *Source:* Chris Barry, 'UK: Council May Get Stake in Blues', *Manchester Evening News*, 23 September 1999. These are up-and-in American barrier call warrants, way out of the money, showing perhaps sophistication in the council and ManCity regarding exotic option valuation (see Rich, 1994, and Paxson, 1997). At a then share price of around 100p, the equivalent exercise prices were around 140p and 180p, with barriers at the same prices.

19. Option arrangements between Stoke City F.C. and the local authority were used in the funding of Britannia Stadium.

20. See Anjos (1999).

Valuing a power plant under uncertainty

by *Mustafa Cavus*[1]

6

Editor's introduction:

This case values a generator by treating it as a bundle of call options to produce electricity in future times. Initially the writer assumes that fuel costs of operating the generator during any one-hour time period are fixed, and that electricity selling prices (only) undergo a random walk. Later he assumes that both the electricity selling prices and the fuel buying prices are random, leading to a model of the generator as a bundle of spread options (i.e. one option to exchange fuel for electricity in each potential operating period less a fixed charge for operating at all).

The decision: *to sell or buy operating assets (generators) of known physical generating efficiency, in a randomly evolving market.*

Option-like features: *one call option to produce electricity at a known avoidable cost, or one spread option to exchange gas for electricity output, at a known physical rate, in each relevant hour of the generator's operating life.*

Equation: *standard Black–Scholes (with one random factor) and standard Margrabe (with two random factors, specifying two volatilities and their correlation). The latter treats the ratio between the two random quantities as a single random factor.*

Boundary conditions: *fixed upper and lower boundaries at S = 0 and S = infinity. Terminal boundary condition is the payoff function for the call option to produce in each future operating hour. Spread or exchange option has in principle a two-dimensional payoff, depending on both gas and electricity prices, but it and its boundary conditions are modified by specifying the problem in terms of the ratio between the two random factors.*

Solution method: *standard analytic solutions for the call (Black–Scholes) and the exchange (Margrabe).*

Potential enrichments of the models: *to allow for the costs of starting and stopping production; to allow for the costs of supporting the asset when idle, both inside and outside the likely peak period for production.*

The importance of cutting-edge valuation tools in competitive markets

The marketplace for electric power is experiencing dramatic change worldwide as regulatory and technological advances have paved the way for competition in the generation of electricity. For example, relatively early in the US the Public Utilities Regulatory Policies Act of 1978 opened the door for electricity producers which use alternative technologies to sell their power into the existing transmission and distribution grid; and the Energy Policy Act of 1992 opened up the generation of electricity to non-utility producers.[2] The Federal Energy Regulatory Commission has also promoted competition for wholesale power by requiring utilities to open up their transmission lines to other power producers.[3]

As a result of deregulation, a fully competitive and transparent[4] marketplace has emerged, where prices are no longer set by a cost-recovery pricing structure but are market-based. With these fundamental changes in market structure, and uncertainties in fuel and electricity prices, all asset management decisions have become more complex. The tools necessary to manage price and investment risks (i.e. for valuing assets) in competitive markets take on a new urgency. It becomes pivotal to have asset management and investment decision tools that can handle uncertainty in a competitive market.

Conventional net present value tools cannot handle uncertainty in the marketplace. For key strategic investment and asset management decisions, the conventional tools yield inadequate and fundamentally misleading results. Real option tools, on the other hand, provide a market player with cutting-edge methodology for making decisions in a competitive industry beset by uncertainty. This case study intends to illustrate this fact for some decisions faced by a non-utility electricity producer.

Asset management decisions faced by a non-utility electricity producer

This case study values a power plant owned by a non-utility producer. The owner of the plant needs to make decisions of fundamental importance in managing this asset. Analysis will be carried out using both NPV and real option methods. As we will see, the decisions suggested by conventional NPV methods are completely different to those of real options. Using the correct tools, therefore, may make the difference in staying ahead of the competition. Consider the following setup.

The plant is a simple gas-fired turbine (SGT) plant that burns gas in order to generate electric power.[5] Its technology is relatively old; it is inefficient in comparison to newer generation units. A modern combined-cycle gas turbine (CCGT), in comparison, would need less fuel per generated megawatt hour (MWh) of electricity.[6] Variable costs of generating electricity are the cost of operating a plant to produce electricity and consist of fuel costs plus variable operation and maintenance costs. The SGT has a variable cost of $44/MWh whereas the comparable figure for the CCGT is $39/MWh.[7] For the rest of the analysis, we will assume that the cost of maintaining the plant at times when it is not operating is negligible.

On being generated, the electricity is immediately sold in the market. The market for electricity is very competitive and prices have been volatile over recent years (the average volatility is assumed to be 50 per cent, although there were periods of even higher volatility[8]). The power plant is assumed to be operated only during the southern US peak month of July, when peak prices exceed the variable operating costs. On each day in July there are only 12 hours (8am–8pm) where the peak prices exceed this plant's variable operating costs. The average price in July last year was $46/MWh. In all other months, the price of electricity is not sufficiently high to cover this plant's variable operating costs.

> **The market for electricity is very competitive and prices have been volatile over recent years.**

The plant owner is faced with the following possible decisions.

1. Sell the SGT plant for a scrap value of $1 million and quit this volatile business.[9]

2. Continue the business until the end of the remaining useful life of the SGT plant, which is expected to be three years given the industry average.

3. Expand the generation business by acquiring a CCGT plant with a remaining operating life of ten years, which would be a significant strategic decision, since the existing SGT has a capacity of 500MW whereas the CCGT under consideration has a larger generating capacity of 960MW. This

CCGT can be bought from another non-utility electricity producer for $25 million. Should he buy and expand rather than quit the business?

4. Any other strategy that he has not thought of yet.

Assume that the risk-free rate of interest is 5 per cent; the risk-adjusted discount rate is 10 per cent.

Decision making using traditional net present value analysis

When to run the plant. The plant should be run whenever the prevailing price of electricity exceeds the variable generation costs (fuel and variable operating and maintenance costs). There are no other costs to the plant owner. At this stage we assume that we can turn the plant on and off at any time without any problems or associated costs.

What is the value of a power plant? The NPV analysis values a power plant as the net present value of all expected earnings for the entire remaining lifetime of the generation capacity. The NPV per MW generation capacity per hour, i.e. NPV/MWh, is equal to the NPV of the (expected) power price, S, minus the variable operating costs, E.

$$NPV \ per \ MW \ per \ hour = \$ \frac{1}{MW} \times \frac{1}{h} = \frac{\$}{MWh} NPV \ of \ (S - E) \tag{1}$$

Then the NPV of the entire power plant is simply the NPV of the generation capacity of the plant, which is equal to the sum of all the NPVs in $/MWh times the number of MWs of the plant (i.e. the capacity of the plant).

$$NPV \ of \ a \ plant = \sum NPV \ of \ (S - E) \times h \times Megawatts = \frac{\$}{MWh} MWh = \$ \tag{2}$$

What is the SGT worth?

Assume the date (t) today is 1 January 2000. We want to calculate the NPV of the generator from its generation capacity until the end of its remaining economical life, which we assume to be three years. For that, first we calculate the NPV of $(S - E)$ for each hour using equation (1). Then we calculate the NPV of the entire plant using equation (2).

The average price of electricity (S) in July last year was $46/MWh, whereas the generation costs (E) specific to the SGT plant were $44/MWh. Assuming that there is no inflation to electricity price and generation costs, the NPV for each hour is simply NPV of $S - E$. The NPV of $S - E$ is the properly discounted value of $S - E$. We have to discount $S - E$ from the time of generation (and immediate delivery to the market) to today. Assuming continuous discounting, one can discount any future $ value by the following formula:

$$\$ \cdot e^{-r \cdot (T-t)} \tag{3}$$

where e is a constant 2.718282, r stands for the appropriate discount rate and $T - t$ denotes the time difference in years. For example, $100 we receive in a year's time (i.e. $T - t$ equals 1) by 10 per cent discount rate (r) is today worth only (see Appendix 1):

$$\$100 \cdot e^{-0.1 \cdot 1} = 90.48$$

Similarly, the NPV per MWh of electricity generated on 1 July 2000 will be calculated as follows.

$$(46 - 44) \cdot e^{-0.1 \cdot (0.4986)} = 1.9027$$

where the time difference between today (1 January 2000) and 1 July, 2000 is 0.4986 years. That means any MWh of electricity generated on that future day has an NPV of $1.9027/MWh. Note that the NPV method discounts with the risk-adjusted interest rate rather than the risk free rate. For the risk-adjusted discount rate we assumed 10 per cent.

In the same fashion we can calculate the NPV of $S - E$ on any other day in July 2000 (see Table 6.1).

Table 6.1	NPV per MWh in July 2000				
Generation day	1/7/00	2/7/00	3/7/00	....	31/7/00
$T - t$	0.4986	0.5014	0.5041	....	0.5808
$S - E$	2	2	2	....	2
NPV (using equation (1))	1.9027	1.9022	1.9017	....	1.8871

The sum of all the NPVs per hour (1.9027+1.9022+...+1.8871) in July yields $58.7426/MWh. Since we assumed that there are 12 peak hours during which the electricity price exceeds the cost of generation on each day in July, the sum of all the NPVs in July 2000 is $704.91/MW (= $58.7426/MWh * 12h).

In a similar fashion, the sum of all NPVs in July 2001 is $637.83/MW. For July 2002 (in the last year of the remaining life of the plant), we have $577.13/MW. Adding up these three values we have $1,919.87/MW, which equals the first term on the right-hand side of equation (2), $\sum NPV\ of\ (S - E)h$. Since the capacity of the SGT is 500MW, we have to multiply this sum by 500MW, which is the second term on the right-hand side of equation (2). Hence, for the value of the SGT we have \$959,936.47 (= \$1,919.87/MW * 500MW) (input numbers are shown rounded).

Given the volatile nature of the electricity market (on average 50 per cent which exceeds the much lower levels of volatility of other markets such as equities or bonds), the owner is asking himself whether to use a risk-adjusted discount rate higher than the 10 per cent assumed so far. So he wants to know what the value of the SGT would be at a discount rate of 12 per cent. Making the same calculations as before but using 12 per cent rather than 10 per cent as the discount rate, he now calculates the NPV of the SGT he owns as \$932,190.87, which is lower than its NPV at a 10 per cent discount rate.

The owner of the SGT feels it is not worthwhile staying in a risky business like electricity generation, so, given the volatile and competitive market, selling the plant for the scrap value of \$1 million seems to be a good idea.

At the same time, he has just been invited by another non-utility owner to buy for \$25 million a relatively new combined-cycle gas turbine (CCGT) plant with a generation capacity of 960MW which has a ten-year remaining operating life and a lower generation cost (\$39/MWh) than the SGT he currently owns. Buying the CCGT rather than quitting the business would be a total reversal of policy.

What is the value of the CCGT?

One can value the CCGT plant similarly to the calculations performed above. The differences are that the generation cost of the new plant is \$39/MWh; the generation capacity is bigger (960MW); and the remaining life is ten years rather than three years as for the SGT plant.

Using equation (1), the NPV/MWh generating capacity, a sample calculation for the first three days in July 2000 looks as in Table 6.2.

| Table 6.2 | NPV per MWh of the CCGT plant for July 2000 |

Generation day	1/7/00	2/7/00	3/7/00	....
$T - t$	0.4986	0.5014	0.5041	....
$S - E$	7	7	7	....
NPV (\$/MWh)	6.6595	6.6577	6.6559	....

The sum of all the NPVs per MWh (6.6595+6.6577+....) in July yields \$205.599/MWh. Since we assumed that there are 12 peak hours per day in which the electricity price exceeds the cost of generation, during each day in July, the sum of all the NPVs in July 2000 is $2,467.19/MW (= $205.599/MWh * 12h). Table 6.3 shows the NPVs for July in the other years.

Table 6.3	NPV per MW generation capacity for the economical life of the CCGT									
2000	2001	2002	2003	2004	2005	2006	2007	2008	2009	sum
2,467.19	2,232.40	2,019.96	1,827.74	1,653.35	1,496.02	1,353.65	1,224.83	1,107.97	1,002.53	16,385.65

The sum of the NPVs per MW for 2000–2009, $\sum NPV \ of \ (S - E)h$, gives $16,385.65/MW. This equals the first part on the right-hand side of equation (2). Since the CCGT has a generation capacity of 960MW, the NPV of the CCGT is found by multiplying $16,385.65/MW with 960MW which equals $15,730,225.91 (input numbers are shown rounded).

The CCGT plant is offered for $25 million. However, the NPV method yields a much lower value for the CCGT plant. Based on NPV calculations, the SGT owner would not be willing to consider buying the CCGT. Since power generation is a risky business he may even want to discount at a higher rate than 10 per cent. Repeating the same calculations for the CCGT plant at a discount rate of 12 per cent yields an NPV of $14,476,943.69.[10] In order to justify the purchase cost of $25 million he would need to discount the CCGT's earnings at a discount rate of 0.01 per cent,[11] which is implausible given the 5 per cent rate for risk-free investments. For the SGT owner it makes much more sense to invest his money in a risk-free investment rather than buying the CCGT and expanding the generation business. Hence, based on the NPV analysis, he would under no circumstances acquire the CCGT.

Summing up, we have seen how the power plant owner faces some key strategic questions which he attempts to answer with NPV methods. Based on the results of the NPV method, expansion by acquiring the CCGT plant does not make sense, since the CCGT plant is being offered for $25 million, whereas the NPV method yields a value of $15.73 million for this plant. The SGT he owns at present could be sold immediately for a scrap value of $1 million, whereas the NPV method yields a value in use of $959,936.47. Hence, based on the NPV method, the rational decision would be to sell the SGT plant immediately and to quit the business.

Notice that both of the plants were valued using a discount rate of 10 per cent. At any higher discount rate, the value of either plant will decrease. This is a risky business and the SGT plant owner does not want to use a much lower discount rate than 10 per cent, which directly affects the valuation. To the plant owner, increased risk seems to have an adverse effect on the value of the power plant.

However, the valuations provided by real option analysis contradict the results provided by the NPV method, as we will explain below.

Establishing equivalence between a power plant and a series of call options

Before we attempt to provide answers to help decision making, we need to establish the framework necessary to use real option analysis for asset valuation in electricity generation. The framework here is an analogy between a power plant and a series of call options. Owning a power plant is equal to owning a series of call options, where each option gives the right but not the obligation to acquire (generate) electricity by paying the necessary exercise costs (generation costs consisting of gas as fuel input and variable operating and maintenance costs).[12] This is similar to a call option commonly found in financial markets. A call option gives the holder the right but not the obligation to acquire the underlying commodity/asset by paying the exercise price. In the following, we will show the equivalence between a single call option and a future hour of generation capacity. Owning generation capacity gives the owner the right (but not the obligation) to generate electricity by spending the necessary costs of generation. It is not an obligation, since the owner may decide not to generate electricity if it is not profitable to do so.

Owning a power plant (i.e. megawatt capacity) is equivalent to holding a series of hourly European call options. The options are of the European nature (i.e. the decision to exercise can only be taken on a specific time, at maturity, in the future rather than at any time between now and at the end of the maturity of the option, as in an American option). Each call option value has two components: the **intrinsic value** and the **time value**. The intrinsic value is the value of the call option for any given electricity price at the moment of expiry. The extra value enjoyed by an option because it still has some time until the decision to exercise can be made is called the time value of the option.

First consider the equivalence to an option in terms of the intrinsic value of each option to produce. Observe that owning a power plant enables the owner to generate electricity in any hour if it is profitable to run the plant. It is profitable to generate electricity whenever the hourly price (market clearing price) for electricity in the market is equal to or greater than the generator's variable cost of operation. The variable cost of generating electricity is the cost of operating a plant to produce electricity, consisting of fuel costs plus a variable operation and maintenance costs.

Hence, profit from running the plant is equal to revenue from generating electricity (i.e. the electricity price on the market) minus the variable costs of generating electricity. In option language, the price of one MWh of electricity is the price of the underlying commodity (i.e. S); the variable cost of operating the generator to produce one MWh is the exercise price (i.e. E); the profit in each hour is the payoff function of a call option (i.e. $\max[0, S - E]$). So at each hour, depending on the level of the price of electricity at that time, our profit will be at least zero. It can be larger than zero, but it cannot be negative (a loss). When the electricity price is less than the cost of generation, the plant will not run.

In Figure 6.1 (see also Figure 2.1) we see the payoff from this hourly call option (i.e. generating capacity). The x-axis denotes a range of possible electricity prices and costs of generation. At the level where the cost needed to generate electricity exactly matches the electricity price, the value of the hourly generating capacity (i.e. the call option) is at break even. In option language the call option is at the money. If the electricity price S is higher than the cost of generation (exercise price E), the call option is in the money. Conversely, if the electricity price is lower than the generating cost, the call option is out of the money. The higher the electricity price over the exercise price, the higher the payoff (the payoff rises along the 45-degree line $S - E$).

We stated that a call option's value consists of two components: the intrinsic value and the time value. We have already established the nature of the intrin-

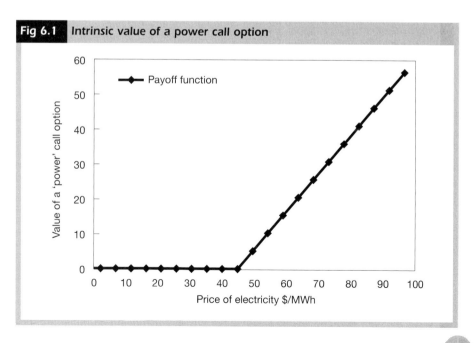

Fig 6.1 Intrinsic value of a power call option

Value of a 'power' call option (y-axis), Price of electricity $/MWh (x-axis)

Payoff function

sic value in the potential profit from hourly generating capacity. Consider now the nature of the time value of hourly generating capacity in the future.

Assume that currently the electricity price equals the exercise price, i.e. the call option to produce is at the money. The intrinsic value of the option then is equal to zero. A rise or a fall in electricity prices will not equally affect the value of the generating capacity (i.e. the call option). A fall in the electricity prices cannot make the value of the call less than zero. Given a 50 per cent chance that the electricity price in the future will fall below the current price, there is a 50 per cent chance that call option value will stay worthless at zero. However, there is also an equal chance that the electricity price will rise above its current value. We know that if an option still has some time to go until the decision of exercise (or not exercise), and is at the money now (so that it would be worth zero if it were to be exercised now), half of all possible futures leave the option still worth zero at expiry, and half of the possible futures leave the option worth more than zero at expiry. So taking the average over all these possible futures, the option must be worth more than zero now, i.e. more than its intrinsic value of zero. This extra value enjoyed by an option because it still has some time to run is called the time value of the option. This is extra to the intrinsic value of the option. The value of the call option is the sum of these two components. This is shown in Figure 6.2 (see also Figure 2.2).

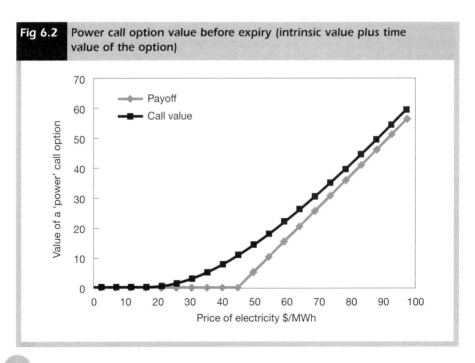

Fig 6.2 Power call option value before expiry (intrinsic value plus time value of the option)

As can be seen in general for options that still have some time until exercise (i.e. before expiry), the option has relatively lower time value if it is far from the money – that is, if the price of electricity (i.e. the underlying commodity) is well above or below the cost of generation, the option has small time value. Conversely if the current price of electricity is exactly at the exercise price – that is, the time value is greatest when the option is at the money. In other words, the time value of an option, which is the value of waiting for more information, is greatest when we are in maximum doubt over whether the value of the generating capacity (i.e. the power call) will be profitable. The price of electricity is not fixed, but tends to follow a random walk over time. The random change in prices is caused by unforeseeable supply and demand conditions in the electricity market arising from both inside (e.g. change in technology to generate electricity) and outside the industry (e.g. change in government regulations, weather and usage patterns for heating, power and cooling).

Decision making using real option analysis

What is the SGT plant worth?

Earlier we calculated the value of the currently owned SGT plant using the NPV method. Having established the equivalence between a power plant and a series of hourly European call options, we will now calculate the value of the same SGT plant with real option techniques. Additional information needed for option calculation is the volatility (which we assumed to be 50 per cent) and the riskless rate of interest (assumed to be 5 per cent). Above we have established that owning generating capacity is equal to holding a call option.

$$c = \text{call option to generate one MW of electricity for one hour} = \$ \frac{1}{MW} \frac{1}{h} = \frac{\$}{MWh} \quad (4)$$

Then a power plant is equivalent to the sum of this series of call options times the number of hours times megawatts available (i.e. the size of the plant).

$$\text{Value of a power plant} = \sum c \cdot \text{Number of MWhs} = \frac{\$}{MWh} MWh = \$ \quad (5)$$

For the first three days in July 2000 we have the following hourly European call values (see Appendix 1 of this chapter for the details of the values and the Black–Scholes formulas behind the calculations). Note that Table 6.4 is the direct equivalent of Table 6.1.

Table 6.4	Call value per MWh of the SGT plant for July 2000 (volatility = 0.5, risk-free rate = 0.05)			
Generation day	1/7/00	2/7/00	3/7/00	....
$T - t$ (time to maturity in years)	0.4986	0.5014	0.5041	....
S ($/MWh)	46	46	46	....
E ($/MWh)	44	44	44	....
Call value ($/MWh)	7.89	7.91	7.93	....

Table 6.4 shows the value of hourly call options for each generation day in July 2000. For example, the value of a call on 1 July is $7.89/MWh. The intrinsic value of the call option is only $2/MWh. This equals 46 minus 44, which is the payoff function of the option at maturity. The remaining value of $5.89/MWh comes through the time value of the option. Note the increasing time value of call options for increasing time to maturity $(T - t)$. That is, all things being equal, a European call option to acquire (generate) electricity is more valuable the longer the time to expiry. So the time value of the option to produce that expires on 2 July is larger than for the similar option that expires a day earlier.

The sum of all the call values in July (7.89+7.91+7.93+....) yields $253.48/MWh. Since we assumed that there are 12 peak hours, where the electricity price exceeds the cost of generation on each day in July, the sum of all call values in July 2000 is $3,041.76/MW (= $253.48/MWh * 12h). Similarly, for July 2001 and 2002 we have $4,980.99/MW and $6,336.01/MW, respectively. Hence, the value of the entire SGT plant simply is equal to $7,179,381.25 (i.e. $14,358.8/MW times 500MW, which is the capacity of the currently owned SGT) (input numbers are shown rounded).

For the plant owner, it makes sense to stay in the generation business rather than quitting the business.

Using NPV analysis on the same plant, however, we calculated a value of only $959,936.47. That is, calculations based on real option analysis yields a seven-fold larger value for the same plant. The NPV method suggested that selling the SGT plant for its scrap value was a good decision. Now, real option analysis suggests that selling the plant for $1 million would be a considerable loss. For the plant owner, it makes sense to stay in the generation business rather than quitting the business. If we relied on the NPV method, we would have sold the power plant for its scrap value and quitted the electricity business. The real option method, on the contrary, suggests that we should keep the power plant. Hence, using real option analysis yields a totally different answer to that provided by the NPV method.

Where does this value come from? Let us consider the date of 1 July 2000. What is the generating capacity worth, to produce a MWh of electricity? NPV says it is the discounted value of electricity price, S, minus the exercise price, E. For 1 July 2000 this equals $2/MWh (= $46/MWh – $44/MWh) discounted to today. If today were the last instant for deciding whether to generate electricity on 1 July, i.e. if there was no time until the exercise decision, our call option to produce immediately would have a value of $2/MWh. This is the payoff at the option expiry, i.e. its intrinsic value. The extra value $5.89/MWh (= 7.89 – 2.00) comes from the time value of the option. A fall in the electricity prices cannot make the value of a call option less than zero. Given a 50 per cent chance that the electricity price in the future will fall below the current (profitable) price of $46/MWh, there is less than a 50 per cent chance that the fall will be large enough to wipe out our profit, leaving the option to expire worthless at zero. However, there is also an equal chance of 50 per cent that the electricity price will rise above $46, thus increasing our level of profit from the $2 we would get today. It is this upside potential which drives the value of the call option to produce in future.

The main assumption behind the call option pricing calculation is that electricity prices follow a random walk. Since electricity markets are competitive, we can assume that the behaviour of the electricity prices is indeed a random walk. So, the underlying market price of electricity is likely to rise or fall between now and any instant in the future. That is, if the market price of electricity is at $46/MWh now, our best forecast for all future times is $46/MWh. Our best and only forecast is always the current price of electricity, since a rise is just as likely as a fall over any possible future period (i.e. always 50 per cent).[13]

What is the CCGT plant worth?

The value of the CCGT plant is calculated in a similar fashion. Table 6.5 shows sample calculations for July 2000 and is directly equivalent to Table 6.2. As we can see, the only difference to Table 6.4, where we calculated the call value of the SGT, is in the generation cost, E (i.e. the exercise price of the call option). In the case of the SGT the exercise prices of the call options were closer to the market price of electricity, S (exercise price and market price were $44/MWh and $46/MWh respectively). In option terminology, we would say that the call option is only slightly in the money.

The CCGT has a lower cost of generation at only $39/MWh. Since the exercise price per MWh electricity for the CCGT is now much lower than the market price of $46/MWh, the call option for it is deeper in the money than the SGT (higher intrinsic value). But the 'moneyness' of an option changes the time value of the option. We have already explained that the time value is greatest when the option is at the money. For options that still have some time until exercise (i.e. before expiry) the option has relatively lower time value if they are far from the money (see, for example, Figure 6.2). For the SGT plant, the time value of a single call option expiring on 1 July 2000 was $5.89/MWh (= 7.89 – 2). The same option for the CCGT has a smaller time value of $3.69/MWh (= 10.6 – 7), although its intrinsic value is larger.

Table 6.5	**Call value/MWh of the CCGT plant for July 2000** (volatility = 0.5, risk-free rate = 0.05)			
Generation day	7/1/00	7/2/00	7/3/00	....
$T - t$ (time to maturity in years)	0.4986	0.5014	0.5041	....
S ($/MWh)	46	46	46	....
E ($/MWh)	39	39	39	....
Call value ($/MWh)	10.69	10.71	10.72	....

Following the same steps as in the valuation of the SGT plant, and noting that the remaining operational life of the CCGT is ten years and its capacity is 960MW, we find that the value of the CCGT plant is $83,354,309.46. This is well above the $25 million for which it is being offered. The NPV method valued the same plant to be worth only $15.73 million, and suggested that it would not be a rational decision to buy the CCGT. Real option analysis, however, suggests that the offer of $25 million is below the CCGT's 'fair value' of $83.35 million.

Hence, based on real option analysis we would go ahead and buy the CCGT since it represents a clear opportunity. In contrast, the NPV method suggested that the CCGT was worth only $15.73 million, and the owner of the SGT plant should not invest in the CCGT. As already noted, NPV suggested the plant owner should quit the electricity generating business by selling the existing power plant for its scrap value of $1 million. In the present case, the results of the real option analysis totally contradict the suggestions of the NPV method. The SGT plant owner should keep the existing plant; indeed he should expand the business by acquiring the CCGT under consideration.

Are there other strategies which the plant owner has not thought of yet?

So far, we have focused on decisions of whether to sell the existing SGT plant or to continue operating the plant, and whether to expand business by acquiring the CCGT or not. Based on the real option analysis, the plant owner has another strategy that he has not thought of yet. It is the idea of 'arbitrage'.

Since for the CCGT plant real option analysis yields a value of $83.35 million, the plant owner could make an arbitrage profit by acquiring the CCGT plant for the value he has been offered ($25 million) and selling it later to another party for the much higher price of $83.35 million, which is the theoretical fair value of the CCGT plant. Hence, using real option analysis a market player may realize arbitrage opportunities in the market.

Improving the realism of the model in the real option analysis

In the real option analysis we have made various assumptions and simplifications. Let us address some of them and suggest ways of improving the realism of the model framework. We will directly estimate the effect on value (and on recommended decisions) of relaxing some of the assumptions we have made so far.

Constraints

For our real option analysis, we have so far assumed that there are (i) no startup constraints or costs and (ii) no physical constraints, such as minimum uptime and downtime constraints. We have assumed that there are no startup delays, that is, a generation plant can be started up instantly whenever the market price for electricity exceeds the variable generation costs. Although the response time is only several hours, a certain lead time for the commitment decision is, however, necessary to start up a power plant, and the costs associated with startup depend on how long the plant has been down.[14] A gas-fired power plant cannot be switched on and off arbitrarily. Once a plant is shut down, it is required to stay off-line for a minimum period (minimum downtime) before it can be started up again. Similarly, once a power plant is started up, it is required to stay on-line for a minimum period (minimum uptime) before shutting down again. Furthermore, a power plant can become unavailable because of planned (e.g. for maintenance purposes) or forced (i.e. unplanned) outages (e.g. as a result of component failure). Tseng and Barz (1999), for example, demonstrate through Monte Carlo simulations that startup costs and physical constraints may result in a difference of up to 6.5 per cent in power plant value.

Assumption of the random walk for electricity prices

As we have explained, the main assumption behind the calculation of call option values is that electricity prices (which are the underlying asset for the option) follow a random walk – that is, the best and only forecast is always the current price of electricity, since a rise is just as likely as a fall over any possible future period. Note, however, that random walk is not the only assumption for modelling the underlying electricity prices. For example, Deng, Johnson and Sogomonian (1999) assume mean reverting price processes to derive the value of the spark spread call option.[15]

Commodities have often been observed to follow a mean reverting evolution (see Appendix 5 and Chapter 10). Likewise, electricity may be assumed to follow a mean reverting behaviour over time, (i.e. random short-term deviations from a long-term mean, but with a tendency of prices to revert to the long-term mean). This is reflected in a decaying term structure of volatility.[16] That is, the longer the time to maturity, the lower the volatility. Hence, it would make sense to find out what effect a decaying volatility has on the value of a plant. In order to find out the sensitivity of the values for SGT and CCGT to mean reversion we have performed the same calculations as before except for the decaying term structure of volatility. That is, instead of a constant volatility of 50 per cent we inputted lower volatilities for increasing maturity options (see Appendix 2 of this chapter). This resulted for the SGT plant in a 14.74 per cent lower value than our initial real option calculations of $7.18 million. Similarly, for the value of the CCGT plant with mean reversion we have 23.31 per cent lower value than the $83.35 million initially calculated.[17] These results are consistent with those of Hamdan (1999).

Random walk assumes that the price change for electricity is normally distributed. This also implies that changes in prices are mostly small for very small dt. When there are jumps in the market price of electricity, discontinuities in the evolution of the price process emerge. Shocks to future demand and supply generate relatively large changes in short-term market prices in comparison to the long-term market prices. Responses to shocks that affect future demand and supply are more pronounced in the short-term dynamics of the market.[18] Supply and demand shocks in energy commodities tend to create much higher price-dependent volatility and price discontinuity than in other markets.[19] In particular, very high volatility occurs when prices are much higher than average. This leads to so-called 'fat tails' in the probability density function of energy prices – extreme events have higher probability than implied by the normal distribution.[20]

Generation costs

We have assumed that there are only variable costs of generation – that is, the fixed costs of keeping the plant are negligible. This may be realistic for a portfolio of power plants where a single power plant only marginally contributes to the overall fixed costs. If a non-utility owner has, however, only a single plant, the fixed costs may be important. With regard to variable generation costs (i.e. fuel, operation and maintenance costs) we have assumed that these are constant and depend on the type of the power plant. Because operation and main-tenance costs constitute a relatively small part of generation costs (less than 10 per cent), it may be safe to assume that these are constant over time. The same assumption is not valid for fuel prices, however. Natural gas prices have experienced high levels of volatility since deregulation. For example, the aver-age annual volatility of the spot price of the natural gas between the inception of Henry Hub natural gas trading on the New York Mercantile Exchange on 3 April 1990 and 31 March 1997 was 49.45 per cent.[21]

If we relax the assumption of constant fuel costs, and allow for uncertainty in natural gas prices, we cannot use the simple call option formula of Black and Scholes (see Appendix 1 for its specifications) to value a call option (and a power plant). Rather, we would then need to use a formula which takes into account the uncertainty in generation costs.[22] This suggests using the exchange option formula of Margrabe (see also my Appendix 1) in order to value the right to exchange in the future between two randomly varying commodities, namely gas fuel and generated electricity. We have applied the exchange option model to value both the SGT and the CCGT power plant. Using as before a volatility of 50 per cent for the price of electricity, and assuming 40 per cent volatility for the fuel price, and a correlation of 40 per cent between electricity and gas prices,[23] the real option analysis yields a value of $6,425,917.69 for the value of the SGT plant. Earlier, using the simple call option model, we valued the same plant at $7,179,381.25. Similarly, for the same input parameters, the value of the CCGT is calculated to be $73,894,340.76 (versus $83,354,309.46 before).[24]

The results provided by the option analysis using an exchange option model rather than the simple call option are, however, highly sensitive to the level of cor-relation assumed between electricity and gas prices. We ran a sensitivity analysis showing the effect of different correlation levels for the value of the SGT plant. As we can see in Figure 6.3, correlation adversely affects plant value. That is, the lower the correlation between the price of electricity and price of the generation costs, ceteris paribus, the higher the value of the plant. For example, a negative correlation of –0.4, ceteris paribus, yields a value of $9.2 million for the plant.

To price power call options we need to make assumptions regarding the cor-relation coefficient. Although in general correlations between natural gas and electricity prices are positive, most of the time this correlation is unstable.[25] Empirical research in energy prices, such as Johnson and Barz (1999), show this unstable evolution of the correlation between electricity and gas prices, which may range from –0.3 to 0.9.

Note, however, that the main conclusions about the decisions faced by the SGT owner stay the same even after we adjust the calculations to allow for operating constraints, for mean reversion in electricity prices, and for uncer-tainty in fuel costs.

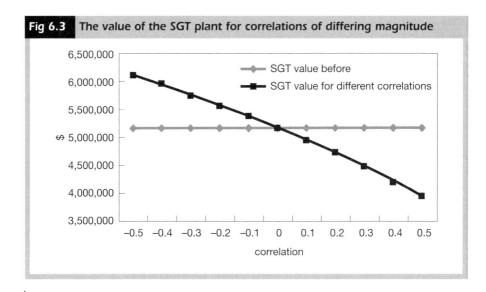

Fig 6.3 The value of the SGT plant for correlations of differing magnitude

- Based on real option analysis we would still go ahead and buy the CCGT since it represents a clear opportunity (allowing for uncertainty in generation costs and a positive correlation of 40 per cent between electricity prices and gas prices, the value for the CCGT is at $36,621,714.93, which represents almost a worst-case scenario, versus its offer price of $25 million).

- We may even be able to immediately sell the CCGT for an arbitrage profit.

- Quitting the business would be the wrong strategy. Allowing for uncertainty in generation costs and a positive correlation between electricity and gas prices, the SGT currently owned is worth $4,225,965.52 which is well above its scrap value of $1 million.

- In summary, the results of the (improved) real option analysis still totally contradict the suggestions of the NPV method, which were to quit the generation business.

Other methods of computation than closed-form (analytic) solution

We have calculated option prices using closed-form solutions. One can also value a power call option using Monte Carlo simulation methods. The basic idea is to use random numbers to simulate possible price paths for the underlying asset prices. The simulations are repeated many times, and for each price path the payoff is calculated and discounted back to the present. The advantage of Monte Carlo simulation is that one can relatively easily improve realism by increasing the complexity, for example, by incorporating startup constraints and physical constraints, such as minimum uptime and downtime constraints.[26] The main drawback of the method is in the large computation time necessary for convergence.[27]

Other complications outside of the model

So far, we have only discussed factors that are implicitly assumed in a model. Other complications may arise outside of the model's framework. There may be market frictions that influence the level of prices, such as transmission constraints. We have assumed that the generated electricity can be brought to the market, but this may not be true when there are transmission problems, such as congestion or other problems in the transmission network.

In addition, sudden shocks to supply and demand may cause shifts to the relative prices and long-term conditions in the market. Changes in regulation influence the level and the volatility of electricity prices. These as well as other supply and demand shocks will affect the evolution of prices. For example, new technologies for power plants may change the level of efficiency and the relative costs in the market. The same is also true for environmental and political risks (e.g. the demand by the Greens to shut down all nuclear power plants and to promote alternative electricity generation).

Conclusions

This case study has evaluated the decisions faced by a non-utility power plant owner using NPV methods and real option analysis. A power plant is equivalent to a series of European call options to produce, and these can be valued using Black–Scholes models borrowed from financial markets. We have performed both NPV and real option analysis to evaluate some key decisions faced by a plant owner, namely whether to sell the plant and quit the volatile electricity business, or to expand by acquiring a second plant.

The recommendations of the NPV method, which suggested quitting the business, were opposite to those of real options analysis. Although this case study is simplified, it shows that conventional NPV methods are not adequate for dealing with uncertainty in a competitive market such as electricity. For important strategic investment and asset management decisions, arriving at wrong recommendations, even in

> **Conventional NPV methods are not adequate for dealing with uncertainty in a competitive market such as electricity.**

cases less extreme than those illustrated here, can cause a market player to lose competitive ground. Conversely, understanding and using real option analysis may make the difference in staying ahead of the competition.

The marketplace for electricity is deregulating rapidly. With all the changes and resulting competition in electricity generation, asset valuation takes on a new urgency and a new dimension.

The application of real option analysis to the electricity industry is not limited to the types of decision evaluated here. Other applications of real option analysis include optimization of plant dispatch, valuation of transmission assets (transmission options), product pricing and structuring, and various aspects of risk management.

Appendix 1

This appendix shows the formulas used in the main text. These are the formulas for a simple call option of Black and Scholes and a call exchange option of Margrabe.

The value of a simple call, c, is expressed in closed-form solution by Black and Scholes (1973) as follows.

$$c = S \cdot N(d_1) - e^{-r(T-t)} E \cdot N(d_2) \tag{6}$$

where

$$d_1 = \frac{\ln\left(\frac{S}{E}\right) + \left(r + \frac{\sigma^2}{2}\right)(T-t)}{\sigma\sqrt{T-t}} \tag{7}$$

$$d_2 = d_1 - \sigma\sqrt{T-t} \tag{8}$$

where

$S =$ current market price of the asset (e.g. of electricity)
$E =$ price of the exercise[28] (e.g. costs of generation)
$r =$ riskless rate of interest
$\sigma =$ volatility of the underlying asset
$T - t =$ time to maturity, time to expiry
$N(\cdot) =$ cumulative normal distribution.[29]

The value of a call option to exchange one asset for another, i.e. to exchange E for S, is expressed in a closed-form solution by Margrabe (1978) similar to a simple call option.

$$c = S \cdot N(d_1) - E \cdot N(d_2) \tag{9}$$

$$d_1 = \frac{ln\left(\dfrac{S}{E}\right) + \left(\dfrac{\sigma^2}{2}\right)(T-t)}{\sigma\sqrt{T-t}} \tag{10}$$

$$d_2 = d_1 - \sigma\sqrt{T-t} \tag{11}$$

where

$$\sigma = \sqrt{\sigma_S^2 + \sigma_E^2 - 2\rho\sigma_S\sigma_E}.$$

In comparison to the simple call option, the volatility of the call exchange option consists of the market price volatility, σ_S, and the volatility of the exercise price, σ_E, whereas the Black and Scholes formula assumes that the only uncertain variable is the market price of the asset, S, and everything else is constant. This formula assumes that both S and E are uncertain variables, each with a different uncertainty level. The correlation between S and E is measured by the correlation coefficient, ρ.

Appendix 2

This appendix shows the results of the sample calculations for valuing the SGT and CCGT plant in the main text. Note that calculations are carried out in Excel. The spreadsheets for the calculations can be obtained from the author on request (mustafa@cavus.de).

Table 6.4   **Call value per MWh of the SGT plant for July 2000 (see the main text)**

Generation day	1/7/00	2/7/00	3/7/00	......
$T-t$	0.4986	0.5014	0.5041	.....
S	46	46	46	.....
E	44	44	44	.....
d_1	0.37	0.37	0.37	.....
d_2	0.02	0.02	0.02	.....
$N(d_1)$	0.65	0.65	0.65	.....
$N(d_2)$	0.51	0.51	0.51	.....
Call value	7.89	7.91	7.93	....

Table 6.5	Call value/MWh of the CCGT plant for July 2000 (see the main text)			
Generation day	1/7/00	2/7/00	3/7/00	......
$T - t$	0.4986	0.5014	0.5041	.....
S	46	46	46	.....
E	39	39	39	.....
d_1	0.71	0.71	0.71	.....
d_2	0.36	0.36	0.36	.....
$N(d_1)$	0.76	0.76	0.76	.....
$N(d_2)$	0.64	0.64	0.64	.....
Call value	10.69	10.71	10.72	......

Table 6.6	Call value per MWh of the SGT plant for July 2000 (volatility = 0.5, riskless rate = 0.05)			
Generation day	1/7/00	2/7/00	3/7/00	......
$T - t$	1.50	1.50	1.50	.....
S	46	46	46	.....
E	44	44	44	.....
d_1	0.50	0.50	0.50	.....
d_2	−0.11	−0.11	−0.11	.....
$N(d_1)$	0.69	0.69	0.69	.....
$N(d_2)$	0.46	0.46	0.46	.....
Call value	13.22	13.23	13.24	......

Effect of decaying volatility term structure

We assumed that the volatility was decreasing as follows:

Year	2000	2001	2002	2003	2004	2005	2006	2007	2008	2009
Volatility	0.5	0.4	0.35	0.3	0.25	0.2	0.2	0.2	0.2	0.2

Whereas we have a volatility of 50 per cent in 2000, for our calculations of call options in 2001 we use 40 per cent volatility, 35 per cent in 2002, and so on. We keep everything else the same. This means for July 2000 the calculations are exactly the same as before (see Table 6.4). For July 2001, for example, our calculation for July 2001 yields the results provided in Table 6.7.

Table 6.7	Call value per MWh of the SGT plant for July 2000 with volatility of 40 per cent			
Generation day	1/7/01	2/7/01	3/7/01	......
$T - t$	1.50	1.50	1.50	.....
S	46	46	46	.....
E	44	44	44	.....
d_1	0.49	0.49	0.49	.....
d_2	0.00	0.00	0.00	.....
$N(d_1)$	0.69	0.69	0.69	.....
$N(d_2)$	0.50	0.50	0.50	.....
Call value	11.23	11.24	11.25	....

The effect of the decreasing volatility can be seen when we compare the results in Table 6.7 with those of Table 6.6. For example, the call value for 1 July 2001 is $7.88/MWh, whereas the same call with a volatility of 50 per cent in Table 6.6 was $9.01/MWh.

Incorporating uncertainty in generation costs

Table 6.8	Call value per MWh of the SGT plant for July 2000 to 2002 (volatility of S and E are assumed to be 0.5 and 0.4 respectively; correlation is assumed to be 0.4)			
Generation day	1/7/00	2/7/00	3/7/00	......
Call value	7.36	7.37	7.39	....
Generation day	1/7/01	2/7/01	3/7/01	......
Call value	11.85	11.86	11.87	....
Generation day	1/7/02	2/7/02	3/7/02	......
Call value	14.85	14.86	14.86	....

Notes

1. Mustafa Cavus works as a senior analyst in the trading and risk management advisory group of Capstone Global Energy, a consultancy that applies financial analysis to the energy industry.

2. A corporation, person, agency, authority, or other legal entity or instrumentality that owns electric-generating capacity and is not an electric utility. Non-utility power producers include qualifying co-generators, qualifying small power producers, and other non-utility generators (including independent power producers) without a designated franchised service area.

3. See, for example, Thierer (1997) for an overview of the deregulation impact.

4. Price transparency is being achieved in the futures and forwards markets for electricity. The New York Mercantile Exchange began trading monthly electricity futures contracts in April 1996. Both Dow Jones and McGraw-Hill have introduced a series of electricity price indices, quoting daily and weekly prices in a number of trading locations. Electricity brokers are offering an increasing array of price quotes for a variety of terms and locations.

5. The amount of electric energy produced is usually expressed in watt hours (Wh), kilowatt hours (kWh), or megawatt hours (MWh). One kilowatt hour equals one hour of using electricity at a rate of 1,000 watts. Three-and-a-half kilowatt hours will provide enough power to keep a 150-watt light bulb on for an entire day. One megawatt hour equals 1,000 kilowatt hours (1,000 kWh).

6. A combined-cycle system is the most efficient way to use gas by combining two means of producing electricity. Hot gases from the combustion chamber spin the gas turbine and the generator to make electricity. The system then pipes the still-hot exhaust gases leaving the combustion turbine to a 'waste heat' steam boiler where their heat produces steam. The steam turns a turbine, connected to a second generator, to produce electricity. Condensers convert the steam to water that returns to the boiler to repeat the cycle. Because steam turbines can be built larger than gas turbines, a combined-cycle system often uses several gas turbines to feed hot exhaust to one steam boiler.

7. The amount of fuel that a particular power plant requires to generate a given amount of electricity is summarized in its heat rate. The lower the heat rate, the more efficient the facility.

8. The volatility of the (electricity) price is a measure of how uncertain we are about the future price movements. As volatility increases, the chance that the price will go a considerable way either up or down increases.

9. Power plants are bought and sold all the time. For example, according to the Energy Information Administration, Office of Coal, Nuclear, Electric and Alternative Fuels, US Department of Energy there were 122 electric utility plants sold in 1999 (see *Electric Power Monthly*, March 2000, http://www.eia.doe.gov/cneaf/electricity/epm_sum.html).

10. Obviously, the choice of the correct discount rate is key in the NPV method. But what should the discount rate be in a volatile market like electricity?

11. For a discount rate of 0.01 per cent the NPV of the CCGT would be $24,985,800.22.

12. This is often referred as a 'spark spread' option.

13. Strictly speaking this assumption of random behaviour is valid for the logarithm of the electricity price, since electricity prices cannot go negative. We are also assuming that any non-random 'seasonality' of electricity prices within the day has already been allowed for. Delta hedging will of course eliminate its effects anyway (see main text Appendix 3).

14. This is, for example, due to the fact that the water in a gas-fired plant must be heated before electricity can be generated. The longer the generator is down, the more heat is lost and the longer it takes – and the greater the expense – to reheat the water.

15. The authors use closed-form solutions in conjunction with information from futures and options markets to value generation assets. When futures and options markets for the underlying commodity are liquid enough, one should make use of such information. For simplicity, the present case study assumes that electricity futures and options markets are not liquid enough.

16. Term structure of volatility refers to volatility functions, which describes the volatility as a function of maturity. That is, the longer time to maturity, the lower the volatility. For this reason, it makes sense to find out what effect decaying volatility has on the value of a plant.

17. See also Table 6.7 in Appendix 2 of this chapter for a sample calculation showing the effect of the decaying volatility term structure.

18. Although the demand shock is permanent, the current market price increases more than expected market prices because anticipated supply and demand responses mean that part of the effect of the shock on the current price is temporary.

19. See, for example, Putney (1999) and Joy (1999).

20. According to Hamdan (1999), the spike-like increases in electricity prices are mainly due to the starts of expensive peaking units that are turned on during periods of unusually high loads and outages in baseload and marginal generating units. His results demonstrate that incorporating jumps into electricity prices increases the option value (hence the value of a power plant).

21. Note that this estimation is based on historical price data from for the nearest to maturity futures positions traded on NYMEX.

22. This means modelling option prices using a multi-factor (i.e. multi-uncertainty) model rather than a single-factor model used in the analysis so far.

23. This assumption is based on Deng, Johnson and Sogomonian (1999).

24. See also Table 6.8 in Appendix 2 of this chapter for a sample calculation.

25. Low correlation may arise, for example, during the summer season when natural gas prices are low while those of electricity peak.

26. See, for example, Tseng and Barz (1999).

27. See, for example, Putney (1999) for application of Monte Carlo methods for energy derivatives.

28. Note that the exercise price consists of fuel cost plus operating and maintenance costs.

29. $N(d)$ is the probability that a normally distributed random variable will be less than or equal to d.

Two case studies on real estate development

7

by Jose Antonio de Azevedo-Pereira

Campero

Editor's introduction:

This simplified real estate problem gives an interesting example of an asset that is wasting (here a lease) so that its terminal value on expiry is zero in all possible states of the market. The analysis shows how easily such a decision can be formulated and solved using a binomial tree.

The decision*: at what price to offer a lease, which will give the right to operate a holiday resort for ten years.*

Option-like features*: uncertainty in future rental income – an option exists not to operate in any year in which rental income is too low to cover avoidable operating costs. Hence the lease is a bundle of European calls to operate.*

Equation and model*: single random factor (rental prices). Finite bundle of calls to produce. No dividend or fixed period costs.*

Boundary conditions*: terminal boundary condition is that the lease has a value of zero under all states of the random factor on expiry date T. No other fixed boundaries are encountered up to time T. Boundary for the decision to operate in each year is simply the avoidable cost of production as that year's option to operate expires.*

Solution method*: numerical solution by binomial tree.*

Implications*: value of lease is much higher than simplistic NPV would suggest.*

Possible data biases*: estimated volatility is very high.*

Potential enrichments of the model*: random changes in interest rates; frictional costs of opening and closing the resort; fixed costs of owning a non-operating resort; intermediate levels of occupation between empty and full.*

The decision problem

Leasimo, SA is studying the possibility of buying a lease on the Campero holiday resort for the next ten years. Campero is a top-quality tourist resort of 15,000 square metres located in the Algarve and owned by Fenapu. In order to maintain high standards, Campero's operating costs are high compared to those incurred by competing resorts.

According to experts, the annual operating costs of Campero should average €220/m² during the next ten years. Such costs will be incurred only if the resort actually operates, so whoever runs the resort has an operating option to open the resort or not in a given year.

At the moment Campero generates annual gross revenue of €500/m² based on the rents charged to holidaymakers. Given the quality of the resort and the past demand, it is expected that Campero's capacity can be fully occupied during the next ten years.

The risk-free interest rate is 10 per cent.

Fenapu's chief financial officer wants to set a price on the lease. Accordingly she wants to know the net present value of the total rents a holiday operator could charge during this period, net of operating costs.

Deterministic framework

Initially, she is prepared to assume that during the next ten years the rent income will inflate at 18.4 per cent on average, but operating costs per square metre will stay unchanged. The latter are based on a known and fixed average operating cost. Since the expected rent increase is in fact risky, it should be discounted at a suitable risk-adjusted rate. Fenapu believes that a rate of 25 per cent is appropriate.

Using a standard NPV approach and using an assumed risk-adjusted cost of capital of 25 per cent, the value of the lease will be:

$$Lease = \sum_{t=1}^{10} \frac{15,000m^2 \times Revenue\ per\ square\ metre}{(1.25)^t} - \sum_{t=1}^{10} \frac{15,000m^2 \times 220}{(1.25)^t}$$

$$= (15,000m^2 \times 500) \times \left[\frac{1}{0.25 - 0.184} - \frac{1}{0.25 - 0.184} \times \left(\frac{1.184}{1.25} \right)^{10} \right]$$

$$- (15,000m^2 \times 220) \times \left[\frac{1}{0.25} - \frac{1}{0.25} \times \left(\frac{1}{(1.25)^{10}} \right) \right]$$

$$= €35.72\ million$$

Risky framework

Although we have noted that the initial rent would be €500/m^2 a year, it is not possible to predict exactly what is going to happen to rent during the whole period of ten years. According to experts, it is possible that in each year the price will suffer an increase of approximately 38 per cent (with a probability of 70 per cent) or a decrease of approximately 27.5 per cent (with a probability of 30 per cent) compared with the previous year. This gives the average or expected increase per year of 18.4 per cent.

The average annual rent chargeable to clients will be known at the beginning of each year, but the payment will only take place at the end of the same year.

By taking all this information into consideration, it is possible to find the (present) value of the rent stream using an option pricing framework. Given the large capital value at stake, Fenapu's chief financial officer wants to make a second valuation of the lease, using such an option pricing procedure.

Assuming price efficiency in the Portuguese rental market, it is possible to use a binomial lattice framework to represent the rental prices per square metre that it will be possible to make during the next ten years.[1]

Using an annual time step, and allowing for the possible price changes but ignoring their probabilities, the following lattice of possibilities is determined for the level of rents in each individual year. If Leasimo takes the lease, it will be able to operate during years one to ten.

											12553.7
										9094.8	
									6588.9		6588.9
								4773.4		4773.4	
							3458.2		3458.2		3458.2
						2505.4		2505.4		2505.4	
					1815.1		1815.1		1815.1		1815.1
				1315.0		1315.0		1315.0		1315.0	
			952.6		952.6		952.6		952.6		952.6
		690.2		690.2		690.2		690.2		690.2	
Rental value per m²	500.0		500.0		500.0		500.0		500.0		500.0
		362.2		362.2		362.2		362.2		362.2	
			262.4		262.4		262.4		262.4		262.4
				190.1		190.1		190.1		190.1	
					137.7		137.7		137.7		137.7
						99.8		99.8		99.8	
							72.3		72.3		72.3
								52.4		52.4	
									37.9		37.9
										27.5	
											19.9

The rental value of the Campero resort depends on two randomly evolving factors – the future rental prices to be charged to tourists, and the future interest rate. Consequently, if the interest rate can be assumed to be fixed, the present value of the Campero rental stream can be valued as an asset which is a derivative (only) of the rental prices.

The lease will run only for the next ten years. Consequently, at the end of the tenth year, the value of future rents will be zero in all the nodes. At the end of the ninth year, the value of the future rents will correspond to the net cash flows to be made in the tenth year, discounted back to the end of the ninth year.

The value of the rent collected at the end of each year is given by the product of the rental price per square metre for that year (determined at the beginning of the same year) less operating cost per square metre, multiplied by the number of square metres to rent. Consequently, the value at the top node will be:

$$Lease\ value = 15,000m^2 \times \left[\frac{(9094.8{-}220.0)}{1.1} \right]$$

$$\cong €121.02\ million$$

Similarly, at the bottom node in the ninth year, the present value of the rents to be made, if the resort is kept open, will be:

$$Lease\ value = 15,000m^2 \times \left[\frac{(27.5 - 220.0)}{1.1} \right]$$

$$\cong €{-}2.63\ million$$

However, all operating costs are avoidable and Campero's management team is not compelled to keep the resort open. Consequently, management holds an option to open or to close the resort, according to conditions in the tourist rental market. Hence, in the event of rental prices as low as 27.5, Campero will remain closed, and the value to consider in the bottom node of the lattice will be zero. In a similar way, values of the resort's income are found for the other possible levels of rents during year nine.

Assuming price efficiency in the Portuguese rental market, the risks of the two possible outcomes that follow any node in year eight can be hedged away, and the value of the hedged amount is given by weighting the two possible outcomes, using the so-called risk-neutral probabilities.

Using the data given above, the weighting on the favourable outcome (upward move in price) is:

$$q = \frac{1 + r - d}{u - d}$$

$$= \frac{1.100 - 0.725}{1.380 - 0.725}$$

$$\cong 57.25\%$$

For any node in the previous year (eight), the value of the total rental stream will be given by the sum of two components: the net cash flow that can be made during year eight and the hedged net value of the two possible rental streams in year nine, valued using risk-neutral probabilities.

The same type of procedure can be implemented recursively to determine the following lattice of possible total values in all years:

Present value of hedged future plus current rentals (in million euros):

Time (years)	0	1	2	3	4	5	6	7	8	9	10
											0.0
									121.0		
								174.0			0.0
							187.1			62.1	
						178.2		88.6			0.0
					158.3		94.3			31.2	
				134.1		88.5		43.8			0.0
			109.5		77.1		45.6			14.9	
		86.3		63.6		41.5		20.3			0.0
PV of the	65.7		49.8		34.6		20.0			6.4	
future rental	48.2		36.9		26.6		16.8		7.9		0.0
stream		26.0		18.9		12.3		6.7		1.9	
			12.2		8.0		4.4		1.6		0.0
				4.7		2.4		0.8		0.0	
					1.4		0.4		0.0		0.0
						0.2		0.0		0.0	
							0.0		0.0		0.0
								0.0		0.0	
									0.0		0.0
										0.0	
											0.0

Subject to minor rounding error

On this basis the present value of the Campero rental stream is €48.2 million, a significantly different amount from the €35.7 million calculated using the traditional NPV approach.

There are two reasons that underlie this difference. In the first place, the option value takes into account all possible changes in the future, and secondly, it allows for the fact that the operator has an option not to open the resort (or equivalently, has

The option value takes into account all possible changes in the future.

a call option to open the resort in any year, whose exercise price is the avoidable operating costs of opening). Traditional NPV takes the forecast outcome as fixed, then discounts it at a risky rate and does not take into account the value of the operating options, such as the one that allows Campero's management team to keep the site closed if conditions are not good.

Since the nature of the cash flow distribution associated with an option of this type is asymmetric, the final values of the traditional NPV valuation and of the options-based valuation must differ – in this case by a substantial amount. The value of the option is higher than its traditional NPV even though that higher option value can be locked in by hedging deals, and hence it can be valued (and delivered) as if it were risk-free, subject to the availability and costs of the hedging transactions themselves. Notice also that the value of the option on this basis would not change if the relative probabilities of growth and decline at any step were changed.

Constrói

A case study on the valuation of an option to defer

Editor's introduction:

This is an interesting case of an American call option to invest in developing a site which is combined with an American put option to sell the same site to the local council, both of which expire in five years' time. There is also a fixed annual payment required to keep this option alive.

The case shows how easy it is to use a binomial tree to formulate this fairly complex problem. Fixed boundary conditions exist, but they cause no difficulty as they are not encountered during the binomial calculations (compare with the discussion of the finite difference method in Appendix 4). It would be a fairly tedious task to make a continuous time model of all of these effects in the form of the Black–Scholes continuous equation, plus boundary conditions, then linearizing this model (using Taylor's theorem) before implementing it in discrete time. In contrast, the binomial method, being in discrete form already, allows the essential events and decisions at each node to be defined immediately in an intuitively obvious way, and any fixed boundaries that are not encountered during the specific calculation can be ignored (though the analyst should always be alert to their existence).

The solution: *give decision rules for whether and when to exercise the option, and at what price to sell it at any stage before exercise.*

Potential enrichments to the model: include a wider range of possible values at the end of each year (achievable by splitting the year into a larger number of branching binomial steps). This would probably increase option value.

Introduction

Almada is a small city on the outskirts of Lisbon. Fifty years ago all the land around Almada was agricultural, mostly used for grain or cattle pasture. Recently that landscape has been changing. High rates of economic development, and in particular a large number of biotechnology firms that have chosen to set up their headquarters and labs in Almada, have created the need to build on an increasing number of farms. The land has been used not only for business headquarters but also for associated houses and commercial areas. During the past decade most of the farms near the city have been developed.

Constrói, SA, a real estate developer based in the north of Portugal, bought a farm some time ago close to Almada and can start to develop it for housing as soon as it wishes. The farm is derelict, so that unless large and economically irrational investments are made in the near future, it will not be possible to conduct any type of farming on the site.

A potential development of the farm immediately would cost €10 million (in present value terms). The present value of the farm after its redevelopment is estimated at €12.5 million (so the option to develop it is in the money by 12.5 − 10 = €2.5 million). However, successive cycles of expansion and crisis in the high technology sector have affected the real estate market in the city, where the volatility of developments has been significantly high. During the next year there is a probability of 65.4 per cent that prices will increase by 50 per cent. Alternatively, prices might drop by approximately 33.3 per cent, with a probability of 34.6 per cent. The same pattern of price evolution is expected to continue for some years.

The risk-free interest rate is 10 per cent a year.

Constrói's management team is worried by the market uncertainty, and is studying the possibility of delaying the beginning of the development, since if the market falls the company may not be able to recover the investment made. However, a decision to delay might result in higher costs. Development costs are expected to grow at the specific inflation rate of the real estate sector in Portugal, 10 per cent p.a. during the next five years. Simultaneously, simply in order to retain the land, Constrói faces an annual fixed cost (administrative expenses, taxes, insurance, security) of €500,000.

Constrói is aware that it cannot postpone the start of the development process for too long. If development does not start during the next five years, it is expected that development in the neighbourhood of the farm will become so dense that the city council may declare the farm site to be of public utility. In other words, if development is not started within the next five years, the farm will probably be expropriated to create public open space. The council has already submitted an offer, which will expire in five years, to buy the farm for €1.2 million. After that deadline the council admits that it will use its legal powers to force Constrói to sell for €0.5 million.

Constrói's management team is trying to decide whether to start the development now or wait until the situation in the real estate market becomes clearer.

If the problem is to be solved using a binomial lattice framework, the first step consists in finding a binomial lattice that represents the possible evolution of the market value of the development during the next five years. There is a 65.4 per cent chance that the prices will go up by 50 per cent. Consequently, working in annual time steps, if the market goes up, the value of the developed property will be €18.8 million (1.5 times €12.5 million) in one year. Alternatively, if the market goes down, the value of the developed property will fall by 33.3 per cent to €8.3 million (0.667 times €12.5 million), also in one year. Following the same type of reasoning for the whole period, the following lattice can be determined for the possible values of the development (ignoring the probabilities of these values):

Development value, ignoring the defer option (P)

Time	0	1	2	3	4	5
						94.9
					63.3	
				42.2		42.2
			28.1		28.1	
		18.8		18.8		18.8
Values	12.5		12.5		12.5	
		8.3		8.3		8.3
			5.6		5.6	
				3.7		3.7
					2.5	
						1.6

The costs of carrying out the development, C, will not vary with house prices – their level is merely a function of expected inflation. Consequently, at each moment in time the expected value of the development costs will be given by:

$$C_t = C_{t-1} \times (1 + inflation\ rate)$$

In these circumstances, the corresponding lattice will be:

Development cost versus year of development and state of real estate market

Development costs (C)

Time	0	1	2	3	4	5
						16.1
					14.6	
				13.3		16.1
			12.1		14.6	
		11.0		13.3		16.1
Values	10.0		12.1		14.6	
		11.0		13.3		16.1
			12.1		14.6	
				13.3		16.1
					14.6	
						16.1

Knowing the value of the development costs C, it is possible to determine the net present value each moment in time of an immediate investment of C in developing the farm. In order to do this, we need only subtract the value of C from the value of P at each node. The following lattice represents the expected evolution of $(P - C)$:

Value of immediate development $(P - C)$

Time	0	1	2	3	4	5
						78.8
					48.6	
				28.9		26.1
			16.0		13.5	
		7.8		5.4		2.6
Values	2.5		0.4		-2.1	
		-2.7		-5.0		-7.8
			-6.5		-9.1	
				-9.6		-12.4
					-12.2	
						-14.5

Assuming price efficiency in the Portuguese housing market, the next step consists of finding the risk-neutral probabilities for the evolution of the development value in the next five years, assuming the option to develop is exercised rationally.

Using the data given above, the risk-neutral probability (or weighting) to be given to the value that would occur after any upward movement is:

$$q = \frac{1 + r - d}{u - d}$$

$$= \frac{1.100 - 0.667}{1.500 - 0.667}$$

$$\cong 0.52$$

The weighting to be applied to a downward movement is $(1 - q)$. Now we can derive a valuation framework based on the following decision rule: invest whenever the immediate value of the developed land is bigger than the value of the option to wait, in order to develop later.

After termination in five years, the €1.2 million offer to purchase the farm will be withdrawn. The council will thereafter pay only the legal price of €0.5 million. Consequently, the value of the whole project, V, at termination ($t = T = 5$) will be given in millions by:

The next step consists of finding the risk-neutral probabilities for the evolution of the development value in the next five years.

$$V = max\ [(P - C), 1.2]$$

Prior to that date, the value of the farm given the option to defer, V, will be given by:

$$V = max\ [(P - C), (D - M), 1.2]$$

where D represents the value of the option to defer the development of the land, and M represents the maintenance costs of €0.5 million a year needed to keep the option alive.

This reasoning can be used recursively, working from the expiry date towards the origination date (i.e. the present date), in order to determine the present effective value of the land, allowing for the option to defer investment.

Time T corresponds to the last moment at which it will be possible to start the development of the land, at which time it will no longer be possible to defer a decision. Consequently, the value of land then (if not already developed) will be given by the maximum of $(P - C)$ and the offer made by the council (€1.2 million).

At time $T - 1$, at each node, it is necessary to start the valuation of the option to defer by taking the expected (hedged) value of the developed land at time T using the weights q and $1 - q$ on the two possible values that follow each node, and then to discount this hedged value by the risk-free discount rate. Also, in order to adjust the value of the option to defer, D, we must subtract the maintenance costs to be paid, in case of deferral over that year.

V at any moment will be given by the maximum of three choices: the value of immediate development, $P - C$; the value of the option to defer, D; and the value of the purchase offer proposed by the council, €1.2 million. The same valuation procedure will be repeated backwards along the lattice towards the initial moment in time. The resulting lattice is the following:

Opportunity value V= max [$(P - C)$,$(D - M)$, 1.2]

Time	0	1	2	3	4	5
						78.8
					48.6	
				28.9		26.1
			16.0		**13.5**	
		8.4		6.4		2.6
Values	4.1		3.1		1.3	
		1.5		*1.2*		*1.2*
			1.2		*1.2*	
				1.2		*1.2*
					1.2	
						1.2

The nodes in bold are those combinations of housing price and time at which immediate development is the best solution, i.e. (P – C) > (D – M) or 1.2. The nodes in italics are cases in which immediate acceptance of the council's offer is the best course of action. The nodes in plain characters are those in which the best course of action is to defer (wait for further price evolution) because (D – M) > (P – C) or 1.2.

We see from the lattice that in the current situation the best choice is to wait before investing, as the value of the option to defer – which is the option to invest 'now or later' – is higher (at 4.1) than the expected net present value of investing immediately (at 2.5) as shown in the lattice for P – C.

Note

1. There is more on the binomial method in Chapter 4 and Appendix 4.

DixPin Biotech plc – a simple example of a binary option

8

by Andrew Stark

Editor's introduction:

In this example Andrew Stark introduces several important points about binomial options, i.e. options where there are only two possible future states. Such options are sometimes important in their own right (e.g. if there are two possible outcomes of a law suit) but also, by subdividing possible future states into a larger number of binomial branches, they can simulate any other kind of option, including continuous ones.

In this example we have the chance to invest in a new product for health care. A major government decision on health care will be taken next year, which will make our product's prospects either very good or rather mediocre.

In Chapter 4 we introduced the binomial option using a rather similar (though much simplified) example, and on that occasion we priced the option by hedging away its risks. In this case study Andrew gives much more detail about the company and its decision, and he also introduces a new and related method of valuing a binomial option, namely by using a portfolio of traded assets which exactly mimic *the risks of the option (as opposed to hedging, in which we use a portfolio of traded assets, some of which exactly* reverse *the risks of the option). In neither case do we directly need to know the probabilities of the two states, and our valuation does not directly depend on them (though in the case of the process by which the matching asset itself gets valued, objective probabilities are probably being used indirectly). If the market is complete and efficient, both routes ideally give the same value for the option, since by the principle of no arbitrage all identically risky portfolios must give identical returns, as must all risk-free portfolios.*

Our possible decisions within this problem are that we can delay our decision to invest until next year and then invest only if the government decision is favourable, or we can invest immediately. If we invest immediately, and if next year's government decision turns out to be unfavourable to us, we will have the option next year either to keep the operation going or to scrap it. We could simply invest now and keep operating.

Andrew shows that the best policy is to wait for a year, and invest only if the government decision is favourable; the second best policy is to invest now, but to scrap after a year if the government decision is unfavourable. The worst policy is to invest immediately and to keep the operation going.

In practice it can be hard to identify either matching assets or delta hedges, but the fact that these can exist in principle is an important support for the standard methods of option valuation.

***The decision:** whether and when to invest.*

***Option-like features:** call option to invest, plus a put option to disinvest.*

***Equation:** one random factor; binomial method avoids having to formulate the problem in continuous time, since the model is already in a differenced form.*

***Solution:** replication of the portfolio's risks and returns by a portfolio of traded assets – option must have the same value as a matching risky portfolio which gives identical returns to the option under the various possible future states.*

***Implications:** as stated – wrong investment timing can destroy part of the firm's value.*

***Potential enrichments of the model:** a wider range of policy choices, taking into account uncertainty over a longer time frame.*

Introduction

DixPin Biotech has a good new product which is protected by patent for at least 15 years, but it is subject to price uncertainty in a binary form, i.e. there are two possible outcomes.

In one year's time a political vote will take place, which will have powerful effects on the level of funding of DixPin's main potential customers for the foreseeable future. If the funding of the company's main customers turns out to be generous, DixPin Biotech will be able to charge a higher price and demand will be larger. If the funding of its main customers is less generous, DixPin will only be able to charge a lower price and will sell less to them. Given this uncertainty, DixPin is discussing whether it would be better to invest in the project now or wait for a year.

The details of the project are as follows:

- if investment takes place now, the company expects to sell 100,000 units of product in the first year at a price of £100 per unit;

- variable costs are expected to amount to £25 per unit for the foreseeable future;

- annual fixed costs are expected to amount to £100,000 per annum for the foreseeable future;

- in one year's time it is expected that, with equal probability, either:

    - demand will rise to 150,000 units per annum and the price to be charged will rise to £120; or

    - the price will fall to £50 per unit and demand to 30,000 units per annum.

    These levels are expected to stay constant for the life of the project, although some uncertainty will exist about future price-volume combinations;

- the project is expected to last for 15 years, although the actual life of the project will depend upon the ability of competitors to produce and patent a better product than the current one. Hence, in one year's time, the expected life of the project is 14 years;

- for each year of the project's life *subsequent* to the funding outcomes arising from the health service decisions mentioned above, its risk is thought to be similar to that of a share with a β of 1.2. The risk-free rate of return is expected to be 5 per cent per annum in all future years and the market risk premium is expected to be 10 per cent per annum in all future years, suggesting that a cost of capital of 17 per cent is appropriate for those years. DixPin is uncertain, however, about the appropriate level of risk in the year prior to the funding outcomes being revealed. Nonetheless, its financial advisers suggest that Robavanish plc, a company which is also exposed to the uncertainties surrounding funding outcomes, has a current share price of 49.25p with forecasts of share price at £1.0175 if the funding outcome is generous and 13.5p if the funding outcome is less generous. In its private evaluation of the project DixPin has performed a conventional net present value analysis of the project using a 17 per cent rate of interest for all years of the project, which results in a valuation of the opportunity at £14.4 million;

- the cost of acquiring the necessary equipment to establish a manufacturing facility is £25 million whether the facility is acquired this year or next year. The manufacturing facilities are very specialized and could not be used for any other purpose without incurring high conversion costs. If the project is abandoned, the manufacturing facility would have a value in alternative use of approximately £10 million if abandonment took place quickly. If not, its value in alternative use would quickly fall to zero;

- DixPin BioTech is perfectly happy to finance the project with equity – it believes that for a project with high asset specificity and the potential risks of this one, equity financing is the best way forward.

Because of DixPin BioTech's position at the speculative end of the stock market, it takes care to keep the market reasonably well informed about the company's new product, its underlying cost structure and the short-term uncertainty surrounding the price-volume possibilities available. Recently, DixPin has been told by market analysts that the new product opportunity contributes more than £20 million (a substantial proportion) to the current market value of the firm. Clearly, the decision as to when to invest in the project could have a substantial impact on the value of the firm's shares.

> **The decision as to when to invest in the project could have a substantial impact on the value of the firm's shares.**

The firm is undecided how to proceed. It believes that if it invests now, the project has a substantial NPV, but not one as large as the value the stock market appears to be attaching to the project. As a consequence, if investment were to take place now, it fears a substantial drop in the firm's stock market valuation.

Evaluation

To evaluate the investment opportunity outlined above, we can see that there are real options embedded within it. First, there is an abandonment (put) option, provided abandonment takes place quickly after investment. Second, there is a timing or deferment option – investment is being considered either immediately or in one year's time.

Now we turn to the cash flow benefits associated with the opportunity. If we refer to 'now' as the end of year 0, the information above suggests that the expected cash flow from operating the project in year 1 is £[100,000(100 – 25)

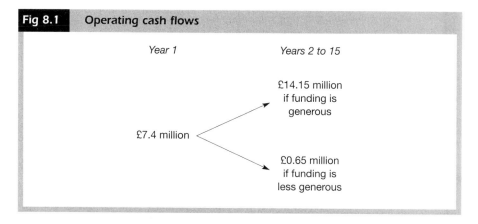

Fig 8.1   Operating cash flows

Year 1   Years 2 to 15

                                     £14.15 million
                                     if funding is
                                     generous

£7.4 million

                                     £0.65 million
                                     if funding is
                                     less generous

– 100,000] = £7.4 million. For years 2 to 15, expected cash flows will reflect the generosity of the funding outcome. If the funding outcome is generous, expected cash flows will be £[150,000(120 – 25) – 100,000] = £14.15 million in years 2 to 15. If the funding outcome is less generous, expected cash flows will be £[30,000(50 – 25) – 100,000] = £650,000 (see Figure 8.1).

Given that there is an equal probability of the funding outcome being generous or less generous, the overall expected cash flow in years 2 to 15 is £[(0.5)14.15m + (0.5)0.65m] = £7.4 million. The benefit of immediately investing in the opportunity project and operating it for the full 15 years is an annuity of cash flows equal on average to £7.4 million. If 17 per cent is used in taking the present value of this annuity, as has been done by DixPin in its private evaluation of the project, the present value of these expected cash flows is £39.4 million, resulting in an NPV of £(39.4m – 25m) = £14.4 million. This is the figure given above for the value attached to the opportunity by DixPin – it has performed a 'passive' NPV calculation which ignores the real options embedded in the project.

To apply a real options approach, we adopt the general principle of no arbitrage in well-functioning capital markets. This suggests that if a set of payoffs from a new opportunity under consideration can be replicated by a portfolio of existing opportunities, the value of the new opportunity must be equal to the value of the replicating portfolio. If not, a riskless arbitrage opportunity would exist.

We use this approach to first evaluate the true 'passive' PV of the project. This requires that we use the information contained within the knowledge of the current price of Robavanish plc and its forecasted price movements. Diagrammatically, this information can be represented as in Figure 8.2.

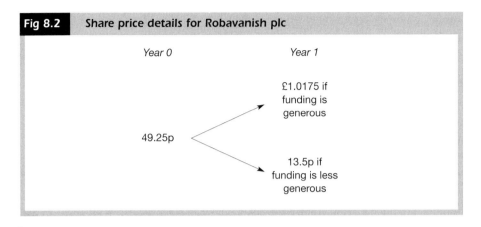

Fig 8.2   Share price details for Robavanish plc

Year 0

Year 1

49.25p

£1.0175 if
funding is
generous

13.5p if
funding is less
generous

First, we observe that the information for Robavanish plc is in terms of a set of outcomes at year 1. DixPin's opportunity, however, has cash flow outcomes over 15 years. Hence, we need a way of reducing DixPin's opportunity to an equivalent one with payoffs at year 1 which fully represent the opportunity. We do this by observing that the project, at year 1, produces a cash flow of £7.4 million together with an annuity of future income flows whose value depends upon whether the funding outcome has been generous or not. If the funding outcome is generous, the PV of the opportunity is equal to the PV of a 14-year annuity of expected cash flows equal to £14.15 million using 17 per cent as an appropriate interest rate. Under these circumstances the remaining life of the project is valued at the end of year 1 at £74 million. Alternatively, if the funding outcome is less generous, the PV of the opportunity is equal to the PV of a 14-year annuity of expected cash flows equal to £650,000 using 17 per cent as an appropriate interest rate. Under these circumstances the remaining life of the project is valued at the end of year 1 at £3.4 million.

Hence, the year 1 payoffs that totally encapsulate DixPin's opportunity are as given in Figure 8.3. Now, we can observe that the year 1 payoffs in DixPin's opportunity can be replicated by owning 80 million shares in Robavanish plc. For if funding is generous, owning 80 million Robavanish shares gives wealth of £(80m × 1.0175) = £81.4 million, whereas, if funding is less generous, the value of 80 million shares of Robavanish plc is £(80m × 0.135) = £10.8 million. As a consequence, the PV of DixPin's opportunity viewed passively must equal the current value of 80 million shares in Robavanish plc, which equals £(80m × 0.4925) = £39.4 million. This leads to an NPV of the project of £(39.4m – 25) = £14.4 million – equal to the value estimated by DixPin.

Why is this? It is because the expected return on Robavanish plc's shares is 17 per cent. Remembering that the two funding outcomes are equally likely, the expected value of

Is the opportunity more valuable abandoned than kept?

the year 1 share price for Robavanish plc is $£((0.5)1.0175 + (0.5)0.135) = 57.625p$. This represents a 17 per cent expected return on an investment of 49.25p. As a consequence, 17 per cent is an appropriate cost of capital to use in year 1 in evaluating the passive PV of the opportunity, as well as for years 2 to 15.

Now we turn to evaluating the opportunity taking into account one of the real options available within the project – the opportunity to abandon. If we invest at year 0, an opportunity to abandon the project exists at year 1. Further, if abandonment occurs, proceeds of £10 million will be realized. In thinking about abandonment at year 1, the appropriate question to ask is: is the opportunity more valuable abandoned than kept? This requires a comparison of the value of the project if kept *versus* its abandonment value. Figure 8.3 suggests that if the funding outcome is generous, the project is better kept (£74 million > £10 million). By contrast, if the funding outcome is less generous, the project is worth more abandoned (£10 million > £3.4 million). As a consequence, if abandonment possibilities in year 1 are taken into account, the payoffs of the opportunity are as indicated in Figure 8.4.

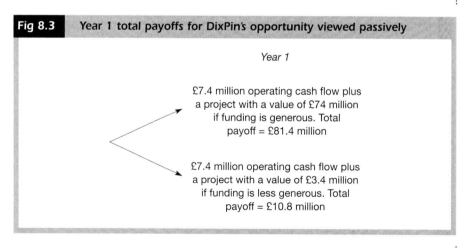

Fig 8.3   Year 1 total payoffs for DixPin's opportunity viewed passively

Year 1

£7.4 million operating cash flow plus a project with a value of £74 million if funding is generous. Total payoff = £81.4 million

£7.4 million operating cash flow plus a project with a value of £3.4 million if funding is less generous. Total payoff = £10.8 million

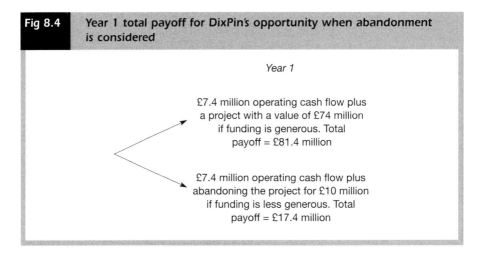

Fig 8.4 Year 1 total payoff for DixPin's opportunity when abandonment is considered

Year 1

£7.4 million operating cash flow plus a project with a value of £74 million if funding is generous. Total payoff = £81.4 million

£7.4 million operating cash flow plus abandoning the project for £10 million if funding is less generous. Total payoff = £17.4 million

We can replicate the payoffs indicated in Figure 8.4 by a suitable chosen combination of holding shares in Robavanish plc and borrowing/lending at the risk-free rate. Suitable calculations suggest that we need to hold 72,521,246 shares in Robavanish plc and lend £7,247,268 at 5 per cent. The total cash outflows to implement such a replication strategy equal £(72,521,246 × 0.4925) + £7,247,268 = £43 million. Therefore, £43 million must represent the PV of the opportunity if investment takes place at year 0 and abandonment possibilities are taken into account at year 1. This suggests that the strategy of investing at year 0 and taking into account abandonment possibilities has an NPV of £(43m – 25m) = £18 million.

We can note two things from this. First, taking into account abandonment possibilities increases the value of the opportunity if investment takes place at year 0. The value of the abandonment option equals £(18.0m – £14.4m) = £3.6 million. This is the increase in the value of the project (assuming investment has taken place at year 0) that is due to allowing abandonment at year 1.

Second, if we had taken the expected value of the payoffs at year 1 given in Figure 8.4 and taken its present value, using 17 per cent as the appropriate rate of interest, the wrong answer for the PV of the opportunity would have resulted. The expected value of the payoffs is £((0.5)81.4m + (0.5)17.4m) = £49.4 million. Dividing this by 1.17 to get its PV at 17 per cent gives £42.2 million, an understatement of the PV of the opportunity described in Figure 8.4. The reason for this is that we cannot replicate the payoffs using shares in Robavanish plc alone. If we could, as with the payoffs in Figure 8.3, the appropriate rate of interest to be used in the PV calculation for year 1 payoffs would be 17 per cent. But to replicate the payoffs in Figure 8.4, a portfolio is needed of lending at the risk-free rate plus holdings of Robavanish plc shares. For this portfolio the appropriate rate of interest is 15 per cent, reflecting the fact that the portfolio is less risky than a pure position in Robavanish plc's stock, due to the presence of the lending which yields interest at the risk-free rate.

There is one more piece of analysis needed for valuing the investment opportunity facing DixPin. This is to value its option to delay the decision to invest until year 1. Given the values of the project PVs at year 1, as indicated in Figure 8.5, it is clear that an investment at a cost of £25 million would be profitable only if the funding outcome was generous (£74 million > £25 million whereas £3.4 million < £25 million).

Again, we can value the option to wait by replicating it with a suitably chosen portfolio which combines holdings of Robavanish plc with borrowing/lending at the risk-free rate. In this case, a replication requires holding 55,524,079 shares of Robavanish plc while borrowing £7,138,810 at the risk-free rate of 5 per cent. The net cash needed to buy this portfolio is £(55,524,079 × 0.4925) − £7,138,810 = £20.2 million. Therefore, the value of the option to wait must also be £20.2 million.

Again, we can observe that if we calculate the present value of the expected payoff of the option to wait of £(49m + 0)/2 = £24.5 million using 17 per cent as the rate of interest we get the wrong value (£20.9 million). This overstates the value of the option to wait because the option to wait is more risky than a pure holding in Robavanish plc – as indicated by the requirement to take a leveraged position in Robavanish plc to replicate the payoffs of the option to wait. In fact, the expected return on the risky option to wait needs to be 21.2 per cent.

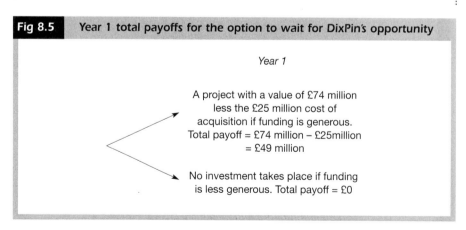

| Fig 8.5 | Year 1 total payoffs for the option to wait for DixPin's opportunity |

Year 1

A project with a value of £74 million less the £25 million cost of acquisition if funding is generous. Total payoff = £74 million − £25million = £49 million

No investment takes place if funding is less generous. Total payoff = £0

Finally, we can identify the best strategy for DixPin. Waiting until year 1 to invest gives the highest value for the opportunity – a value of £20.2 million. This value is similar to that placed on the opportunity by the well-informed market, suggesting that the market, in this case, fully understands the value of waiting. If investment takes place at year 0 (now), it would seem that even if the market then sensibly assumes that abandonment will take place at year 1, if the funding outcome turns out to be less generous, a fall will immediately take place in the company's market value of £20.2m – £18m = £2.2 million.

Conclusions

We can make a number of final points. First, in this example, the strategy of waiting was best, despite the fact that the strategy of investing immediately and retaining had an expected NPV of £14.4 million, and the strategy of investing now and abandoning, if necessary, after 1 year had an even higher expected NPV of £18 million – either earned on an investment of £25 million.

Second, waiting had particular value because of the wide disparity in the two cash flow streams depending on the funding outcome. This illustrates the general point that the value of waiting will increase as the disparity in outcomes (volatility) increases, *ceteris paribus*, as will, indeed, the value of the abandonment option.

Third, the example is inevitably simplified relative to opportunities in practice. The possibility of waiting might not be confined to one year. Abandonment possibilities might also span longer periods. This increases the complexity of the analysis – although a suitably programmed spreadsheet can cope – because of the increase in the number of strategies.

Fourth, the example assumes that DixPin has the management information systems available to track the progress of the investment opportunity. To do this is easy in the simple example above. However, it is not clear that, in practice, such systems exist for more complex projects which contain extended real options. In the absence of such information systems, it would be irrational for a company to value an opportunity as if the systems were in place, since this would inevitably overstate the value of the opportunity and could lead to the incorrect timing of investment, followed by a fall in the value of the firm.

Finally, the example assumes that the firm's managers have the same set of interests as the other shareholders. In practice, the interests of managers and shareholders are not perfectly aligned. How to align the interests of managers and owners with respect to the exercise of real options has not been much addressed in the literature on real options.

Real urban development options at Canary Wharf

9

by *Kanak Patel and Dean Paxson*

Editor's introduction:

Kanak Patel and Dean Paxson value the Canary Wharf development on the basis of data given in the flotation prospectus. As often in this book, real option methods give a higher valuation than the traditional NPV value, but sometimes the real option value is short of what the market was prepared to pay for this opportunity at a particular point in time. Similar effects have been noted in the valuation of oil reserves, and they raise important questions: was the market valuing the opportunity rationally, but in ways we are not yet aware of (for example because the market perceived a richer set of options than the authors) or was the market 'implying' a higher volatility to the development options than the authors did at a different date?

The decision: *what to pay for Canary Wharf and when.*

Option-like features: *American call options to develop and to redevelop sites, where both the development costs and the developed rental values are following random walks.*

Model: *perpetual American option to invest, at a randomly varying exercise price, in order to acquire an asset of randomly varying value. Treated as an exchange option, and the two random variables are transformed to a single random variable, the ratio between them, giving a univariate differential equation which has an analytic solution.*

Boundary conditions (given in sources): *values under extreme conditions of the random variables; value matching and smooth pasting conditions for the decision to invest; suitable boundary conditions are derived from these to apply to the transformed variable of investment value over investment cost.*

Solution: *standard analytical solution.*

Implications: *value of equity, on the chosen option basis, is far below the actual market capitalization soon after issue.*

Potential model enrichments: *include allowing for dividend payment (rents foregone by delaying development); allowing for options to redevelop.*

Introduction[1]

Real urban development options are characteristic real options in transforming urban sites into developed office properties, as illustrated in the story of the Canary Wharf Group. First, decisions are required on the type, density and timing of the property development. Then, stages of planning, construction and letting (and the development costs) are appropriately modelled as real options if the development costs and property values are uncertain.

Valuation is problematic in the case of Canary Wharf. In the *Listing Particulars*, D.C. Martin of CB Hillier Parker, and W.A.C. Newsom of FPDSavills, offered stages of valuation for 'properties under construction': open market value (OMV), open market value when completed, and net realizable

Valuation is problematic in the case of Canary Wharf.

value (NRV). These valuers are aware of the option element in some of these valuations, since for two of the properties under construction there are arrangements with Citibank, which have several complex option elements.

Furthermore, there is substantial variation in stock market analysts' valuation of the Canary Wharf properties and development programme,[2] where the shareholders' funds, adjusted for the valuers' assessment of open market value, might be £1 billion pounds *less* than the current market capitalization. The consolidated balance sheet as of September 1998 consisted of £1,457 million fixed assets, £709 million current assets, £1,589 million total liabilities, and shareholders' funds (equity) of £577 million. The company in the share placing raised a net £577 million.

We study two phases of urban development in Canary Wharf: the construction and leasing stage (3.6 million square feet) and the prospective development stage (5.2 million square feet). We provide some hypothetical solutions for the construction options, and for the development options. Is it plausible that these option values constitute around one-third of the entire stock market valuation of Canary Wharf?

We describe the Canary development properties and the methodology used by Martin and Newsom for valuation, then survey some of the literature on deferred development options for property. We then apply some of this theory in attempting to value the development options at Canary Wharf, using some of the specifications in the listing particulars, and implied volatilities for traded options on property and construction securities. Finally, we summarize the costs and benefits of valuation approaches supplementary to the open market and net realizable valuation methodologies.

Canary Wharf development properties

'The strategy of the Canary Wharf Group is to create shareholder value by controlling and actively managing all aspects of the development and operation of the Estate, including property development and construction, marketing and leasing and management of its property portfolio'.[3] There are three categories of properties excluding those developed and to be developed which have been sold to occupiers or developers:

- completed properties held for investment;

- properties under construction;

- properties held for development (see Table 9.1).

The primary property held for investment is One Canada Square, completed in 1991, with major tenants including accountants, four banks, two newspaper groups, and Canary Wharf Group itself, with 50 floors and more than 1.2 million square feet. There are seven properties under construction, ranging from relatively small retail outlets to the massive 25 Canada Square (which is almost equal in size to One Canada Square), half leased to Citibank and scheduled for completion in 2002.

The OMV given in the listing particulars is carried out in accordance with the Royal Institution of Chartered Surveyors (RICS) manual published in 1995. The OMV assumes a willing seller, a proper marketing of the interest, and no purchaser with a special interest. Since some of the tenants receive nil or reduced rent periods, the 'net annual rents receivable' (R_Rec) reflect the 'present nil rents passing under those leases'. The 'estimated net annual rent' (NAR) assumes 'the best rent at which a letting of an interest in the property would have been completed at the date of valuation'.

For properties under construction, the OMV is £572 million, and for properties held for development it is £622 million. For properties under construction,

165

Table 9.1 Canary Wharf property valuations

Held as investments

No.	Address	Sq ft	R_REC	NAR	OMV	NAR/OMV	OMV/Sq ft
1	7 Westferry	175,000	3,065,527	4,170,000	61,000,000	6.84%	349
2	10 Cabot	635,900	6,393,111	19,050,000	227,500,000	8.37%	358
3	20 Cabot	558,400	6,125,465	16,300,000	228,500,000	7.13%	409
4	One Cdn	1,235,200	23,536,234	38,573,000	600,000,000	6.43%	486
5	25 North	365,800	135,000	11,000,000	137,000,000	8.03%	381
6	30 South	294,500	3,394,990		119,000,000		404
7	Cabot R	96,300	2,432,568	2,430,000	38,000,000	6.39%	395
	Car parks		2,090,000	2,300,000	19,000,000	12.11%	
Total		3,335,100	45,082,895	91,523,000	1,411,000,000		415

Under construction

No.	Address	Sq ft	Rent	OMV	Completion cost	OMV(C)	NRV	NAR/OMV(C)	OMV(C)/Sq ft
1	17 Columbus	198,000	6,100,000	63,000,000	23,500,000	95,000,000	72,000,000	6.42%	480
2	20 Columbus	275,000		65,000,000	30,000,000	107,500,000	75,000,000		391
3	33 Canada	560,000	16,655,698	125,000,000	84,000,000	230,000,000	139,000,000	7.24%	411
4	Cdn Sq R	65,000	4,275,000	12,000,000	31,000,000	57,000,000	26,000,000	7.50%	877
5	15 Westferry	155,000	4,975,000	17,000,000	41,000,000	65,000,000	37,000,000	7.65%	419
6	8 Cdn Sq	1,100,000		140,000,000	257,000,000	490,600,000	193,000,000		446
7	25 Cdn Sq	1,220,000	44,456,000	150,000,000	310,000,000	625,000,000	365,000,000	7.11%	512
Total		3,573,000	76,461,698	572,000,000	776,500,000	1,670,100,000	907,000,000		467

Held for development

No.	Plots	Sq ft	Area	NRV (Area)	NRV/Sq ft
1	DS1	498,000	Central	495,000,000	312
2	DS3	506,000			
3	DS4	395,000			
4	DS8R	190,000			
5	HQ1	283,000	Southern	780,000,000	288
6	HQ2	930,000			
7	HQ3	300,000			
8	HQ3R	100,000			
9	HQ4	300,000			
10	HQ5	800,000			
11	BP1	440,000	Eastern	220,000,000	235
12	BP2	215,000			
13	BP3	280,000			
Total		5,237,000		1,495,000,000	
Total total		12,165,100			
Sold		1,361,400			
Gross		13,526,500			

the valuers have 'relied upon the total anticipated construction cost estimates provided by the company and confirmed as reasonable by AYH Partnership'. For properties held for development, valuers have assumed a phased development as disclosed.

Note that the largest part of the properties under construction consists of two buildings to be partially occupied by Citibank, 25 and 33 Canada Square. There are several complex option arrangements between Citibank and Canary Wharf (CW).

(i) Citibank has the *option* to require CW to take a lease of up to 100,000 square feet at 33 Canada Square for a term of 15 years or (at CW's *option*) up to 20 years, at £20/square foot up to 2004, £27 up to 2009 and thereafter at open market rent, *if higher*.

(ii) Citibank has an *option* to take up to an additional 200,000 square feet of space on the estate for a term of 15 years or (at Citibank's *option*) up to 20 years, at £20/square foot up to 2004, £27 up to 2009, and thereafter at open market rent, *if higher*.

(iii) Citibank has the *option* to require CW at any time up to May 2001 to accept a leaseback of up to 150,000 square feet in 25 Canada Square on the same terms as the lease granted to Citibank.

(iv) Citibank has the *option* until January 2003 to take up to two additional floors of 25 Canada Square at open market rent.

These options might be characterized as (i) and (iii) out-of-the-money puts, (ii) in-the-money calls, (iv) at-the-money capacity or quantity calls.

For the properties held for development, the valuers 'have allowed for the exercise by Citibank of their contractual rights to take further office space with the properties'.

The valuers have also given an opinion as to the net realizable value of the development properties. As defined in the RICS manual, NRV 'consists of the sale proceeds that it is anticipated will be received from the eventual disposal of the stock ... less the further costs to be incurred in getting the stock into marketable condition'. The valuers estimated future values and future costs using forecasted growth and inflation during the project, and discounted the NRV back to the date of assessment. A phased development programme was considered, including the developers' profit and finance costs (and risks) on holding the site.[4]

The valuers' estimated development programmes ranged over the next seven years, covering 13 buildings (5.2 million square feet) but excluding properties under construction. For properties held for development, construction costs were estimated at between £198.96 to £209.32 per square foot. The estimated rental value of office accommodation, applied to the net internal area, ranged between £30 and £36 per square foot, and the equivalent yield at practical completion ranged from 6.25 per cent to 7.25 per cent. The valuers assumed that the Canary Wharf benchmark rental was £36 in 1999, and that it would grow by a declining schedule starting at 5.6 per cent (1999), 7.9 per cent (2000) down to 3.5 per cent (after 2005). It was assumed that initially there would be a 25 per cent City of London premium rent over Canary Wharf in 1999, declining to slightly less than 15 per cent in 2005.

Theory of real property development options

There are several characteristic real property options, ranging from 'vanilla' option models assuming a simple stochastic process, to combination or compound options, including complex stochastic processes, assuming uncertain cost and uncertain developed property values.

Real property options

Ward (1982) appears to be the first to apply an option model to British property. He analyzed 'practical rent review clauses' which restricted rent reviews to 'upwards-only' changes. Ward applied both the Black–Scholes and the binomial option pricing models to the European call option that the lessor holds, with the option of exchanging the rent in the post-review period for the full market rent. Also he noted the same models could be applied to leveraged UK property companies. For both, however, he believed the usefulness of option models 'will depend on the effectiveness of the investment market in creating specific instruments that will facilitate the arbitrage and investment process'.[5]

Titman (1985) believed he was the first to propose a land pricing model that considered uncertainty, acknowledging that others had modelled the option value of irreversible investment decisions. He suggested a simple binomial model of vacant land, with constant costs to construct a building of various units. The vacant land was considered a derivative security that is derived from the future price of building units. He noted that the binomial model is solved by backward induction from the end-period states and prices; and the vacant land value increases with the uncertainty of those future building prices, which in turn increases the optimal waiting time before construction. Perhaps the most interesting aspects of Titman's work are the concluding comments that (a) a government-induced uncertainty in housing prices may lead to a decrease in building activity and (b) option models can be used to determine optimal reconstruction and renovation policies and the optimal durability of buildings.

Stochastic investment cost and property values

Several authors have developed models for stochastic investment or development (conversion) costs plus stochastic development values. Sick (1989), Dixit and Pindyck (1994) and Paxson (1997) survey several such plausible models and solutions. Williams (1991) extended the vanilla option models to both investment cost and development value uncertainty, assuming constant variance of each factor and a constant correlation between the stochastic elements (or in his case, between the rates of growth in costs and rents). He emphasized that he derived novel results only for the optimal and maximum densities of development.

Quigg (1993) utilized Williams' model for an 'empirical test' of the difference between the intrinsic value of undeveloped land and the option-theoretical value. Quigg's empirical element was based on hedonic estimation for five different types of properties in one city, with dummy variables for location and sale period, with reservations as to 'observation errors'. Using stochastic models, she then assumed that the risk-adjusted drift parameters for cost and development value are constant, and that the variance of investment cost is constant and uncorrelated with development value. Then, she 'derived' the implied volatility of development value from sales prices of undeveloped land.

Capozza, Sick and Li (1994) extended the stochastic models, assuming construction costs are constant but relaxing the assumptions as to the density (intensity) as well as the timing of development, and illustrated the relationship between land values and the location of the land, relative to the city centre. They show that the intensity value increases significantly as the volatility of the prospective rent increases. Their equations can be used to derive the 'rent vega', that is the sensitivity of hurdle rents (required rents before the development option would be optimally exercised) to the volatility of prospective rents.

Sequential development options

Grenadier (1992) valued three stages of property development, including the option to develop, the option to construct at optimal densities and times, and the option to change the mix of tenants. Williams (1997) valued the option to redevelop, assuming that office buildings have finite lives. Patel and Paxson (1998) valued several sequential European embedded options in a property development, including options to defer construction, to contract or to expand development programmes and, in the event of eventually declining demand for specified property, to switch property use.

The evolution of real property option literature involves relaxation of early assumptions as to the diffusion processes of rents and prices, and allows some of the property development variables such as investment and transaction/search costs to be considered as stochastic processes.

169

Real construction options

Consider the case of a real property construction option, where the construction cost (X) follows a stochastic process, as outlined in Williams (1991) and Quigg (1993):

$$\frac{dX}{X} = \alpha_x\, dt + \sigma_x\, dz_x \tag{1}$$

where α_X is the increase of construction costs over time and σ_X is the volatility of construction costs. Also assume that the value of the developed property P follows a similar process:

$$\frac{dP}{P} = (\alpha_P - \beta)dt + \sigma_P dz_P \tag{2}$$

where α_P is the increase of property values over time, β is the carrying cost of holding the undeveloped site, σ_P is the volatility of the values and $P = \sigma_{XP}\, dt$ is the constant correlation between dz_X and dz_P. Other assumptions made in Quigg (1993) are that the drift rates of X and P are adjusted for risk as υ_X and υ_P by multiplying the respective volatilities by risk aversion coefficients for X and P, λ_X and λ_P.

The value of the property construction option V(P,X) obeys:

$$\frac{1}{2}\sigma_X^2 X^2 V_{XX} + \sigma_{XP} XP V_{XP} + \frac{1}{2}\sigma_P^2 P^2 V_{PP} + \upsilon_X XV_X + \upsilon_P PV_P - iV + \beta P = 0 \tag{3}$$

where i is the risk-free rate.

For simplification, let z = P/X and W(z) = V(X,P)/X, the relative value of the property construction option to the construction costs, and

$$\omega^2 = \sigma_X^2 - 2\rho\, \sigma_X\, \sigma_P + \sigma_P^2 \tag{4}$$

Then equation 3 is simplified as:

$$\frac{1}{2}\omega^2 z^2 W'' + (\upsilon_P - \upsilon_X)zW' + (\upsilon_X - i)W + \beta_z = 0 \tag{5}$$

In solving this ordinary differential equation, assume there is a ratio of property value to the construction costs z*, at which it is optimal to build, and that there are certain other boundary conditions.[6]

One solution (offered by Quigg, although there are other closed-form solutions, given slightly different assumptions) is:

$$V(P, X) = X(Az^j + k) \tag{6}$$

where

$$A = (z^* - 1 - k)(z^*)^{-j} \tag{7}$$

$$z^* = \frac{j\,(1 + k)}{(j - 1)} \tag{8}$$

$$k = \frac{\beta z}{(i - \upsilon_X)} \tag{9}$$

$$j = \omega^{-2}\,(0.5\omega^2 + \upsilon_X - \upsilon_P + [\omega^2\,(0.25\,\omega^2 - \upsilon_P - \upsilon_X + 2i) + (\upsilon_X - \upsilon_P)^2\,]^{0.5}) \tag{10}$$

The intrinsic value of the option (V^I), that is the limit of equation 6, as ω tends to zero, is:

$$V^I\,(X,P) = P - X \qquad z \geq 1 + k \tag{11}$$

$$V^I\,(X,P) = \frac{\beta P}{(i - \upsilon_X)} \qquad z < 1 + k \tag{12}$$

The real property development options are positively related to the eventual developed property value, P, negatively related to the construction cost, and the sensitivity to the construction cost volatility and value volatility may be mixed, depending on the risk parameter values relative to the exchange option values reflected in equation 10.

Illustration of real development options at Canary Wharf

We estimate the real option value of both the properties under construction and the properties held for development at Canary Wharf.[7] As illustrated in Table 9.1, there are around 3.6 million square feet in the first category, in various stages of development, and around 5.2 million square feet in the second category.

The real option estimation model requires an estimate of the volatility of both development cost and developed property value. The expected volatility of properties similar to those constructed at Canary Wharf is proxied, in this case, by the (relatively short-term) traded call options for Land Securities on the London International Financial Futures Exchange (LIFFE), which reflects at least the marginal investors' expectations of the volatility of a securitized portfolio of prime (mostly London) office properties.

The real option estimation model requires an estimate of the volatility of both development cost and developed property value.

The expected volatility of construction costs for properties similar to those constructed at Canary Wharf is proxied by the (relatively short-term) traded call options for Tarmac on LIFFE Equity, which reflects at least the marginal investors' expectations of the volatility of a securitized portfolio of construction contracts. The correlation between returns on Tarmac and Land Securities is based on the daily share prices from 1 January 1994 to 1 January 1999. The correlation between the costs and values is assumed to be around 0.0083, and the volatilities are assumed to be around 26 per cent (value) and 26.3 per cent (cost).

The costs to develop are estimated from the listing particulars as £217 per square foot, which is the average completion cost per square foot of the properties under construction. The development value is £467 per square foot, which is the average open market value of the properties under construction.[8]

Real option value of CW properties under construction with the parameters assumed above, and at the current date implied volatility proxied by traded options on Land Securities and Tarmac shares, is around £967 million.[9] At the assumed development value and cost to develop per square foot, the approximate deterministic present value is around £893 million.

Figure 9.1 shows the picture of development value volatility against development cost volatility, at an assumed correlation of 0.083. The 'value-cost volatility' surface is rather flat at high-value volatility for the CW properties under con-

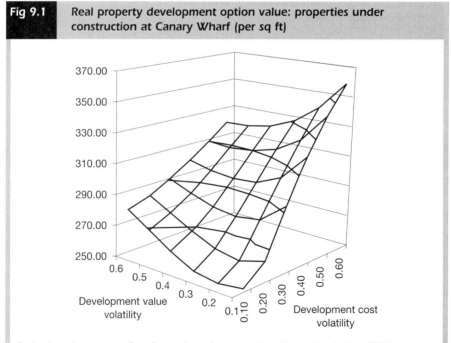

Fig 9.1   Real property development option value: properties under construction at Canary Wharf (per sq ft)

Real option value per square foot of properties under construction, with a cost to develop of £217 per square foot, development value of £467 per square foot, cost drift 3 per cent, value drift 3.5 per cent, interest rate 5 per cent, value and cost volatilities simulated from 10 per cent to 60 per cent.

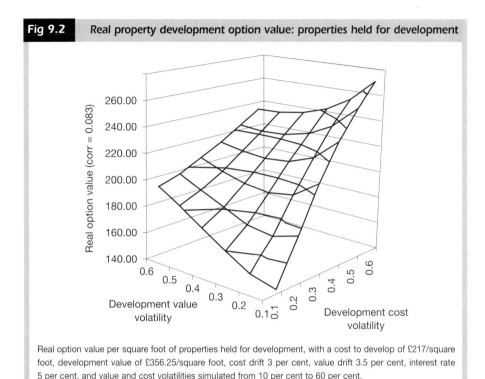

Fig 9.2 *Real property development option value: properties held for development*

Real option value per square foot of properties held for development, with a cost to develop of £217/square foot, development value of £356.25/square foot, cost drift 3 per cent, value drift 3.5 per cent, interest rate 5 per cent, and value and cost volatilities simulated from 10 per cent to 60 per cent.

struction because the 'real option' is 'in the money', that is the deterministic net present value of the development is substantial. That construction will be completed at current rental values and costs of construction equates to the call option being exercised. The low real option value at low cost and value volatility is £252, while the high is £361 at low value and high cost volatility (compared to a difference between expected property value and construction cost of 250 per square foot).

For the properties held for development, the costs to develop have been estimated also as £217 per square foot (although the average construction cost per square foot in the listing particulars is around £202). It has been assumed that the development value is £356.25 per square foot, which is the 'estimated market value' of the properties held as investment times a probability of success factor of 75 per cent. (Note for the properties held for development, the approximate average net realizable value is around £285 per square foot. The 'estimated market value' is the average expected rental value divided by the average equivalent yield at practical completion, or around £475 per square foot.) The net present value is based on the square footage times the development value less the construction cost, divided by (1+interest rate),[3] assuming an average three years to completion.

Figure 9.2 shows the picture of development value volatility against development cost volatility, at an assumed correlation of 0.083, for the CW properties held for development. The 'value-cost volatility' surface is slightly 'shapely' for the CW properties held for development because the 'real option' is not too far in the money, that is the deterministic net present value of the development is not as high a ratio of development costs as the 'properties under construction'. The properties may or may not be developed in the future, at uncertain future rental values and costs of construction, which is similar to a call option that is not very certain to be exercised. The low real option value at low cost and value volatility is £144, while the high is £268 at low value and high cost volatility (compared to a difference between expected property value and construction cost of £139 per square foot). The ratio of the highest simulated real option value for properties held for development to the net present value is 193 per cent (compared to 144 per cent for the properties under construction).

Table 9.2 shows the real option value of CW properties held for development assuming all of the above parameters, except that the correlation between value and cost ranges from 0.6 to –0.6. At 0.6 correlation, the real option value is around £814 million; but at –0.6 correlation, the real option value is around £1,092 million. Note that this is consistent with the characteristics of a spread option, as higher correlation results in a lower spread call option value.

Table 9.2	Canary Wharf real development option: properties held for development (correlation variation)

11 August 1999

Total real option value	814,739,572	878,748,102	933,658,571	981,103,082	1,022,626,006	1,059,394,747	1,092,278,846
Correlation	0.6	0.4	0.2	0	–0.2	–0.4	–0.6
Real option value	155.57	167.80	178.28	187.34	195.27	202.29	208.57
Square feet	5,237,000						
NPV @	729,252,250						

Real option value of properties held for development, with a cost to develop of £217/sf, development value of £356/sf, cost drift of 3 per cent, value drift 3.5 per cent, interest rate 5 per cent, cost and value of 26.3 per cent and 26 per cent, correlation simulated.

Conclusion: comparative valuation of Canary Wharf development options

We have reviewed the traditional valuation methodologies used in the valuation of properties under construction and properties held for development in the listing particulars for the flotation of Canary Wharf Group plc in April 1999. Then, we surveyed some of the relevant literature on real property options, especially concerning development, where the developer has several financial, strategic and operational options before the developed property is fully constructed and let.

Assuming that both construction costs and developed property values at Canary Wharf are uncertain, we used a simple real option valuation (ROV) approach to arrive at values which can be compared to deterministic net present value approaches.

In summary, the various valuation approaches for Canary Wharf are as follows (in millions of pounds):

	OMV	NPV	ROV	NRV
Under construction	572	893	967	907
Held for development	622	629	962	1,495
TOTAL	1,194	1,522	1,929	2,402

The valuers have not argued that the OMV or NRV approach should be (or is) used for stock market valuation. A disadvantage of the NPV and ROV approach used herein is that it lacks the detailed specification, construction and rental information available to the valuers. One advantage of the real option valuation approach is the specific focus on the volatility of both construction cost and property values over the valuation horizon, but naturally this should be property specific rather than based on general assumptions and proxies. Whether any of the NPV, ROV or NRV approaches to valuation adequately account for the Canary Wharf stock market valuation over time depends on, among other matters, the consistency between security market and property market analysts and appraisal methodologies.

Notes

1. Thanks for comments on the first version of this chapter by D.C. Martin, W.A.C. Newsom and participants in the RICS Cutting Edge Conference at the University of Cambridge, September 1999. The usual disclaimer applies. We gratefully acknowledge the financial support of the RICS Research Foundation.

2. *Wall Street Journal*, 25–26 June 1999. These 'reported' valuations range from (per share) 330 pence (Hugh Rice, CCF Charterhouse), 443 pence (Merrill Lynch, 'even if the company obtained commitments to lease all of the 5.3 million square feet of properties held for

development'), 351 (Peel Hunt), 375 pence (Credit Lyonnais), 414 pence (George Iacobescu, CEO Canary Wharf), with a quoted market range of 328.5 to 460.5 pence in 1999. The share price range times the outstanding ordinary shares translates into a low of £2,201 million (the initial issue price of 330 pence) to a high of £3,071 million.

3. *Listing Particulars*, p. 21.

4. Several other factors were considered as disclosed in the *Listing Particulars*, pp. 111–115.

5. Ward (1982), p. 104. Presumably he was referring to tradable long and short positions in 'rent' futures/forwards, and long/short positions in securitized properties.

6. At the hurdle ratio z^* the option value equals the intrinsic value so that $W(z^*) = z^*-1$. The smooth pasting condition assumes that the option will be exercised when $W'(z^*) = jAz^{*j1} = 1$.

7. These estimates are provided as illustrations only (at this stage) since the costs and values per square foot have been 'abstracted from the *Listing Particulars*' as averages. Also it is possible some of the developments have special construction and rental arrangements (and other embedded options like those accorded Citibank) which have not been considered in these valuations, Also there is no direct link between the Land Securities and Tarmac traded option implied volatilities and the expected volatilities for values and development costs at Canary Wharf, or evidence that the correlation between the two securities is an adequate proxy for the correlation of construction costs and property values at Canary Wharf. Land Securities is not a portfolio of London Dockland properties, and Tarmac has recently demerged its construction arm. Clearly there is scope for empirical research on appropriate proxies for this case, or better still for direct estimates, which are available to the valuers.

8. These values are based on the OMV of properties under construction. The valuers also estimated the OMV when completed and let for four properties under construction. The estimated OMV for 25 Canada Square was 15 per cent higher. A 15 per cent increase in the average development value for properties under construction and held for development would result in an increase of the ROV of £427 million (or 22 per cent), showing the leverage effect of call options.

9. Note that because for several of these properties construction has already commenced, it is questionable whether this simple real option model is then appropriate. Presumably there are other real options in changing the pace of construction and even modifying the construction in process to suit changing rental and cost objectives.

Options embedded in house mortgages: a valuation with two random walk factors **10**

*by Jose Antonio de Azevedo-Pereira,
David P. Newton and Dean Paxson*

Editor's introduction:

Valuing a mortgage (either as an asset for the lender or as a liability for the borrower) depends on two random factors: house prices and interest rates. Free boundaries exist for the borrowers' decisions whether to repay early or to default. There are also practical complications in handling jump discontinuity conditions whenever a payment falls due. Interesting in its own right, the case is an example of how numerical methods can be used on any two-factor problem. The description given here is brief, and sources are quoted for the fuller technical details. The latter include the technique of 'upwind differencing' for explicit finite difference, and also fuller theoretical details, such as the market clearing and other conditions required to derive stable prices.

The decision: *whether to borrow; whether to repay early; whether to default on the loan.*

Option-like features: *American option to repay early and a series of European options to default, leaving the lender to take possession of the house.*

Equation: *two-factor model, with two volatilities and their correlation.*

Boundary conditions: *fixed boundary conditions under extreme values of the random factors and terminal payoffs. Numerous jump discontinuity conditions at repayment dates.*

Solution: *explicit finite difference, applied to transformed versions of the variables, and using 'upwind differencing' to avoid instability problems.*

Implications: *decision rules for default and prepayment; guidance on setting penalties for pre-payment; valuation of the loan and its associated insurances.*

Possible extensions: *variable rate mortgages; penalties for early repayment in more complex forms.*

177

Introduction

It might be thought that a house mortgage is a perfectly straightforward arrangement, but even the simplest fixed-rate repayment mortgage, in which the loan is paid off in equal instalments, contains valuable options for the borrower against the lender. Since mortgage contracts often last for several decades, it is necessary to model both interest rate and house price as random elements (a two-dimensional random walk).

The value of the mortgage contract to the lender is not just the present value of future payments promised by the borrower but is reduced by the value of the borrower's options to prepay (eliminating the debt early) or to default (reneging on the debt and turning over the house to the lender). Valuation depends on future interest rates. If market interest rates rise, the borrower is protected by the fixed rate, but if interest rates fall it may become financially optimal to pay off the debt early (perhaps by remortgaging with another institution). If house prices ever collapse, it may become optimal for the borrower to default on the debt, letting the lender repossess the now very cheap house so that the lender bears the loss of value on it, while the borrower switches to renting, or buys another house at a lower price.

In the mid-1990s British fixed-rate, 20-year mortgages were offered by NatWest Bank at around 10 per cent per annum interest. These were taken by housebuyers who were unwilling to risk increases in variable rates for mortgages. If variable rates had risen, these borrowers would have been happy, but in the following few years rates fell significantly. It became financially attractive for borrowers to remortgage, either with a new, lower fixed rate or with a variable rate. Not surprisingly, the bank's original contract included a penalty for exercising this prepayment option (the penalty was around 10 per cent of the debt outstanding at the time of prepayment) in order to destroy the value of the borrower's prepayment option at the time. The bank was also then willing to substitute a new mortgage, in competition with other mortgage providers, even negotiating rate reductions for the two subsequent years in order to discourage switching. Of course, over a 20-year period it may yet become profitable for these borrowers to have held on to the original fixed rate, since interest rates may rise high enough and for long enough to make the original fixed-rate deal more attractive after all.

Thus, a borrower faces an optimal early repayment decision, which is not automatically triggered as soon as it becomes profitable to pay off early at the current rates since these rates are liable to change. Valuation, even of an apparently simple fixed-rate mortgage, requires that the uncertainty in future interest rates be taken into account.

The two variable factors, interest rates and house prices, must both be modelled if we wish to get a correct mortgage valuation which allows for

The exercise of one option eliminates the other.

options held by the borrower. For valuation purposes, it is assumed that the borrower can legally exercise both options, and that a borrower will exercise either option if it becomes financially rational to do so. The exercise of one option eliminates the other. In consequence of this interaction between the two options to terminate the loan, they cannot be considered separately.

Repayment mortgage

We will consider a 'repayment mortgage'. An individual borrows from a lender (such as a bank) a large sum of money with which to buy a house and makes equal monthly payments such that with the final payment the loan is discharged. This means the lender has been promised a fixed rate of return by the borrower. We will refer to this as the 'coupon rate' in order to avoid confusion with the rate we will use in valuations, which we will continue to call the 'interest rate'. The monthly payments are easily calculated but the value today of all these future payments to the lender depends on the changing interest rate on investments, of comparable risk, as time passes. To demonstrate the uncertainty in value today, suppose that after the mortgage has been arranged interest rates rise and remain generally high during the period of the loan. The lender will receive a lower return than would have been made from a variable-rate agreement, whereas if rates fall and remain generally low the lender will receive a valuable set of cash flows giving a high return relative to the alternative, variable-rate investments. In addition, the borrower has options to prepay or to default and these options' values depend on both the interest rate and the house price.

A more sophisticated model than ordinary diffusion for interest rates is needed in order to obtain a modestly realistic model (for a comprehensive treatment of interest rate modelling, see James and Webber, 2000). We model the short-term or 'spot' interest rate as a function of time, r, as a 'CIR' mean-reverting square root process (Cox, Ingersoll and Ross, 1985b) and the house price as a function of time, H, as a lognormal diffusion process (Merton, 1973). The random process for the house price is of the same type as we have seen before for an asset paying a 'dividend'. We represent these in equations (1) and (2). Stochastic elements are modelled by two standardized Wiener processes, X_r and X_H, which are correlated as in equation (3). Since living in the house has benefits (which would otherwise have to be paid for separately), we incorporate a 'service flow' from the house, considered mathematically equivalent to a dividend from shares of stock in a company.

$$dr = \kappa(\theta - r)dt + \sigma \sqrt{r} dX_r \tag{1}$$

$$\frac{dH}{H} = (\mu - \delta)dt + v dX_H \tag{2}$$

$$dX_r dX_H = \rho dt \tag{3}$$

where:

κ = speed of adjustment in the mean-reverting process

θ = long-term anticipated mean of the interest rate

σ = instantaneous standard deviation of the interest rate

X_r = standardized Wiener process for the interest rate

μ = instantaneous average rate of house price appreciation

δ = 'dividend type' per unit service flow provided by the house

v = instantaneous standard deviation of the house price

X_H = standardized Wiener process for the house price

ρ = instantaneous correlation coefficient between the Wiener processes.

It is known from standard arguments in finance that the partial differential equation (PDE) for the valuation of any asset $F(r,H,t)$, whose value is a function only of interest rate, r, house price, H, and time, t, takes the following form (Cox, Ingersoll and Ross, 1985a,b; Epperson *et al.*, 1985; Kau *et al.*, 1992, 1993):

$$\tag{4}$$

$$\frac{1}{2} H^2 v^2 \frac{\partial^2 F}{\partial H^2} + \rho H \sqrt{r} v \sigma \frac{\partial^2 F}{\partial H \partial r} + \frac{1}{2} r \sigma^2 \frac{\partial^2 F}{\partial r^2} + \kappa (\theta - r) \frac{\partial F}{\partial r} + (r - \delta) H \frac{\partial F}{\partial H} + \frac{\partial F}{\partial t} - rF = 0$$

For a problem of this level of complexity, analytical solutions are not available but, nasty as this partial differential may seem at first, it can be solved using finite difference techniques. An introduction to the finite difference method, for one random variable, is given in Appendix 4 and details of (4)'s solution, including boundary conditions, can be found in the financial literature on mortgages (Azevedo-Pereira, Newton and Paxson, 2000a).

We will illustrate using results for a 25-year 12 per cent p.a. mortgage for 95 per cent of the house value, with a spot interest rate of 10 per cent p.a. and a 10 per cent p.a. long-term mean rate, interest rate volatility, σ, 10 per cent p.a. and service flow, δ, 7.5 per cent p.a. (for further details, see Azevedo-Pereira, 1997). Values will be expressed as multiples of the house value.

The results shown are for a repayment mortgage without an early termination penalty but this is readily included. Additional features such as 'mortgage indemnity guarantees', 'coinsurance' and 'endowment' mortgages have been valued (Azevedo-Pereira, Newton and Paxson, 1999, 2000b).

Figure 10.1 shows the value of the contracted future payments to the lender, assuming that all will be paid and ignoring the borrower's options.

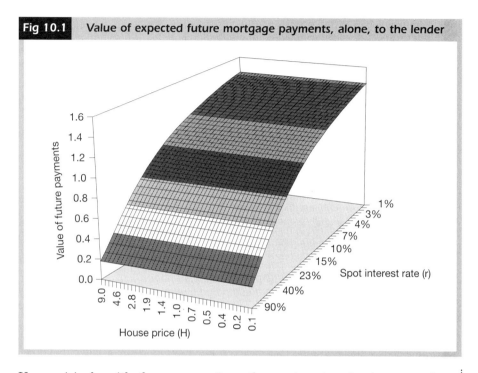

Fig 10.1 Value of expected future mortgage payments, alone, to the lender

Unsurprisingly, with these assumptions, the mortgage's value is seen to be independent of the house price. We can imagine the shape of this curved surface modified to take into account the borrower's two interacting options, which will lead us to Figure 10.4.

Figure 10.2 shows the value to the borrower of the option to default as a surface in a three-dimensional plot. The plot has been rotated to show the surface more clearly. The surface results from calculations which must be done using a PC but the general features make sense (if they did not, the calculations would need to be checked!). The highest value drawn corresponds to a low spot interest rate and a house price one-tenth of its initial value. In these circumstances, the borrower has a house of little value and a contract requiring monthly payments calculated with a relatively high fixed interest rate. If the borrower were to choose to continue with payments, without default, until the end of the contract, then the present value of these, to the lender, would be high. However, recall that we assume financial rationality on behalf of the borrower and that default is legal and so the value to the borrower of being able to default is correspondingly high. Looking at the rest of the surface, we see that higher house prices reduce or eliminate the default option's value and that higher spot interest rates reduce default option value, and extremely high rates eliminate the default option's value even at very low house prices. This makes sense (though

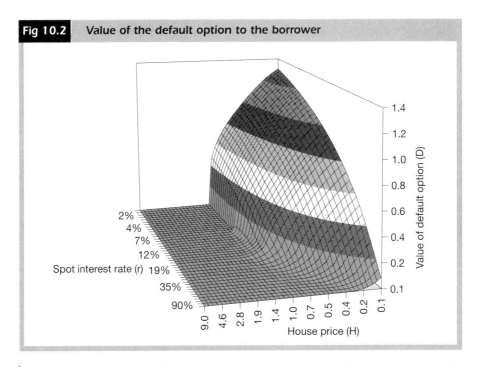

Fig 10.2 Value of the default option to the borrower

it depends on the volatility of the interest rate) since a high current spot rate implies high future spot rates for sufficient time to dramatically lower the value of future fixed repayments.

Figure 10.3 shows the value to the borrower of the option to prepay. Prepayment is a valuable option as long as the house price is sufficiently high and the option's value increases with falling market interest rates. It is no surprise, therefore, that mortgage lenders are concerned to impose penalties for early payment in mortgage contracts.

Figure 10.4 shows the combined value of the contracted future payments to the lender less the value lost to the borrower's options. The flat top on the surface maps an area of house price versus spot interest rate where the lender does not lose value but, conversely, does not gain value either if spot rates fall, when faced by a financially rational borrower. Outside this region, the lender faces quite rapid loss of value (notice that although house prices and interest rates are taken to very high levels in the figure, the mortgage value starts to fall away at moderate levels of either). For this reason, of course, lenders create mortgage products not only with penalties for prepayment (if these are allowed by the law of the country in which the mortgage originates) but also with various forms of insurance to cover all or part of the potential losses they might incur on default. These, too, can be valued within the framework described here (Azevedo-Pereira, Newton and Paxson, 1999, 2000b).

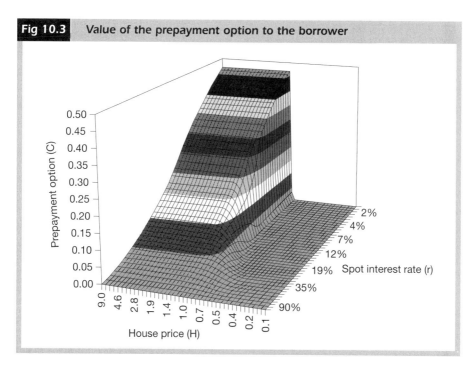

Fig 10.3 Value of the prepayment option to the borrower

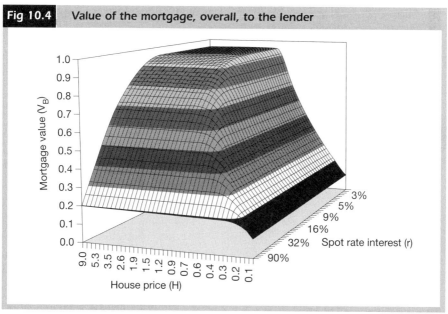

Fig 10.4 Value of the mortgage, overall, to the lender

Technical note

The results plotted in the figures were obtained by solving the partial differential equations, with boundary conditions, using the finite difference method and programming in Fortran.

Finite difference solution

We give a basic introduction to the techniques of finite difference solution in Appendix 4, where we demonstrate the method for a single underlying variable which has a random element of price variation.

In that appendix, we describe how value can be determined by a two-dimensional 'grid' of input data, namely one dimension for the single random factor (asset price) and the other for time. We also explain that calculations begin at the future terminal (payoff) value condition, at the time of expiry of the option, and then proceed backwards along the time dimension, from the future towards the present. Pictorially, you can think of this as a series of lines of option value (against asset value) working backwards in time. Successive lines at different times, when plotted together, generate a two-dimensional surface, with value (height) a function of asset value and time, as illustrated in Chapters 2 and 3 and Appendix 4. Generally the line defining value at expiry has sharp corners, but the lines at successively earlier times tend to be higher and smoother in shape.

In the valuation of the options embedded in house mortgages, the option values are driven by three different input variables: time, and the current values of the two random factors, house price and interest rate. In effect our outcome variable, option value, is being determined by a three-dimensional grid of possible input variables (time, house price and interest rate). At each instant of time (starting from expiry), we can work out option value across a two-dimensional grid of possibilities for the two random input variables of current house price and current interest rate. This produces a value surface similar to those plotted above. We then work backwards in time, and this successively forms a three dimensional grid of input values in house price, interest rate and time.

> **In the valuation of the options embedded in house mortgages, the option values are driven by three different input variables.**

Typically the value surface at the terminal date is a low and sharp-edged one. As we run time backwards towards the present, the value surface generally tends to rise, and evolves into a more smoothly rounded shape. This is exactly analogous to the behaviour of the value line over time, in the cases shown in Chapters 2 and 3, where there is only one random factor driving the option's value. In this chapter we actually plot the highest and most rounded form of this surface, namely at the moment earliest in time, when the mortgage begins. In principle there are four dimensions to explore: the three input variables of house price, interest rate and actual time remaining to expiry, and the output variable of value. It is not possible to plot all these simultaneously, unless we can imagine a 'nested' set of valuation surfaces. Each would be similar to those we have plotted, but the earlier surfaces would tend to 'nest inside' the later ones. Any fixed boundaries (e.g. at the outside edges of the diagram) would be shared by all these surfaces. This is hard to visualize, so the best we can do in practice is show a 'movie' of how these surfaces grow and evolve with increasing time to maturity. We have plotted the valuation (and sub-valuations) for only one time frame of this movie. This has required us to work through a 3D grid of input-variable possibilities, a time-slice at a time.

The options held by a mortgage borrower are prepayment and default. Rationally, prepayment could become optimal at any time (this is an 'American'-style option). However, default only makes sense on payment dates (e.g. on one of 240 monthly dates during a 20-year mortgage). This is because you can't default before your next payment becomes due, and you would be irrational to give up before then the right to a month's usage of the house which was generated by your last actual payment.

Therefore, the three-dimensional grid of input variables, through which we must work to obtain a solution, is sub-divided into a series of problems: starting from expiry, we work backwards in time, using Black–Scholes diffusion, and allowing for the possibility of prepayment at any instant until a monthly payment date is reached. This date forms a fixed time boundary, at which we must consider the possibility of default. Jump continuity conditions apply across the instant of payment, and the Black–Scholes equation holds only on either side of this instant (unless default or prepayment happens at that instant). The above monthly calculation cycle is repeated until a set of option values is obtained for the possible house prices and interest rates at the current time.

The actual calculation detail is given in the source references. It was necessary to transform the variables and the boundary conditions, and to use the 'upwind differencing' form of the explicit finite difference method, in order to circumvent stability problems.

Some further real options topics   **11**

ost of this chapter is a brief summary and interpretation of research reported by Dixit and Pindyck in *Investment under Uncertainty* on the activation and deactivation of assets, and we also note their treatment of an exchange option to invest at varying cost in an asset of varying value (compare Chapter 9). In addition, David Newton adds brief notes on the application of real options analysis to research and development (R&D).

For the Dixit and Pindyck work we omit the full theory and implementation detail. We aim to provide just enough information so that readers can decide whether they need to consult this significant material, and how.

Options to activate and inactivate resources

As mentioned in Chapter 3, we may face decisions as to when to invest in a new asset and when to scrap an existing asset. An asset may also have an intermediate state of being 'mothballed' or idle. Why and when is it efficient to use the mothballed state? Can we create additional valuable real options, e.g. by redesigning our business system to make it cheaper to move between the active and inactive states? Such decisions can apply to the management of many real assets, including oil refineries, copper mines, electricity generators (Chapter 6), real estate investments, and the hiring and firing of permanent employees.

Dixit and Pindyck report some results which we have already touched on in Chapters 3 and 4, namely that there will be critical levels of the selling market price at which we should change our asset between states, such as the active, inactive, mothballed and scrapped states. There is often a strong inertia against changing an existing state (technically known as hysteresis). A higher volatility of the selling price market makes this inertia still greater. In effect, if we have an idle asset, price must go a long way above avoidable operating cost before we start operating, but once operating, price must fall a fair way below avoidable operating cost before we stop operating.

Some other important relationships are found. For example, a higher (re)investment cost for replacing a plant that has been scrapped makes it less attractive to scrap (this means that higher losses/lower selling prices are tolerated before we should decide to scrap). To a lesser extent, a higher cost of exit, or a lower scrap/disposal value, makes it less attractive to invest in the first place (because the value of the option to exit is lower, therefore the value of the project as a whole at a given market price is lower, and hence a higher market price is needed to induce initial investment).

But even when the costs of entry and exit are small, the threshold prices for activating and deactivating are far apart. In the case of employing a permanent staff member, the costs of entry and exit can be significant (respectively the recruitment and training costs, and any severance payments). This has implications for decisions to change the size of the permanent work force, particularly if the alternatives are using temporary agency staff or overtime.

These factors mean that firms will not be quick to close capacity as prices fall, nor quick to reopen capacity as prices rise. The resulting delay in response can accentuate price swings in the industry, which are therefore affected by the firms' decisions (even though the individual firms see themselves as price takers).

The analysis for the activation-inactivation decision is rather complex, and Dixit and Pindyck make some simplifying assumptions (e.g. that the option is perpetual, and that capacity can only ever be either zero or one unit, and that assets last for ever). To judge from the illustrations they give, it seems that we can suffer more severe losses from taking this type of decision wrongly than if we take a wrong decision whether to exercise a simple 'one-off' put or call option – we saw in Chapter 2 that the latter is rather a 'forgiving' type of calculation.

The analysis for the activation-inactivation decision is rather complex.

Dixit and Pindyck point out that mothballing will only ever be used if the maintenance cost during mothballing is sufficiently low, and/or if having a mothballed asset avoids a sufficiently large fraction of the cost of reinvesting in a completely new asset if and when demand recovers.

Higher costs of maintenance during mothballing will make it less attractive to enter the mothballed state and more attractive to leave it, up to the limit where mothballing ceases to be a strategy at all (thus in turn changing the overall value of the system). If the cost of reactivating a mothballed asset rises, the firm is less willing to scrap a mothballed asset and it loses value overall, and the firm also has greater inertia against moving between the mothballed and active states. Lower volatility makes the firm less likely to use mothballing, since this intermediate state is generally costly. If so, the main value of mothballing is that it offers the option of a cheaper reversal of policy at a later date, between reactivation and scrapping. Lower volatility gives a smaller chance of large changes in either direction and hence reduces the value of this 'option to wait' before deciding between scrapping and activation.

Qualitatively, these predictions of the theoretical model seem to make sense. Dixit and Pindyck's quantitative test of the theoretical model was to apply it to the oil tanker charter industry, using the actual parameter values of 1992. According to the model, charter prices were well within the inertia zone, so that the industry should have invested very little in new oil tankers, and it should also not have mothballed many existing tankers. Dixit and Pindyck found that the industry did indeed have a low actual rate of investment at the time, but they did not mention the actual rate of mothballing.

Clearly the industry was already doing roughly what option theory requires, but because the calculations seemed moderately sensitive, at least compared to 'plain vanilla' American call or put options, even a small improvement in the decision rules for activating, deactivating, investing and scrapping could have added value for the industry.

Option to switch between invested and non-invested states

The decision: at what states of a randomly evolving market should we invest in new capacity, activate previously inactive assets, scrap existing assets, etc.

Random walk variable: level of demand or market price (e.g. for tanker capacity or for mine output).

Option model: exchange option, to move between the active state and inactive state, with or without the option to mothball.

Value added by the option model: better decisions, leading to higher firm value. Better decision rules as to whether and how to have an inactive or mothballed state.

Decision rule for exercising the option: make an upward shift of activity when the selling market price reaches the relevant threshold (i.e. to activate an inactive asset or to invest in a new asset). Make downward shifts of activity when the selling market price reaches the relevant threshold (i.e. to inactivate an existing active asset, or to mothball or scrap an existing inactive or active asset).

189

Duration to expiry: assumed perpetual.

Price to acquire the exchange option: the price or value of the entire option system is not explicitly discussed, but the firm's value depends on its current state (active or inactive) as well as on the current external selling market price.

Exercise prices of the exchange option (without mothballing): four potential exercise prices – zero to active, active to inactive, inactive to active, inactive to scrap (zero).

Terminal boundary: none, because option is perpetual.

Black–Scholes equation: equation for an inactive asset is standard equation for the option to acquire a dividend-paying asset; the equation for an active asset has similar terms, where these now represent the value of the option to stop producing, as opposed to producing unconditionally, plus terms to reflect the value of actual production if continued indefinitely in today's market conditions.

Upper and lower boundaries: zero for S = zero, and S for S = infinity.

Free boundaries: for all feasible changes between any two states, the values of the two states must be equal at the critical value of S (value matching condition), and the slopes of the changes of the values of both states with respect to S must be equal (smooth pasting condition).

Solution method: a general analytic solution is known (which applies to all possible sets of boundary conditions). The various fixed and free boundary conditions which define this particular problem also define a system of non-linear equations, which must be met simultaneously by all the parameter values of the particular analytical solution. This non-linear equation can be solved by numerical methods (e.g. by the non-linear search routines which are now included in most spreadsheets) to find the parameters of the analytic solution.

Random factor: S = price of final product or service.

Dividend rate: current profit rate of alternative state(s) depending on state we are now in (e.g. rate of profit we lose by not presently having an active asset, which an active asset would be earning for us).

Income to the option holder: an active asset is actually making profit (or loss) as well as being an option to move into some other state, and this income is modelled by a term in the Black–Scholes equation.

Volatility: of the price of the final product.

Optimal investment when both investment value and investment cost are varying randomly

The decision: when to invest.

Option-like features: two random walk factors, namely asset value and the cost of acquiring the asset.

This can be treated as a perpetual option to exchange the investment cost for the value of the finished asset.

Decision rule: invest when the ratio of asset value to investment cost exceeds a critical level.

Equation: this problem and its solution are closely related to the exchange option model of Margrabe, if treated as a perpetual option. A joint two-factor equation is defined for the effects on wealth of asset value and investment cost, where both asset and investment are treated as (potentially) paying either a profit (dividend) or some other quasi-payment such as a convenience yield.

Boundary conditions: the boundary conditions must ensure that at the instant of investment the values of the option to invest and of immediate investment are equal (value matching). They must also both have the same slope with respect to changes in both investment cost and asset value so that random change over the next instant cannot change their respective values (smooth pasting).

Further modification: like Margrabe, Dixit and Pindyck derive an equation in the ratio of the two prices, and they transform the boundary conditions so that they apply correctly for this new variable. The result is an ordinary differential equation, which has a known analytic solution. An additional boundary condition is imposed that the solution be positive, and a specific solution is obtained.

In Chapter 2 we touched briefly on real options in R&D. Here David Newton adds further notes on the issues that arise.

Research and development is characterized by uncertainty, since effective R&D requires a complex interaction of variables. Technically successful R&D projects eventually supply a capability to produce new goods or services, and this can be treated as a call option to invest in producing and selling such goods and services commercially, which we need do only if they can be sold at a profit. Technically unsuccessful R&D will not lead to any capability of provid-

Research and development is characterized by uncertainty.

ing goods and services, and it need not be pursued to an investment in production. Hence an investment in R&D may be considered as payment for a call option to invest in future production and sales.

Without the benefit of real options analysis it can be tempting to misapply or misinterpret traditional DCF techniques. This risk is particularly high for longer-term R&D projects that appear to involve high risk. In allowing for uncertainty, companies would traditionally use a high discount rate, and might use a single rate for the whole time period from the initial, uncertain R&D to net cash inflow far into the future, although the latter might by that time actually be far less risky, provided the initial R&D project is technically successful. This calculation will often result in a negative NPV (and a rejected R&D project). Research managers who lack the tools of option pricing must argue for such research programmes without being able to demonstrate their full value. This may lead to 'strategic importance' being used as a justification, with the disadvantage that the same plea may also allow weak projects to be supported.

At its simplest, for a manufacturing company, the present value of an investment in R&D can be valued as if it were the price to be paid for a call option to invest later in plant. The exercise price is the investment cost of the plant. The underlying asset is the value of the net future cash flows from the plant if investment is undertaken. Of course, it is the uncertainty in these returns which gives time value to the option.

A key difficulty is in the calculation of this volatility. In financial markets, historical volatilities are available as a basis for estimation of future volatilities, together with the volatilities implied by a large range of comparable financial instruments, but for R&D the underlying asset (the revenue potential of the newly feasible business venture which will arise after technically successful R&D) does not yet exist (Newton and Pearson, 1994; Newton, Paxson and Pearson, 1996). Companies which undertake many projects and which keep records of the deleted projects are better placed to make volatility estimates. Monte Carlo simulation of several underlying variables has been used in estimating volatility of new projects, and has been used retrospectively to value deleted projects (Doctor, Newton and Pearson, 2001).

The fascinating conclusion of recent work on real options in R&D is that, on the one hand, if an R&D project has a negative NPV it may yet have a positive value and be worth starting, if we can value the project as an out-of-the-money real call option to invest later; but, on the other hand, when that later time comes, it will not always be optimal to exercise an in-the-money call option by investing, even if the investment project seems to have a high current NPV (see Chapter 2).

The pitfalls of real options analysis and how to avoid them

12

Any new and important technique is sure to be overhyped, misunderstood and at times misapplied. All of these risks are strong for real options analysis, since the economic ideas are new and sometimes counter-intuitive, the mathematics is very demanding, and there are no established 'industry standard' softwares to aid implementation.

In order of importance, the most significant mistakes are:

1. using real option analysis when we shouldn't;

2. getting the real options model wrong;

3. getting the model right, but inserting data which bias the answer;

4. getting the model and the data right, but miscalculating the solution.

Using real options when we shouldn't

Real options analysis makes a number of assumptions, and we are in serious danger of error if our real asset decision setting does not tally with these assumptions.

The fundamental assumption of real options analysis is that the relevant uncertainties are random walks, and therefore unforecastable. As we explain in Appendix 3, it need not matter if the random walk has a known trend. In particular, the analysis assumes that we are price takers – no decision we can take will change the future course of the random walk.

These assumptions are violated if there is only a small number of leading competitors (oligopoly). In this case decisions will not be random. Every player's actions can have some effect on price, and all the players will take every decision in the full knowledge of what the possible (and most advantageous) countermoves will be for every other player.

In cases like this, game theory (which makes precisely these assumptions) may be a far more useful guide than real options theory. Nonetheless these things are seldom completely clear-cut. Even in an oligopoly, all the players will face some joint uncertainties which are outside the influence of any or all of them (economic conditions, changes of tastes, emerging competition from outside the present technology, etc.).

> **Even in an oligopoly, all the players will face some joint uncertainties.**

In addition there are special conditions under which game theory itself prescribes that competitors should deliberately take random decisions, and there are other conditions in which competitive economics derives values very similar to those of option theory (see Dixit and Pindyck, 1994).

Another very important assumption of real options theory is that the risks of an option can be hedged away. If hedging is feasible, the option will be priced as if it had been hedged, in which case its return is risk free.

Provided hedging is indeed possible, it does not matter whether any one option is actually hedged or not. If you try to sell an option that you have not hedged (or if the market hears about the option and incorporates its value in your share price), the market will price it as if it had been hedged. If you choose not to hedge, you will increase your risks and you have the chance of making greater (as well as lesser) returns than the risk-free return. But on average the market may not reward you for taking such risks.

As with financial options, the safest route to profit from real options is to arbitrage, i.e. to buy a real option for less than it is worth, or sell it for more than it is worth. Once you have successfully arbitraged, it may be best to encapsulate the arbitrage profit in your share value and to hedge away the option's remaining risk.

Using the wrong real options model

We can easily wrongly assume that our actual decision is 'like' a given real options model, when in reality it is 'unlike'. Warning examples have been given in Chapter 3, but past examples are no substitute for future alertness. In particular, we should strive to think of as many possible different models of the situation, and check how our solution could be biased if we have picked the 'wrong' model.

For example, if we have assumed that interest rates are fixed, would it greatly change our decisions, or our wealth, if interest rates were truly variable? If we have assumed that oil and gas prices vary independently of each other, what would it do to our decision and our wealth if these prices were linked by some economic mechanism? In simplifying, have we actually omitted important types of option, or important additional random factors?

Getting the model right, but inserting wrong values which bias the answer

It is vital to understand what drives option value (and/or optimum decisions) in any particular real option model. We need to check the model for sensitivity to the variables, and understand how errors in the variables could bias the analysis.

For example, call option values are increased if there is a longer time to expiry and greater volatility of the underlying asset. Have we overestimated the length of the available time window for investment? What is the smallest plausible estimate we could use for volatility?

What mistake could an overestimate of option value lead us to make? Will it lead us to overinvest (e.g. by paying a high price for research which is a supposed European call, but which actually 'expires' before we expected) or will it lead us to underinvest (e.g. we overestimate the time value of an American call to build a plant, accordingly we do not exercise early, and we lose the opportunity to invest at all when the option expires slightly before expected).

Sometimes it is useful to put the valuation question in a reverse form: for example we may not know what the jump probability of failure in our research actually is, but are we willing to act as if it were no more than X, since probability above X would reverse our decision (to invest or not to invest)?

Getting the model and the data right, but making mistakes in the solution

Many of the mathematical algorithms in use are in non-standard forms which are hard to use and/or fragile. It may be easy to miss an important variable, or put in a crazy parameter.

Some of the possible mistakes are fairly self-advertising, e.g. we may notice that calculated option values are exploding towards plus or minus infinity, or are oscillating between the two. High numerical craft skills may be needed to avoid this, but there is also no substitute for 'sanity checks' on final results. The results of option valuations are sometimes in conflict with common sense (this is not always bad, since in some problems the greatest benefit of option analysis is precisely that it rejects a plausible intuition). Nonetheless it is vital to make as many logical checks as possible to ensure that the results, and their sensitivities to parameter changes, square with economic rationality. Examples were given in Chapter 4.

There is also no substitute for 'sanity checks' on final results.

The future of real options analysis 13

Real options analysis is evolving fast, and the short introduction given here cannot reach even the existing frontiers of the subject. However, we can foresee at least some of the trends, although in the spirit of real options itself we must accept that many developments remain unforecastable.

One important trend will be the rapid migration of existing financial option skills and models for use on real options. Models for dealing with flexible interest rates, stochastic (i.e. evolving) volatilities and various advanced kinds of exchange options are all waiting to find applications in real asset management. We suspect it will be a long time (if ever) before real options is taught entirely as a branch of applied economics, without reference to financial market instruments.

Alongside this ongoing influence of financial market thinking on real options thinking, there will doubtless be some models and applications which arise entirely within real asset management (such as the activation/inactivation models for ships, mines and workforces which we mentioned in Chapters 3 and 4). Some of these models will doubtless find applications in the financial markets arena, and will trigger further developments there.

Solution methods will also make explosive progress. At the time of writing it is an extremely tedious task to find the early exercise boundary for an American option, particularly if this has, say, two random factors and several modes of exercise. Ongoing progress with algorithms, software packaging and computer speeds will permit vast improvements in speed and in robustness (some of the existing numerical methods can be fragile at times). The present state of computing for real options resembles the early days of econometrics or linear programming, where arcane programs were written by highly technical and specialist users, and machines took all night to solve a calculation that can now be specified and solved in seconds by a non-specialist.

One interesting evolution will take place inside real options itself, namely that nature will increasingly imitate art. That is to say, businesses will increasingly structure their deals to have them make sense in real options terms.

One interesting evolution will take place inside real options itself.

An obvious case of something comparable that has already happened is the way in which businesses and even government have been restructuring in recent years to imitate the arm's length trading, pricing and resource allocation of an efficient market. As a result, operations that were previously internal have been outsourced and sold to the highest bidder; costs have been variabilized by transferring them to external agencies; firms have sought to identify their core competences (usually sustainable technical or marketing monopolies) and have ruthlessly outsourced other services (e.g. dispatch or servicing or training) for which the firm itself has no distinctive advantage of scale or skill.

The comparable next step in real options is that firms will restructure their projects, their deals and even their financial structures to align more closely with the concepts of real options or even financial options.

For example, contracts between businesses will more exactly reflect the features of financial options. Firms may well float individual business projects (as well as ongoing business processes) on stock markets, thus permitting delta hedging of their risks at an earlier stage. However, as with the previous wave of privatizations and float-offs, firms should try to take any arbitrage or mispricing profits on a project before the project is floated. There will be far more, and far more intelligent, deals in which flexibility is created, priced and traded, either as part of a product or as a product in its own right. The results of actual and potential technical research will be more openly and competitively traded.

Similarly, real projects and processes themselves will be more optimally designed as chains of compound options in order to generate maximal overall value. It is not impossible that real option design will become a new academic and professional specialism. It is also possible that some companies will take to real option arbitrage as a corporate way of life comparable to the more traditional trade of asset stripping – that is to say predators may buy and sell companies and projects in such a way as to release value by rationalizing the joint structures of the chains of real options that they possess. Such firms may deploy high levels of mathematical expertise, but as ever there will be no substitute for commercial judgement and common sense.

We will also see increasing links between real option thinking and the broader aspects of business strategy and marketing. Firms will set strategies that optimally create chains of options, and they will offer products and services which make optimal returns from the real option values that they offer to customers. Finally, the loop of activity will close back to the financial markets – firms that find they have unacceptable exposures in the real assets arena might sometimes seek suitable hedges in the financial arena.

The foregoing points all apply to the formal methodology for evaluating options – we have not discussed whether or not this methodology will be used by a single rational decision maker, who acts in the shareholders' best interests. Andrew Stark provides the following notes to introduce what can happen if we discard this assumption. This leads to new forms of the classic agency problem – what if superiors and subordinates (or agents) have different preference functions and different information sets about the same problem? What options do they enjoy against each other? How can agents be optimally motivated, and what information and incentive systems are needed?

The current literature on real options stresses the economic value of the flexibility embedded in business activities and, by implication, in projects under consideration. As discussed earlier, examples of such flexibility include the option to time the acceptance of a project, the options to temporarily or permanently shut down a project or activity after its initial acceptance, the option to change production levels in the light of circumstances, etc. Nonetheless, in discussing the exercise and valuation of flexibility, two important issues are typically ignored that have substantial implications for the usefulness of real options techniques as aids to improved business decision making:

- the availability and cost of information systems capable of providing the necessary data for the appropriate exercise of flexibility,

- the availability of incentive systems capable of motivating managers to exercise flexibility in the interests of shareholders.

Consider the issue of information availability. Suppose a firm is attempting to evaluate the contribution of an abandonment option to the value of an investment opportunity under consideration. Implicit in doing this evaluation is an assumption that the firm will regularly generate information on, at the very least, the economic value of the project, if it is kept, and its abandonment value – values that will be part of the comparison that will tell management whether to exercise the flexibility to abandon the project. This is not necessarily part of the regular information-generating activities of the firm. If the firm, however, has no intention of designing an information system to regularly produce such information, there is little point in attempting to value the project as if it has such an intention. The actual flexibility embedded in a project is *conditional* upon the availability of the information to support the exercise of flexibility.[1]

Naturally, the production of information to support the exercise of flexibility is a costly exercise. As a consequence, firms will rationally think in

A firm could decide to restrict its level of flexibility in order to restrict information system costs.

199

terms of whether the benefits of a particular level of flexibility are worth accessing given the costs of producing the information necessary to support it. Indeed, a firm could decide to restrict its level of flexibility in order to restrict information system costs. For example, it might suggest that it will perform a post-audit of a project after the first two years to decide whether it is worth persevering with but, if the post-audit verdict is to persevere, no further consideration will be given to abandoning the project prior to the end of its economic life. And, at the extreme, if a firm generates *no* information relevant to the exercise of flexibility (e.g. the timing of the acceptance of an opportunity), it is perfectly rational (if not necessarily optimal) for that firm to use conventional, passive, NPV analysis in evaluating opportunities.

Now turn to the issues of motivation. Typically, analyses of the impact of flexibility on the value of opportunities implicitly assume that managers responsible for exercise of this flexibility will do so in the interests of shareholders. As a consequence, motivational issues are assumed away. This seems inconsistent with the emphasis in the popular financial press and elsewhere on ways of appropriately motivating managers at all levels of business organizations to work in the interests of shareholders via vehicles such as stock option schemes, bonus schemes, etc.

If it is accepted that some, if not necessarily all, managers need motivating to work in the interests of shareholders, including the exercise of flexibility, the design of suitable incentive systems becomes a genuine issue in implementing real options-style evaluations and decision making. After all, it is well understood that in, for example, profit or investment centres, retaining fully depreciated assets is valuable to the manager of the centre relative to replacing them. This is because replacing them – assuming that replacement brings no increase in efficiency – produces a reduction in profit or investment centre performance using the normal performance measures for these centres (i.e. profits or a measure of profits related to the level of investment such as return on investment or residual income). Replacement reduces the performance indicator by which the performance of the manager is, at least partially, evaluated.

One response to this issue, it might be thought, is to take away the decision-making rights over the exercise of flexibility (e.g. abandoning the project) from the manager responsible for the operation of a project and let it reside with executives at the top of the organization who, perhaps, are easier to motivate to work in the interests of shareholders by tying their rewards to the market performance of the firm. And indeed, this would make sense as long as top executives are as fully informed as the managers below them about decisions to be made. This is not generally the case, however. Some of the benefits of decentralizing decision making arise from the fact that local managers are better informed about their local circumstances than those higher up the firm's hierarchy. This then suggests that top executives could ask local managers to communicate their information on local circumstances, allowing the former to make the appropriate decisions. This will not necessarily solve the problem, however. If the managers are suspected of taking decisions to further their self-interest, they also would be suspected of communicating information to further their own interests – truthful communication of information cannot be automatically assumed here. As a consequence, motivating honest communication of relevant information is not costless.

In general, the design of incentive systems to motivate managers to work and make decisions in the interests of shareholders is a complex problem. Nonetheless, two general points can be made. First, motivating managers to work (make decisions, communicate information) in the interests of shareholders is costly. To the extent that introducing additional flexibility into managers' tasks increases the difficulties of controlling their actions, it will increase the costs of control. Again, as with information production, the exercise of flexibility has hidden costs that need to be considered in thinking about whether flexibility actually produces net benefits. One possibility is that the costs of controlling the exercise of flexibility outweigh the benefits. Under these circumstances, it would be quite rational for a firm to ignore flexibility and evaluate potential projects using conventional, passive, NPV analysis. Second, the current management control system needs to be examined for whether it actually promotes the exercise of flexibility in an appropriate fashion. If it doesn't, and there is no intention to change it, there is little point in evaluating opportunities as if flexibility will be appropriately exercised.

What the above points out is that real options techniques cannot be treated as independent from other features of the organization. In particular, the virtues of flexibility have to be set against costs arising from possible increased requirements for information production and management control. And, if relevant information is not produced and motivation issues with respect to the exercise of flexibility are not addressed, evaluating investment opportunities using real options techniques has the potential to be positively misleading.

Note

1. L.A. Gordon and A.W. Stark, 2000, 'The value of an investment-monitoring system in a real options environment', unpublished manuscript.

Summary for executives **14**

eal options analysis offers major insights into business economics, business strategy, business operations, general economics, psychology and even in future (we suspect) biology.

Why is real options analysis so powerful?

Its core idea is uncertainty of the random walk type. The random walk is almost the most severe form of quantified uncertainty possible, and it is also the form of uncertainty that we expect in the most competitive markets of all – namely the perfectly competitive markets of economic theory.

Given the increasing globalization of business, and the increasing tendency to split previously internal activities into independent businesses which trade at arm's length, we are certain to see more competitive behaviour in many markets. In turn we can expect more and more businesses to have to pay realistic prices for real options, which they may have to buy at or close to the money, and which they may have to exercise at small margins of profit.

A simple example of the power of real options analysis is how it can explain the high stock market valuation of many Internet and bio-technology companies which are actually loss-making. Shares in these companies are real call options to invest in highly volatile markets. It should be no surprise that such options can have high value even when, as at present, they are out of the money and currently unprofitable to exercise and likely on average to remain so.

Why is real options analysis so important?

Wherever we face the ultimate uncertainty of the random walk, real options analysis offers numerous insights into business decisions. At the level of a company's

> **Real options provokes us to understand the decisions that take a business completely out of its present markets.**

market strategy we have seen how it can increase our willingness to buy into presently unprofitable projects, markets or companies, while it can also warn us against making some investments in apparently favourable market conditions.

Deeper even than market strategy, real options provokes us to understand the decisions that take a business completely out of its present markets; for example put or exchange options that suggest when to scrap operations, when to exit markets, when to sell an asset into an entirely new market, and even when to sell an entire company. Real options offers us integrated tools for taking such decisions, which span both the old and the potential markets, and when both the old and the new markets are subject to random walk uncertainty.

What kinds of business will find real options analysis most and least useful?

Real options analysis may be most useful at two opposite ends of the business spectrum, namely (a) pure competitive commodity businesses and services, or other industries that are becoming intensely competitive; and (b) innovative research businesses, which are striving to create new real options.

How can we best use real options thinking?

Qualitatively

The main value of a real options analysis will often simply be that it provokes us into using one more way of structuring a business problem. Is this situation a real option? If not, why not? What could make it more like a real option? Should we or could we try to make this decision more like a real option? If this decision were a real option, what would be important to us? What would be our most important threats, opportunities and numerical sensitivities?

Even without quantitative analysis, real options analysis can suggest important qualitative insights, e.g.

- deep-in-the-money options have little further upside potential;

- out-of-the-money options can be worth buying, especially under conditions of high uncertainty;

- overestimating volatility or overestimating the time to maturity might bias us either towards or against investing;

- redesigning a chain of options (e.g. into a better sequence of get-out steps, with better stages of data collection in between) can add overall value.

Quantitatively

The most important thing to do is probably a sensitivity analysis: check sensitivity to a slightly different model (more options, more random factors), and within each model check sensitivity to slightly different problem parameters (volatility, expiry date, rate of dividend).

The most important thing to do is probably a sensitivity analysis.

When to use consultants

You may want to use outside help in one or more of the following stages of analysis:

- structuring the decision in general economic terms and in real option terms;

- building the right mathematical model;

- solving the computations and doing the sensitivity analysis and reality checks.

Specialists sometimes make their main career in only one of these three fields. Get insider or outside consultants to tell you which of the three fields they are strong in. Be suspicious if they claim equal strength in all! Get different consultants or individuals to evaluate each other in these three fields, and look for shared opinions.

If your in-house skills are gravely deficient in one or more of the above three areas, you will usually find this easy to recognize. It will be less easy to recognize a problem, and therefore more risky for you, if your internal or external consultants are 'nearly' good enough, but not quite.

If you have read this book you should have a good supply of awkward questions to ask either internal or external consultants. Encourage your team to ask the same awkward questions of each other. If in serious doubt, get an independent source of expertise to put the same questions to them.

In particular, always insist on clear explanations, using the structure that we have followed in this book, namely:

1. Clear narrative of the decision situation in common-sense language (debate the content of this).

2. Clear statement of what options are involved or why (a debate on this could be the heart of the analysis).

3. Clear statement of the decision rule inside the option model, and how this adds value within the assumptions of the option model (e.g. better price to pay, better go/no-go decision). What value would we lose by a 'wrong' decision? Would it matter?

4. Clear defence of what variables are being used in a model and why.

5. Sensitivity analysis to the assumed values for the key variables (especially to variations in expiry date, volatility, dividend rate and probability of jump loss).

6. Clear audit of the evidence (or lack of it) for the values of the key variables.

7. Sanity checks on all results. i.e. does it all make qualitative sense?

For example, ask to see a plot of a wide area of the valuation surface. Demand clear explanations of what is happening all over the valuation surface. Where and what are the boundary conditions? Where does the value surface rise and fall, under changes in time and the underlying asset? How do free boundaries vary over time? To check an estimate of the value of an American option (which may be more accurate in theory, but fragile in calculation), does this differ in the expected ways from the value of the equivalent European option, which is far easier and more robust to calculate?

Always insist on a rigorous analysis as to why (if ever) a real options answer conflicts with seasoned intuition. One of the two is right, and you may stand to lose a lot from backing the wrong side.

APPENDIX 1

Essentials of compound interest and discounted cash flow

by David Newton and Sydney Howell

Discounted cash flow is a way of comparing the values of sums of money expected to arise in different time periods. We reduce each sum of money expected in the future to its equivalent 'present value' today, using a discount rate which we believe is appropriate for the risk of the investment. The total 'present value' of all the expected cash flows can then be found by addition. Mathematically, the way to find the present value of a future sum of money is the inverse of compounding interest (where we find the future value of a present sum of money). We simply substitute a 'discount rate' for an 'interest rate'. If we want to compare values that arise at different points in time, we can discount values back (to show their value earlier in time, e.g. 'present value' at the beginning of a project) or compound them forward (to show their value later in time, e.g. 'terminal value' at the end of a project). Such comparable values can then be summed to give either the total present value (PV) or the total future value (FV) of the entire sequence of payments. The sum of the cash outflow on an investment today and the present value of all expected future cash flows caused by it in future is called the net present value (NPV). Data from capital markets can be used to find the discount rate appropriate for a given risk class (see Appendix 2).

You will see elsewhere in the book that, under certain conditions, option values can be found using the risk-free rate, even though the unhedged option, and its underlying asset, are most certainly not risk free.

We will take you first through the basics of compounding which will lead to 'continuous compounding' and naturally to 'continuous discounting', an especially useful idea in option valuation.

Compound interest

Suppose that today we agree to lend you $100 at 10 per cent interest, compounded annually, and that all money owed should be paid together after four years. The amount which you owed would grow like this:

Time/years	Amount owed/dollars
0	100
1	100(1 + 0.1) = 110.00
2	110(1 + 0.1) = 121.00
3	121(1 + 0.1) = 133.10
4	133.1(1 + 0.1) = 146.41

The present value, PV, is $100, the future value after one year is $110, and after two years it is $121. It is easy to continue this growth projection. For example, to get the value in year 4 take the present value, $100, and multiply four times by 1.1, which is $146.41. We can write this more quickly as $100(1.1)^4$. Since the amount for each year is 1.1 times the amount for the preceding year, the amount for any time t years ahead, is given by[1]

$$FV = 100*(1 + 0.1)^t = 100*1.1^t$$

Generalizing to any interest rate, r, we have:

$$FV = PV(1 + r)^t$$

Notice that if rates are quoted as percentages (e.g. 10) then for a general rate r% the growth factor over n years is $(1 + r/100)^n$. In finance it is more usual to quote interest rates directly as decimal fractions, so the growth factor over n years is $(1 + r)^n$. However, it is always worth checking whether a particular calculation has input the discount rate as a percentage or as a decimal fraction.

Conversion of compound interest rates to different time periods

Suppose that, instead of an annual rate, you have been quoted an interest rate of 0.21 (21 per cent) over two years. You want to know its equivalent compound rate per annum. These are familiar numbers; the first example we looked at for compound interest was 0.10 p.a. (10 per cent p.a.), which compounds to 0.21 (21 per cent) over two years. Clearly, the latter is equivalent to 0.10 (10 per cent) per one-year period. An example closer to home is in credit card interest charged monthly. Interest of 2 per cent per month allowed to accumulate for 12 months would amount to an equivalent annual rate of $(1 + 0.02)^{12} - 1 = 0.2682$ (to four decimal places) or 26.82 per cent p.a. Reversing the calculation, if you are given the annual rate you can calculate the monthly rate as $(1 + 0.2683)^{1/12} - 1 = 0.02$.

The application of compound interest rates converted between different units of time becomes problematic if cash is withdrawn within the total period under consideration. Here's why.

Suppose you have two bonds which give cash payments (called 'coupons') every six months and every year respectively. This will happen for several years (the exact number does not matter, for our purposes), starting with a payment from one bond six months from now, followed by both bonds one year from now. Payments are expressed as percentages of a fixed sum ($1,000): 5 per cent per six-month period and 10.25 per cent per annum. These rates are equivalent, since $1.05^2 - 1 = 0.1025$. However, the bonds are not necessarily equally attractive investments; their worth depends on other interest rates. Consider a one-year period. After six months, one bond pays 5 per cent, ($50). Now, if this is reinvested somewhere at 5 per cent per six-month period, it will earn 5 per cent of 5 per cent ($2.50) and after one year the owner of the bond will have $50 (first coupon) + $2.50 (interest on first coupon) + $50 (second coupon) = $102.50, which is 10.25 per cent of $1,000 and, hence, there is no difficulty. However, if the first coupon ($50) is reinvested at more or less than 5 per cent, clearly the outcome after a year will differ from that from holding the 10.25 per cent p.a. bond. Investors in bonds would not consider the bonds equivalent just because their compound interest rates are equivalent. The equivalence of the compound rates is based on the assumption that interest is accumulated at a constant rate during each year.

Nominal, actual and effective interest rates

Compound interest rates cannot be converted to equivalent rates over shorter periods by simple division. Thus, a rate of 0.21 p.a. (21 per cent p.a.) is equivalent to 0.10 (10 per cent) per six-month period, not $0.21/2 = 0.105$ (10.5 per cent). However, it is common practice to quote compound interest rates using simple multiplication. For example, a nominal interest rate quoted as '10 per cent p.a. semi-annually' is actually a rate of 5 per cent per six-month period. This is not a conversion to an equivalent annual rate as described previously; the amount actually paid is 5 per cent every six months. However, the nominal rate can be converted to an equivalent annual rate, as before:

Equivalent annual rate $= (1+0.05)^2 - 1 = 0.1025$ p.a. (10.25 per cent p.a.)

This equivalent rate is known as the effective interest rate and, if it is an annual rate as here, it is sometimes called the annual percentage rate or APR. The nominal rate may alternatively be called the stated interest rate. As long as you know how to calculate the effective rate, there is no practical problem in quoting a nominal rate.

A nominal rate of 10 per cent p.a., with actual compounding periods of six months, three months and one month, converts into three different effective rates as follows:

semi-annual $\left(1 + \dfrac{0.1}{2}\right)^2 = 1.1025$ Effective rate = 10.25 per cent p.a.

quarterly $\left(1 + \dfrac{0.1}{4}\right)^4 = 1.1038$ Effective rate = 10.38 per cent p.a.

monthly $\left(1 + \dfrac{0.1}{12}\right)^{12} = 1.1047$ Effective rate = 10.47 per cent p.a.

Looking at these three results, it is easy to deduce the general equation for converting nominal rates to effective rates. Taking a nominal annual interest rate which is actually divided into m parts of a year (division by the integer m, say) then paid (and compounded) m times:

$$\left(1 + \frac{r_{nominal}}{m}\right)^m = 1 + r_{effective}$$

$$r_{effective} = \left(1 + \frac{r_{nominal}}{m}\right)^m - 1$$

Continuous compounding

We now have a formula for converting a nominal annual rate to an effective rate, depending on how many times in the year an instalment of interest is paid. Mathematically, a time period can be sliced into as many shorter periods as you wish. Imagine what happens when m is made larger and larger. This increases the power to which the number in parentheses is raised, tending to produce a larger result, but at the same time the number in parentheses becomes smaller, which tends to produce a smaller result. The net effect of these opposing tendencies is demonstrated below, using t = 1 and r = 0.1. The results were calculated, to eight decimal places, using a spreadsheet.

Mathematically, a time period can be sliced into as many shorter periods as you wish.

m	$\left(1 + \dfrac{0.1}{m}\right)^m$
1	1.10000000
10	1.10462213
100	1.10511570
1,000	1.10516539
10,000	1.10517037
100,000	1.10517086
1,000,000	1.10517091
10,000,000	1.10517092

The results obtained increase as m is increased. Notice, however, that they appear to be approaching a limiting value. A proper proof (not attempted here) would show that this is the tenth root of the number given its own symbol, 'e', in mathematics. We cannot express e as a finite decimal number, but is approximately equal to 2.71828. It may be found as a function on calculators and in spreadsheets. On your calculator you will almost certainly find the 'exponential function', shortened to 'exp'. Exp(0.1) means e to the power 0.1, which may also be written $e^{0.1}$. Using a calculator or a spreadsheet you will find the value of $e^{0.1}$, to eight decimal places, is 1.10517092, which is the result obtained by making m sufficiently large. Although this is only a demonstration, not a mathematical proof, you will not be surprised to hear that no matter how large m is made, the result will not exceed the limiting value which is equal to $e^{0.1}$. Generalizing from one year to any time interval t, and generalizing the interest rate per year from 0.1 to r the limit is e^{rt}.

This is called 'continuous compounding'. It follows that future value t time periods ahead with continuous compounding at a nominal rate, r per period, is given by the equation:

$FV = PVe^{rt}$ where r is understood to be the nominal rate

In continuous compounding, the time between successive compounding operations is infinitesimally small; the number of compounding operations over the period of a nominal rate is infinitely large. Described in this way, these are not practical operations to carry out! Yet there is a simple formula for the result and this method of compounding is often practically convenient, particularly in options work. Graphically, lines representing compounding as we use progressively shorter periods shift to higher values of FV but they move no higher than the limit set by the line for continuous compounding. This is demonstrated in Figure A1.1.

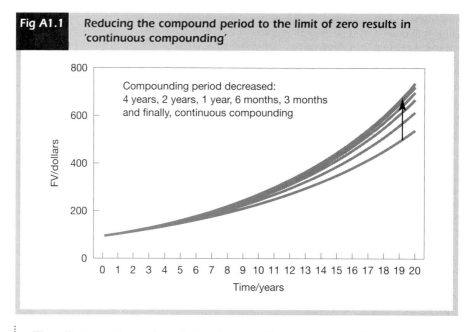

Fig A1.1 Reducing the compound period to the limit of zero results in 'continuous compounding'

The effective rate can be calculated for continuous compounding:

$$e^r = 1 + r_{effective}$$

$r_{effective} = e^r - 1$ where r is understood to be the nominal rate

Conversion of continuously compounded rates to different time intervals is particularly convenient, because multiplication of exponentials simply involves addition of the powers. For example, a continuously compounded rate of 0.10 (10 per cent) per six months is equivalent to a continuously compounded rate of 0.20 (20 per cent) p.a. (recall that the answer would be 21 per cent p.a. using discrete compounding). The time periods must be measured in the same units; thus two six-month periods at rate 0.1 per period but one year at rate 0.2 per period. Labelling the two time measures 'a' and 'b':

$$e^{r_a t_a} = e^{r_b t_b} \quad \text{and so} \quad r_a t_a = r_b t_b \qquad \text{e.g. } (0.1)2 = 0.2(1)$$

For conversion between continuously compounded rates r_a and discrete (not continuous) compounding rates r_b the formula is:

$$e^{r_a t_a} = (1 + r_b)^{t_b}$$

$$r_b = \exp\left[\frac{r_a t_a}{t_b}\right] - 1 \qquad \text{switching to notation whereby } \exp[x] = e^x$$

For example, 10 per cent p.a., continuously compounded, is equivalent to 10.52 per cent p.a. compounded discretely once per annum (i.e. '10.52 per cent p.a')., since $t_a = t_b = 1$ and $e^{0.1} - 1 = 0.1052$ (to four decimal places). It is also equivalent to 5.13 per cent per semi-annual period compounded semi-annually (i.e. just '5.13 per cent semi-annually') since, in this case, $t_a = 1$, $t_b = 2$ and $e^{0.05} - 1 = 0.0513$ (to four decimal places). Notice that if $t_b = 1$, the formula for calculation of the effective rate is obtained. Alternatively, 10 per cent p.a., compounded once per annum discretely, is equivalent to 9.531 per cent p.a. compounded continuously.

Discounting: DCF and NPV

Discounting is the process of calculating the present value of future cash flows, and is a fundamental financial technique. To an investor, a nominal amount of cash does not have the same value at different times; generally, a dollar next year is worth less than a dollar today, since a dollar today could be invested today to repay more than a dollar next year. Discounted cash flow calculation (DCF) is important because it allows the values of future cash flows to be adjusted to a common time. Bringing all values to a common time allows them to be summed so that the total present value of a series of cash flows, to be received at many different times, can be calculated. This allows alternative investments, which have different time patterns of money flow, to be compared.

For example, would you prefer to receive $1 million now or ten years from now? If you take the money now, you can invest it. If you are a cautious investor, you bank the money and receive interest. For simplicity, suppose you receive 10 per cent p.a. compound interest, fixed over ten years. If you leave all the money in the bank, after ten years you will have $1 million times $(1+0.10)^{10}$, which is $2,593,742. Clearly, your financial preference should be to receive $1 million now. If, instead, you are promised $1 million now *and* $1 million ten years from now it would not be sensible to say that your gain in value today is worth $2 million. A better way would be to determine how much money, put in the bank today, would yield $1 million after ten years, then add that amount to $1 million received today. $1 million received ten years from now is the equivalent of an amount in the bank today of $1 million divided by $(1+0.10)^{10}$, which is $385,543 – making the value of the two receipts, measured today, $1,385,543. This is the basis of DCF.

When an initial cash investment is made (a 'negative cash flow'), and is expected to be followed by cash inflows in later periods, the sum of the discounted cash flows is known as the net present value (NVP).

The idea behind NPV follows from DCF and can be shown in a simple example. Suppose a company is considering an investment of $1 million today. Its managers expect to receive a series of cash flows annually for ten years, after which the project ends. They use the method of discounted cash flow to calculate the PV of the future cash inflows. They then compare this PV of inflows with today's outflow of their initial investment. If the PV is greater than the investment, the investment is judged to be profitable. We use the term NPV to express this comparison, and for a $1 million investment we would write NPV = − 1,000,000 + PV. Then if the NPV of the investment is positive we consider that the investment would be profitable. In an efficient capital market, the unexpected news of this deal will raise the company's value by the amount of the NPV. An NPV of zero means that the investment has just broken even on its cost of capital (neither increasing wealth nor decreasing it) and in a theoretically efficient market only zero NPV investments would ever be available.

We already have formulae relating future value to present value. For discrete (i.e. not continuous) compounding this is:

$$FV_t = PV \, (1+r)^t$$

For a single future value, the formula showing discounting is easily obtained by rearranging this formula:

$$PV = \frac{FV_t}{(1+r)^t} = FV_t(1+r)^{-t}$$

A crucial feature of both PV and FV is that present values and future values can be reduced to the values of any date we wish, and when reduced to that date the values arising in different times become additive. If a series of expected cash flows is discounted back to the present date, the present value of the series is the sum of the present values of the individual cash flows. This is important because it allows projects, each with cash flows expected at many different times and in different amounts, to be valued and, hence, compared. The additivity of present values is easily demonstrated.

A cash flow of $110 one year from now, discounted at 0.10 p.a. (10 per cent p.a.), is worth $100 today. Similarly, $121 two years from now is also worth $100 today. Therefore, the series of cash flows, starting today and arriving in consecutive years, $100, $110, $121, discounted at 10 per cent p.a., is worth $300.

$$PV = 100 + \frac{110}{(1+0.10)} + \frac{121}{(1+0.1)^2} = 100 + 100 + 100 = 300$$

There is only one present value for the series, but an infinite set of possible future values, one for each future time. Cash flows are discounted back from future times to earlier times and compounded forward from earlier times to future times. For the series of cash flows in the example, the future value after one year is $330:

$$FV_{1 \text{ year}} = 100(1 + 0.1) + 110 + \frac{121}{(1 + 0.1)} = 110 + 110 + 110 = 330$$

Here, 100 has been compounded forward, 110 does not need to be adjusted and 121 has been discounted back. Similarly, the future value after two years is \$363:

$$FV_{2 \text{ years}} = 100(1 + 0.1)^2 + 110(1 + 0.1) + 121 = 121 + 121 + 121 = 363$$

Here, 100 has been compounded forward two years, 110 has been compounded forward one year and 121 did not need to be adjusted.

Notice how consistent and convenient PV and FV calculations are. The only rule for computing values at different times is that you must convert all cash amounts to the same time before adding them.

The results in the example can be inter-converted by noting that:

$300(1 + 0.1) = 330$ $330/(1 + 0.1) = 300$
$330(1 + 0.1) = 363$ $363/(1 + 0.1) = 330$

Discrete compounding and discounting are more familiar in daily life than continuous (perhaps) but the continuous forms are more useful in option pricing, since the mathematics of the exponential function is particularly convenient in continuous time. The corresponding formulae for continuous discounting are:

Discrete types of compounding and discounting are more familiar in daily life than continuous.

$FV_t = PVe^{rt}$ continuous compounding of PV from time 0 to time t

$PV = \dfrac{FV_t}{e^{rt}} = FV_t e^{-rt}$ continuous discounting of FV from time t to time 0

The annual cash flows 100, 110, 121 can be continuously discounted at 10 per cent p.a. back to the present as follows (to two decimal places):

$$PV = 100 + \frac{110}{e^{0.1}} + \frac{121}{e^{0.2}} = 100 + 99.53 + 99.07 = 298.60$$

Compare this with the different result obtained using discrete discounting (three present values of 100 sum to 300). There is no problem here; the three numbers 100, 110, 121 were chosen to have the same present value (100) with discrete discounting at 10 per cent. But discrete discounting at 10 per cent p.a. is equivalent to continuous discounting at only approximately 9.531 per cent, since more frequent (continuous) interest payments give us a higher return for the same nominal annual interest rate. The proper continuous equivalent to discrete discounting at 10 per cent p.a. is to discount at a continuous rate of 9.531 per cent as follows (accurate to several decimal places in the answer):

$$PV = 100 + \frac{110}{e^{0.09531}} + \frac{121}{e^{2*0.09531}} = 100 + 100 + 100 = 300$$

The mechanics of discounting have been explained, but how is the discount rate r chosen? Different levels of risk make investors require different rates of return, and by using different discount rates for different levels of risk we can value projects, assemblies of projects or even companies. The theory relating risk and return is considered in Appendix 2 but in the next section we will give an overview of discount rate selection.

Choosing the discount rate and understanding NPV

In order to understand NPV it is important to appreciate the way in which the discount rate is related to risk. It is not essential to know the detailed mathematical formulations of risk and rate of return (which are explained in Appendix 2) before gaining this insight.

The discount rate for a particular investment is chosen by considering what else might be done with the cash, instead of committing it to that investment.

For example, suppose you have $1 million in cash, and the best bank rate offered is 0.10 p.a. (10 per cent p.a.). Suppose another, equally 'safe' bank offers 0.0975 p.a. (9.75 per cent p.a.). If you deposit your cash at the inferior rate, after one year you would have $1,097,500. The net present value of this investment at the best bank's rate (10 per cent) would be calculated like this (to the nearest $):

$$NPV = -\$1,000,000 + \frac{\$1,097,500}{(1 + 0.10)} = -\$1,000,000 + 997,727 = -\$2,272$$

This is a negative NPV and shows how much of your present wealth you would be throwing away by investing at the inferior rate: the inferior return on $1 million is only giving you as much as the 10 per cent return on $997,727. Putting your $1 million into the inferior bank is equivalent to throwing away $2,272 of your money and leaving the rest invested in the best bank.

For comparison, the NPV of the $1,100,000 that the best bank will pay you if you deposit there, discounted at the best available rate of 10%, less the value you deposit, is zero. This means you are throwing away zero wealth if you deposit in the best bank.

Now suppose that a third investment becomes available. You might decide to use the same 10 per cent discount rate to value that investment:

Suppose the new investment is for one year and offers a return of $1,600,000 on $1 million invested.

$$\text{NPV} = -\$1,000,000 + \frac{\$1,600,000}{(1 + 0.10)} = +\$454,545$$

This means that if you consider the new investment to be as safe as depositing your money in the best bank, you would confidently expect to receive, after one year, the same amount which you would have received from the best bank had you had $1,454,545 to invest now. In other words, you would expect the alternative investment to bring you additional present value of $454,545 and so you would consider it a very good investment.

This is obvious if you split the numbers as follows:

$1,000,000(1 + 0.10) = $1,100,000
$454,545(1 + 0.10) = $500,000

The first equation is equivalent to the future value of investment of $1 million in the best bank, the second shows the extra future value of $500,000 acquired by investing in the new proposition, which has a present value of $454,545.

If the alternative investment really is only as risky as investment in the bank, then the NPV analysis above is correct. However, what should you do if you think the new investment is more risky? Presumably, you would no longer think it worth an extra $454,545. In general, the more risky the investment, the higher the rate of return required by investors. Suppose, for the moment, you are able in some way to classify investments according to their risk (this will be covered theoretically in Appendix 2). Suppose the risk of the new investment is similar to that of investments requiring a discount rate of 0.30 p.a. (30 per cent p.a.). This means you would deem a return of 30 per cent to be just sufficient, no more and no less, to compensate you for taking the risk of the new investment.

A return of $1,600,000 on an investment of $1 million, discounted at 0.30 p.a. (30 per cent p.a.), gives an NPV of:

$$\text{NPV} = -£1,000,000 + \frac{£1,600,000}{(1 + 0.30)} = +£230,769$$

The NPV is positive; the new investment is a good one, though not as attractive as it would have been if its risk had been as low as an investment in the bank. You would expect to receive $1,300,000 for an investment of comparable risk, but are receiving more than that. In return for investing $1 million at the given risk level, you will be getting a return you could only have expected to get if you had had $1,230,769 to invest, since:

$1,000,000(1 + 0.30) = $1,300,000
$230,769(1 + 0.30) = $300,000

NPV is a tool for decision making. The discount rate is chosen either by direct comparison with another investment yielding a known rate of return and considered to be of comparable risk, or by statistical methods (described in Appendix 2) using data from many investments to define risk and relate it to expected rates of return. A positive NPV is present value in excess of that which you ought to expect, given the level of risk implied by the discount rate. By choosing a discount rate you are, knowingly or unknowingly, also choosing to compare the investment with some other investment (discount rate is sometimes called the 'opportunity cost of capital', which expresses the idea of a return foregone by investing in an alternative project). The comparison could be with a particular investment, such as a similar project already undertaken within a company, or it could be with a theoretical project of the same risk.

Suppose you use the bank deposit rate as the discount rate and obtain a positive NPV for a project. If the project is no riskier than a bank deposit, it is a better investment than depositing with the bank; if not, it merely promises a better return, but no account has been taken of the greater likelihood that its promised cash flows might not arrive in full or on time. In the same way, if you use the rate of return from another project as the discount rate, NPV shows whether the new investment is inferior (negative NPV), equal (NPV is zero) or superior (positive NPV) to that project *if* their risks are equal. This means the project discount rate must be chosen with care. Any one past project may not be typical of either the level of risk or the rate of return realistically required by investors. Rather than comparing with a single past project, therefore, decision makers may set a 'benchmark' rate (a minimum acceptable return) as a practical way of using NPV to rank projects. Compared with this benchmark, zero or positive NPV projects will be acceptable; the higher the NPV, the more valuable the investment.

In order to set a benchmark rate that most truly reflects the risk of a company project, it is necessary to look outside the company since the company's policies on risk, and the actual outcomes of its projects, may not reflect the realistic best alternatives available. Stock price data are readily available for many large companies, and it is possible to determine the appropriate return for a given level of risk for investment in other companies' shares in the same industry on a stockmarket at a particular time (see MBA standard texts on Corporate Finance, such as Brealey and Myers, 2000).

Why does it matter that the rate should as closely as possible match those of other companies facing similar risks? Isn't a rate typical of the company's own past performance perfectly acceptable or even more appropriate? An example will show why.

Two projects are under evaluation. They are equally risky and the correct discount rate, to take this level of risk into account, is 0.20 p.a. (20 per cent p.a.). You are considering the effects of setting a benchmark rate at either 0.10 p.a. (10 per cent p.a.) or 0.30 p.a. (30 per cent p.a.). The cash flows and discounted cash flows are as follows:

Project 1

Year:	0	1	2	3	4	5	
Cash flow:	−250	336	0	0	0	49.77	NPV
Discounted at 10%	−250	305.45	0	0	0	30.90	86.36
Discounted at 20%	−250	280.00	0	0	0	20.00	50.00
Discounted at 30%	−250	258.46	0	0	0	13.40	21.87

Project 2

Year:	0	1	2	3	4	5	
Cash flow:	−250	0	0	0	0	746.50	NPV
Discounted at 10%	−250	0	0	0	0	463.52	213.52
Discounted at 20%	−250	0	0	0	0	300.00	50.00
Discounted at 30%	−250	0	0	0	0	201.05	−48.95

When the correct discount rate is applied, the projects are assessed as having equal value (50.00). However, if the company used a benchmark rate of 10 per cent per annum it would assess Project 2 as considerably more valuable than Project 1 (213.52 contrasted with 86.36). Conversely, if the company used a benchmark rate of 30 per cent per annum Project 2 would be rejected (NPV = − 48.95) while Project 1 would still offer positive value compared with the benchmark (NPV = 21.87).

Assuming that managers use discount rates which properly reflect risk, company shareholders can delegate operations to them with a simple instruction: maximize NPV at the correct rate!

The central idea which has been discussed here is that if the NPV is negative, the investment is not sufficiently attractive to justify the risk taken. If the NPV is zero, the investment gives exactly the return appropriate for the risk taken. If the NPV is positive, an investment has been found which more than compensates for its risk and is, therefore, attractive to an investor.

One consequence is sometimes not understood. Consider two projects, both lasting one year and discounted at different rates in order to reflect their different levels of risk. It so happens that the projects have the same positive NPV. Therefore, they are equally valuable now to an investor. The projects start and finish at the same times. Suppose they are both completed successfully with cash flows as expected. They are *not* then equally valuable. Here are the data:

NPV analysis at the start

	Project 1	Project 2
Discount rate p.a.	0.1	0.6
Initial investment	$100,000	$100,000
Received at end	$132,000	$192,000
NPV	$20,000	$20,000

Outcome if cash flows are as expected

Rate of return	32%	92%

The projects required the same initial investment, were for the same period and had the same NPV, yet one gave a return of 32 per cent while the other gave a return of 92 per cent. On comparing these rates of return, project 2 wrongly seems superior. However, when we allow for risk correctly before the event both projects are equally attractive, and both would produce the same increase in wealth for investors (e.g. increase in the market value of the company) since before the event there is a larger risk that project 2 will not produce returns close to the forecast levels.

Judging projects by 'rates of return' can be seriously misleading. In particular a technique called 'internal rate of return' tries to find a discount rate (there may be more than one) at which the NPV of the project is zero. It can be seriously erroneous to judge projects by their internal rates of return (IRR), but unfortunately the method is still widespread.

You now know the principle behind the selection of appropriate discount rates and the interpretation of NPV. The detail of how to quantify risk and how to relate risk to the rate of return (and, hence, to discount rate) is considered in Appendix 2.

Although NPV analysis incorporates risk (in the discount rate), the missing element is the flexibility available to decision makers as the future unfolds. This can be taken into account, to a degree, by 'decision trees', but these do not satisfactorily account for the changing levels of risk as projects or investments progress (see Doctor, Newton and Pearson, 2001, for an application of both decision trees and options analysis). Instead, the real options methodology provides a way of keeping the NPV concept but adding option values, as you see in the case examples in this book.

Formulae for special cases of PV: annuities, perpetuities and growing perpetuities

There are several well-known formulae which simplify the calculation of PV and NPV in special cases. Some of these are used in Chapter 7.

It is often the case that cash payments are made as a fixed amount at regular intervals; for example, $10,000 on 1 January every year for 15 years. If the discount rate is 8 per cent and the first payment is to be received one year from now, the present value of the expected future cash flows is the sum of 15 terms:

$$PV = \frac{10,000}{1.08} + \frac{10,000}{1.08^2} + \dots + \frac{10,000}{1.08^{15}} = 10,000 \left[\frac{1}{1.08} + \frac{1}{1.08^2} + \dots + \frac{1}{1.08^{15}} \right]$$

A series of equal cash flows equally spaced over time, such as this, is called an annuity. There is no need to add all the terms because there is an elementary formula which gives the same result more easily:

$$PV = \frac{10,000}{0.08} \left[1 - \frac{1}{(1.08)^{15}} \right] = 85,595$$

The general form of this equation with cash flows, C, discount rate as a decimal, r p.a. and over a time, T years, is:

$$PV_{annuity} = \frac{C}{r} \left[1 - \frac{1}{(1+r)^T} \right]$$

A perpetuity is a special case of annuity in which payments are supposed to be made for ever. On reflection, you may find this idea surprising, but nevertheless, perpetuities have been issued. In practice, the issuer may buy back the perpetuity after many years, using the same formula for valuation as when the perpetuity was issued. The general equation for valuing perpetuities is:

A perpetuity is a special case of annuity in which payments are supposed to be made for ever.

$$PV_{perpetuity} = \frac{C}{r}$$

For example, a perpetuity of $100 p.a. at a discount rate of 10 per cent (0.10) is worth $1,000, since:

$$PV = \frac{C}{r} = \frac{100}{0.1} = 1,000$$

Elementary formulae are also available for valuing annuities and perpetuities whose payments increase each period to (1+g) times the amount in the preceding period (in other words, payments increase by 100g per cent each period). A general formula for the present value of the series of growing cash amounts is given below. The series terminates after a finite number of terms if it is a growing annuity or contains an infinite number of terms if it is a growing perpetuity:

221

$$PV = \frac{C}{(1+r)} + \frac{C(1+g)}{(1+r)^2} + \frac{C(1+g)^2}{(1+r)^3} + \text{ ... etc.}$$

The formulae for valuing an annuity and a perpetuity are summarized below, with those for a growing annuity and a growing perpetuity:

	Constant payment C	*Payment grows by g each period*
Annuity	$\dfrac{C}{r}\left[1 - \dfrac{1}{(1+r)^T}\right]$	$\dfrac{C}{r-g}\left[1 - \dfrac{(1+g)^T}{(1+r)^T}\right]$
Perpetuity	$\dfrac{C}{r}$	$\dfrac{C}{r-g}$

Notice that the formulae including growth rate g reduce to those for constant payment if g is made equal to zero. Although there are corresponding formulae for use with continuous discount rates, it is common practice to use these formulae (i.e. discrete rates).

There is one pitfall to avoid in using the formula for a growing perpetuity: the formula is invalid unless the growth rate, g, is less than the discount rate, r. Think what this means. The series can be written as:

$$PV(1+r) = C + \frac{C(1+g)}{(1+r)} + \frac{C(1+g)^2}{(1+r)^2} + \text{ ... for ever(!)}$$

By taking a factor of $(1+r)$ to the left-hand side of the equation, the effect of changing the relative sizes of g and r on the terms in the series becomes easier to understand. If g is less than r, the terms become progressively smaller and they add up to a finite result. However, if g is greater than r, the terms become progressively larger and so the sum of the series increases without limit – it becomes infinite. If g is equal to r, the PV terms stay constant and so, again, the sum of an infinite number of terms of the series increases without limit. If you set g equal to r in the formula for the present value of a growing perpetuity, division by zero results. To a mathematician this could imply an infinite result, which is correct. However, if you set g greater than r, you obtain a negative mathematical result which is not the correct answer (the correct answer is infinite). Beware the second pitfall of believing that the invalidity of the formula when g is greater than r can be proven using the formula itself. The derivation of the formula includes the limitation that g must be less than r and so the formula cannot be invoked to prove its own invalidity outside that condition.

Discounting and probability

A particular requirement for option valuation is an understanding of continuous discounting when there are discrete alternative future outcomes with given probabilities. This is used in binomial and trinomial tree and finite difference methods (see Appendix 4). Here we will give only a brief account, assuming that the reader is familiar with elementary ideas of probability.

Suppose either $50 or $150 will be received six months from now, with equal probability, and that the (continuous) discount rate is 0.1 (10 per cent) p.a.

Future values

The present values of the two amounts, ignoring probabilities, are $150e^{-0.05} and $50e^{-0.05} and so the present value required is ($150*0.5 + $50*0.5)*e^{-0.05} = $100*e^{-0.05} = $95.12 (to the nearest cent). Practically, you could imagine that we offer you $150 or $50, to be given one year from now, according to whether a tossed coin lands with its head or its tail facing upwards. If the coin is unbiased, there is a probability of 0.5 that it will face one way and 0.5 the other. Therefore, you 'expect' to receive on average in one year's time ($150*0.5 + $50*0.5) = $100, whose present value is $95.12.

The same ideas are used when three outcomes are possible. For example, $150 with probability 0.4, $120 with probability 0.2 and $50 with probability 0.4 and discount rate again 0.1 (10 per cent) p.a.

Future values

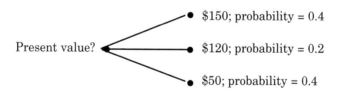

The present value is ($150*0.4 + $120*0.2 + $50*0.4)*e^{-0.05} = $104*e^{-0.05} = $98.93 (to the nearest cent).

Note

1. Note we are using the convention * to indicate multiplication, which is the standard notation in worksheets.

APPENDIX 2

Essentials of the capital asset pricing model

It is intuitively obvious that if we invest money we need compensation for the time delay in receiving the money (we would want this compensation even if the return were risk free). We also need compensation for any unpredictability in the size of the return. We may also need compensation for any risk of outright loss of our investment. The capital asset pricing model tacitly assumes that there is zero risk of outright loss of our investment, though this risk can be modelled as a Poisson jump process (see Chapter 4).

The capital asset pricing model (CAPM) is a basic and extremely important model for measuring risk, and for relating the required rate of return to the degree of risk. The underlying mathematics is extremely subtle, but the inputs and basic outputs are simple.

The model assumes that risk can be quantified as the statistical variance or uncertainty of returns, over some time horizon of interest. Of two investments with equal expected or average returns, the one with the lower variance is taken to be less risky, and therefore preferable. This measure allows for zero or negative returns in any one period, but it does not allow for a 'risk of ruin' (i.e. however uncertain, the income stream is assumed to be at no risk suddenly going to zero for ever).

If risk is defined as variance, the most basic form of the CAPM assumes the existence of a 'risk-free' asset, for which the variance of return can be taken as zero. The nearest real world proxy to this is usually thought to be the 90-day US Treasury bond.

No one would buy an asset of greater risk than zero (i.e. with any variability of return at all) unless (in expectation) it offered a higher average rate of return than a 90-day Treasury bond. The required trade-off between risk and return turns out to be very simple.

It can be shown that portfolios of assets tend to have lower risk than single assets. The most efficient port-

It can be shown that portfolios of assets tend to have lower risk than single assets.

folio (in the sense of lowest risk for a given return) is the entire portfolio of risky assets, i.e. if you want to take any investment risk at all, you should buy the same minute percentage of the total market value every single traded asset. If you wish to take on a level of risk in between those of the risky market and of the risk-free asset, you can divide your investments between holdings in the risk-free asset and holdings in the risky market portfolio.

The extra return that you get from the risky market portfolio, sufficient to compensate you for putting all your wealth in that portfolio, is called the **market premium**. So the total return from investing in the market portfolio is the **risk-free return** plus the **market premium**.

If you want to take higher risks (and get higher returns) than the risk-free return plus the market premium, you should not buy single shares, because although they are riskier than holding the portfolio of all shares, the market does not give them enough return to justify holding any one of them exclusively.

The market will not give you a large enough return on a single share to compensate you for devoting your entire portfolio to it. This is because you could immediately do better still by constructing a portfolio of several similar shares, all with the same overall average return, but with a lower variance of return, due to the portfolio diversification. Since anyone in the market can do this, the market prices all individual shares as if everyone had already diversified.

Therefore if you want to take risk levels higher than putting all your wealth into the risky market portfolio the optimal way to do so is to expand your portfolio by borrowing a quantity of the risk-free asset, selling and investing the proceeds in the risky market portfolio. This adds to your returns (because you are making the market premium on the shares you don't own), but it also adds to your risks, because the fluctuation of your income is now based on the fluctuation of a sum larger than your personal wealth, i.e. larger than the part of the port-folio that you own.

The calculation for the required rate of return on any single asset is based on comparing the variability of the returns to that asset and the returns to the total risky market. The ratio between their movements is called **beta** (the Greek letter β). If beta is less than one, the asset is less risky than the total market and so needs a lower return than the market. If beta is one, the asset is neither more nor less risky than the total market, and if the beta is above one, the asset is riskier than average, and requires higher than average returns. Beta is simply the linear regression coefficient which predicts returns on the individual asset from returns on the market.

The actual effect of the extra risk is itself linear in beta. For any risky asset a, the required return r_a is the risk-free return, plus beta times the market premium, which in symbols is $r_a = r_f + \beta(r_m - r_f)$, where r_f is the risk free return, r_m is the risky market return. The bracketed quantity is the market premium.

There are important links between the capital asset pricing model and option pricing. One is that only a risk-free (delta hedged) option can be priced at the risk-free rate of return (but given that any investor can delta hedge, all options are priced as if they had been delta hedged). This in turn suggests that you should not gamble on unhedged options. The second is that a firm's required rate of return and its beta are both related to the volatility of the firm's stock price, and hence to the value of options on the firm's stock. In option theory the required rate of return on a firm is usually notated as μ, where as stated above:

$$\mu = r_f + \beta(r_m - r_f) \tag{1}$$

This can also be expressed as

$$\mu = r_f + \phi \, \rho_{am} \, \sigma_a \tag{2}$$

where ϕ is the so-called market price of risk (expressed as the market premium required to offset one unit of volatility in the return to the risky market portfolio, i.e. ϕ is the ratio of market premium to market volatility). Also ρ_{am} is the correlation between the return on the market and the return on the individual share, σ_a is the volatility of the individual share, and we will define σ_m as the volatility of the market, i.e.

$$\phi = (r_m - r_f)/\sigma_m \tag{3}$$

or

$$\sigma_m \, \phi = (r_m - r_f) \tag{4}$$

(4) gives a slightly deeper explanation for the market premium itself, since the market premium is driven both by the risk-aversion measure ϕ and by the volatility of the total risky market σ_m which is non-zero by definition. Clearly ϕ and the market premium will be zero if investors are risk neutral (i.e. indifferent to variations around mean earnings). Substitution of (3) in (2) gives:

$$\mu = r_f + \rho_{am} \, \sigma_a \, (r_m - r_f)/\sigma_m \tag{5}$$

But $\rho_{am} \, \sigma_a/\sigma_m$ is simply the regression coefficient beta in (1) so that (5) reduces to (1).

Even the simple form of CAPM above is enough to show that there is a fundamental unity between the principles for pricing the entire risky market, the principles for pricing a single risky stock, and those for pricing an option on that stock.

There is empirical evidence that the above basic CAPM cannot fit real-world data without some enrichment (for example, arbitrage pricing theory suggests that the required rate of return is driven not by a single 'market level of return' factor but by several different variable factors. These might be observable variables, e.g. the returns of specific industry sectors, or they might be abstract, unidentified variables, each of which has some effects on all the sectors, though with different weightings).

It is worth noting an even simpler model, which is implicit in the basic theory of option pricing. This assumes away the problem of relating the stock's required returns to those of one or more underlying market factors. Instead the only relevant variables are thought to be the volatility of the individual stock, σ_a, the market's degree of risk aversion in pricing the volatility of that stock, ϕ_a, and the risk-free rate of return r_f.

Wilmot, Howison and Dewynne show that in this simple world the required rate of return on the stock μ is determined as:

$$\mu = r_f + \phi_a \, \sigma_a \tag{6}$$

Other closely related formulations exist, for example:

$$\mu = r_f + \phi_m \, \sigma_a \, \rho_{ma} \tag{7}$$

This re-expresses (6) by explaining the origin of the stock-specific price of risk ϕ_a as being the product of the stock's actual volatility σ_a, its actual correlation with the market ρ_{ma} and the market price of risk ϕ_m. Likewise it explains the market premium $r_m - r_f$ in (5) as being ϕ_m the market price of risk (return required per unit of market volatility) times σ_m the market volatility.

If a stock paid no dividend, we would expect that all of its required rate of return would be generated by capital appreciation (price increase). Hence its price should drift upwards with time, so as to generate an average rate of capital appreciation equal to μ in (6). Note that μ corresponds to the drift term m in the continuous random walk of stock price so if a stock pays no dividend, its drift m should equal μ in (6) (m here is a drift term as defined by equation (6) in Appendix 3).

However, if the stock pays out part of its return in the form of a continuous dividend, at a constant fraction δ of the stock's current value, the stock's capital appreciation must be smaller than μ in order to prevent the stock from giving an excessive total return for the risk being taken. The rate of capital appreciation or price drift m required for such a stock is $(\mu - \delta)$.

There are, however, certain assets which do not visibly pay any dividend but whose rate of capital appreciation still 'falls short' of the total rate of return μ required to compensate an owner for the risk of owning the asset. If so it is common to express the actual rate of capital appreciation in the form $(\mu - \delta)$ for some δ, where δ is simply the gap between the required total rate of return and the observed rate of capital appreciation m.

There are certain assets which do not visibly pay any dividend.

For such an asset δ is often called the 'rate of return shortfall'. It might be more accurate to call δ the 'rate of capital appreciation shortfall', since an efficient market will always price any asset so that it generates its required total rate of return μ.

The theoretical explanation for when an asset appears to show a 'rate of return shortfall' is that the owner of the asset must be enjoying a 'quasi dividend', at a rate of δ on the asset's current value. For some commodity assets this return might take the form of a 'convenience yield' – for example, there can be an advantage, such as the 'precautionary motive', to being the owner of a quantity of oil or cash, and this advantage is a benefit in return for which the owner would be willing to forego an income (or capital appreciation) rate of δ on the money value invested in the commodity.

An example of this appears in Chapter 10. The rate of return required to compensate a house owner for the risk of owning a house is μ, but the observed rate of price appreciation on the house is a smaller number than this, which we can express as $(\mu - \delta)$ for some δ. The difference δ is the flow of benefits that the owner gets from the mere fact of owning the house. This flow of benefits might seem to be intangible – even sentimental – but in fact it can often be given a money value. For a house owner we can think of the benefit flow δ as the outflow of rent payments which the owner can avoid by choosing to live in the house personally. Alternatively, if the owner chooses to let the house out to a tenant, δ can represent the inflow of cash rent that could be earned from letting the house.

Further reading can be found in standard financial texts such as Hull (2000).

Technical appendix: option mathematics in continuous time

This appendix is intended for a reader who has already met differential equations, perhaps in physics or engineering, but we assume you are not yet familiar with stochastic calculus, or with the economic and financial uses of differential equations.

The key numerical texts in option theory occasionally give only light sketches of why the models are built the way they are, and the manipulations in the standard texts sometimes contain large enough algebraic and statistical leaps to confuse a beginner who is not yet at ease with the conceptual base.

This appendix aims to help you past these initial difficulties. It assumes you have read Chapters 1 to 3. The explanation and notation that follow are largely based on Wilmott, Howison and Dewynne (1995) and could serve as an introduction to that excellent text.

A preliminary: how can we use a differential equation to value an asset in continuous time?

Humans are not indifferent to the passage of time, so we value distant payoffs lower than near or current payoffs. The basic idea of discounting is probably already familiar (if not see Appendix 1) but we now want to use it in a continuous time framework. The required rate of growth of any (risk-free) payment that is delayed into the future (in order to make all its subjective values at any future time equal to each other) is the continuously compounded growth rate r.

This gives a differential equation for the required rate of change in the delayed payment's value V over time:

$$dV/dt = rV \tag{1}$$

Notice that (1) holds for any risk-free payment or asset. It merely states that the asset's value V will grow exponentially over any short increment of time. But it does not say from what value to what value, i.e. (1) does not specify what the asset is worth at any time t, which is its value V(t).

To put this in mathematical language, the solution to the differential equation (1) above is indeterminate unless we also impose a boundary condition, e.g. if we are discounting some payment P_T at future time T back to the present, that future payment is the terminal boundary condition $V(T) = P_T$; conversely, if we are compounding a present sum K_0 forward in time, the initial boundary condition is $V(0) = K_0$.

Of course this differential equation has a simple analytic solution. In the case of discounting a payment P_T back from time T to give the equivalent present value at an earlier time t, the general solution at time t is $V(t) = P_T\, e^{-r(T-t)}$. In economic terms P_T is a model of the final payment at time T, while in mathematical terms, $V(T) = P_T$ is the terminal boundary condition at time t = T.

Conversely, if we are compounding the value of a payment K_0 received at time t = 0 forward into the future to some general time t, the general solution to the differential equation is $V(t) = K_0\, e^{rt}$. In economic terms K_0 is the initial payment at time t = 0, and in mathematical terms it is the initial boundary condition V(0) at time t = 0.

How will we be using this?

Both of the terms of (1) will be part of our final valuation differential equation, unchanged.

We will at times be using both the forward 'compounding' and the backward or 'discounting' implementation of (1). There will be a final payment P at time T, which we need to value at the earlier time t, but a new idea which we will need is that the future payment P will be a stochastic variable rather than a known fixed sum. In fact, P will be a function of a random walk variable S. For concreteness we can use the example of a call option, for which the underlying asset is the stock price S, but the random walk variable S can be far more general than this (e.g. exchange rate, demand rate).

We will need to generalize (1) in the following ways. Since a new variable S enters the model, and since changes in S will affect the value V of our option (or other **derivative** asset), the value of our option V must now be V(S,t), which is a function of both S and t. In turn this means that we will need to set up a **partial differential equation** for the value of the option, reflecting how the value V(S,t) will change in response to changes in both S and t. Of course S is undergoing a continuous random walk. This walk is a **diffusion process**, so we need a formal model of the process for the future diffusion of S, away from its known present value.

As in (1) the final payment P which we will receive at time T is the terminal boundary condition. This future payment is no longer a fixed and known constant but is a function of the value that will be taken at future time T by the underlying asset S (so we will receive at time T the sum P(S,T)). Hence the **payoff function** P(S,T) is the **terminal boundary condition** for our valuation differential equation.

The mathematics that follows aims first to relate changes in the value V(S,t) to changes in the values of S and t (for this purpose we use **Taylor's theorem** and **Ito's lemma**). We also need to eliminate the uncertainty of S from the valuation equation. In this way the resulting payments will be risk free, so that we can use the **risk-free interest rate** r, as in (1) (for this purpose we need **delta hedging**).

We will then have a valuation partial differential equation. On its own, without boundary conditions, the valuation differential equation permits an infinity of possible values V(S,t) for any combination of S and t. By applying sufficient fixed or free boundary conditions we (mathematically) restrict the possible solutions to one unique solution, and also (economically) we make the equation represent the economics of one specific entity (e.g. a European call on a dividend-paying asset). Hence the unique solution V(S,t) is the unique value of that entity for every S,t combination.

This process defines a partial differential equation (PDE), which is known to have a unique solution (i.e. the option will have a unique value V(S,t) for every combination of S and t, because the equation plus boundary conditions is known to have a unique solution) but formulating the problem, as a PDE plus boundary conditions, does not of itself give the required solution.

This appendix will not discuss how we actually find solutions. Some well-known analytic solutions exist for simple versions of the Black–Scholes PDE and boundary conditions, including the epoch-making Black–Scholes formula for valuing the European call (quoted in Chapter 6, Appendix 1). However, the most demanding problems (as in engineering and physics) need numerical solution methods, which are introduced in the financial context in Appendix 4.[1]

> **Some well-known analytic solutions exist for simple versions of the Black–Scholes PDE and boundary conditions**

Our first step in problem formulation is to set up a mathematical model of the random walk of the underlying asset's price S, which will drive the value V of our derivative.

The underlying asset's random walk as a Wiener process

A random walk for asset prices is expected under perfect competition. A continuous time random walk of underlying stock price S can be modelled as a **Wiener process**.

The Wiener process is a combination of a continuous deterministic trend in time (**drift**), and a continuous, unforecastable random element.

The deterministic component (exponential trend in time)

$$dS/dt = mS \tag{2}$$

implies by transposing:

$$dS/S = mdt \tag{3}$$

or equivalently, also by transposing:

$$dS = mSdt \tag{4}$$

which describes continuous exponential growth or decline in S.

The random component of a Wiener process

Define dX as a random variable drawn from a normal distribution, where the mean of dX is zero and the variance of dX is dt (and hence the standard deviation of dX is $\sqrt{dt}$). Hence the bigger the interval of time dt before we sample dX, the larger the cumulative jump X will on average have made. The standard deviation for the cumulative jump in X grows wider as dt lengthens, but at a decreasing rate. (This is simulated by Figure A5.1, and the complete probability distribution for future X is shown in Figure A4.4. Confidence intervals are not marked on figure A5.1, but it is easy to visualize them as horizontal parabolas: uncertainty leaps outwards in the first few instants after the current 'now' price, but widens more slowly thereafter.)

X must make some jump over any infinitesimal time dt, and each of these jumps (being normally distributed) is unbounded. Hence the length of the path that X will travel over any finite time increment is infinitely long, and dX/dt has no finite value at any instant.

Why must we make the variance of dX linear in time? The reason is that we want X to follow a random walk in order to model prices in a perfectly competitive market. The property we need is the Markov property, which is that in order to forecast a future price, no price earlier than the current price will ever be needed.

This means that the variation of price over any interval of time must be independent of its variation over any other, earlier or later (non-overlapping) interval of time. But if any two random variables are independent, the variance of their sum is the sum of their variances. So if the random variations over any two periods of time of, for example, two minutes are independent, the variance of their total period of four minutes is the sum of the variances of each of the two-minute periods. If we recall that this includes the case where the two periods of two minutes follow each other consecutively, and if we generalize the argument to time periods of any standard finite length, variance must be linear in time.

Equivalently, the random variable dX, which is the size of the jump that X makes over the time increment dt, is $z \sqrt{dt}$, where z is a drawing from the standard random normal deviate. This as in statistical tables has a mean of zero and variance 1, so $E(z^2) = 1$ where $E()$ is the expectation operator for a random variable.

In general, in order to give dS a variance $E(dS^2)$ per unit of time other than 1, we scale its variance by multiplying dX by σ where σ^2 is the required variance per unit of time (required expectation of dS^2).

Hence the random part of the increment to the Wiener process over the time increment dt is σdX (or equivalently $\sigma z \sqrt{dt}$ where z is the standard normal deviate).

How does the normal random increment dX change the stochastic asset price S? We normally assume a multiplicative or geometric growth model, often called geometric Brownian motion. This defines the random component of change to S itself over the time interval dt as $dS = S\sigma dX = S\sigma z \sqrt{dt}$.

The effect of multiplying S by the random normal increment dX is equivalent to adding a random increment to the log of S, so that if the asset price S starts at zero, it will remain zero for ever, but if S starts above zero, it can never become negative (this reflects the limited liability feature of stocks and shares – they can never be worth less than nothing). It also means that large upward movements in S are more likely than large downward movements, and therefore the stock price S has a skewed distribution resembling a log normal. This is also empirically realistic.

Notice that the expectation of this random change for S over the time interval dt is $E(S\sigma dX) = S\sigma E(dX) = S\sigma E(z \sqrt{dt}) = S\sigma 0\sqrt{dt} = 0$. The variance of this random change is $E(S\sigma dX - E(S\sigma dX))^2 = E(S\sigma dX - 0)^2 = E(S\sigma dX)^2$ (because $E((S\sigma dX) = 0)$. But by previous assumption the variance of dX over the time interval dt is dt, therefore the variance of the random change of S over the interval dt is (in the absence of a fixed trend):

$$E(dS)^2 = E(S\sigma dX)^2 = S^2\sigma^2 E(dX)^2 = S^2\sigma^2 E(z\sqrt{dt})^2 = S^2\sigma^2 dt \qquad (5)$$

We can now add the deterministic component mentioned above to the random component, so that the complete Wiener process for a stock price with both a deterministic trend and a multiplicative or geometric random walk (also called geometric Brownian motion) is:

$$dS = mSdt + \sigma SdX \tag{6}$$

Notice that because the next increment dX is random and unforecastable, our best forecast of dX is its expectation of zero. This is why the best forecast for a pure random walk (without trend) is simply its most recent value, with zero predicted for all random changes in the future.

We next need to make a link between the above model of the price S of our underlying asset, and the value V of our derivative asset. We need to find a (stochastic) differential for the option price V as a function of the above (stochastic) differential of the stock price S in (6).

To do this we need the basic tool of stochastic calculus: Ito's lemma.

An essential tool for modelling functions of stochastic variables: Ito's lemma

This lemma is based on Taylor's theorem for expanding a function around a chosen point (which we'll call the evaluation point). For a general function f of the random variable S, Taylor's theorem gives the following series, describing the variations of f around the evaluation point, as a function of S:

$$df = (df/dS)dS + 0.5 \, (d^2/dS^2) \, dS^2 + \text{terms in } dS^3 \text{ and higher......} \tag{7}$$

In normal calculus (and in most numerical applications) we ignore terms in dS^2 and higher because their limit as dS falls is vanishingly small compared to that of dS. However, recall the definition of dS, and then see the effect of squaring it to dS^2 (which we need to do within the second term of the RHS of (7)):

$$dS = mSdt + \sigma SdX \tag{8} = (6) \text{ repeated}$$

The expected value of squaring both sides of this expression is:

$$E(dS^2) = E(mSdt + \sigma SdX)^2 \tag{9}$$

Multiplying out the brackets on the RHS:

$$= E(S^2\sigma^2 dX^2 + 2\sigma SmSdtdX + m^2 S^2 dt^2) \tag{10}$$

We can ignore the terms after the first, since they are of order higher than dt.

$$= S^2\sigma^2 \, E(dX^2) + ...\text{terms of higher order than dt} \tag{11}$$

But by the definition of the variance of dX the expectation of the random element $E(dX^2) = dt$, therefore as in (5):

$E(dS^2) = S^2\sigma^2 \, dt + ...$terms of higher order $\qquad\qquad$ (12)

It can also be proved that as dt tends to zero, the expectation operator disappears, so that with certainty:

$dS^2 = S^2\sigma^2 \, dt$ $\qquad\qquad\qquad\qquad\qquad\qquad\qquad\qquad\qquad$ (13)

This is the substitution we use in the Taylor's theorem expansion of df (repeated from (7) above):

$df = (df/dS)dS + 0.5 \, (d^2f/dS^2) \, dS^2 + ...$ $\qquad\qquad\qquad$ (14)

Making the substitution $S^2\sigma^2 \, dt$ for dS^2, which is (13) into (14):

$df = (df/dS)dS + 0.5 \, (d^2f/dS^2) \, S^2\sigma^2 \, dt + ...$ $\qquad\qquad$ (15)

Hence f is a process which evolves in two dimensions, since the change in f (namely df) responds to changes dt in time, and to changes dS in S (here S can be the stock price, or more generally, any other random factor which drives an asset value f in some way). This equation for f is equivalent to a diffusion process, e.g. the diffusion of heat or of chemical particles along a pipe.

The reason for this is that in a diffusion process, individual particles are assumed to follow random walks from wherever they start. Distributions of energetic particles spread out, particles of fluid spread out, and likewise distributions of stock price 'spread out' from the fixed starting point of today's price, so that we become less and less certain of stock prices further into the future (see Appendix 5).

The second term on the RHS of (15) emerges naturally from the algebra, but it also has intuitive interpretations. One is that if (d^2f/dS^2) is non zero, f is a curved function of S, which is true of all non-trivial differential equation solutions.

For example, if (d^2f/dS^2) is positive, f is rising for variations in S on both sides of the evaluation point (relative to a straight line tangent to f at the evaluation point which is of course the first term in (15)). S is certain to make positive and negative random variations dS around its value at the evaluation point over any time increment dt (strictly speaking the variations of the log of S are unbounded, and extend from minus infinity to plus infinity). When these variations are applied to d^2f/dS^2 and averaged (integrated) out over the whole probability distribution, they jointly contribute a net positive term to the expected value of df at the end of time dt, since the most minute change in dS will raise f relative to the tangent line at S, which is the first term in (15).

A simpler form of the same intuition is that the expectation of dS^2 for a stochastic S is simply the variance of dS, so this expectation is positive (proportional to dt) for any small but finite interval dt.

We should notice some important generalizations of this model.

We should notice some important generalizations of this model. We have seen that for the single random variable S, the second order term $\sigma^2 dX^2$ is retained in the Taylor's expansion, because Ito's lemma shows that this is equivalent to the first order term $S^2\sigma^2$ dt. This generalizes to higher dimensions (larger numbers of independent S variables). For example, if the option f (or the instrument f or portfolio of instruments f) is a function of more than one random walk (S_1, S_2, S_3........), Ito's lemma means that all the second order random terms between all the random variables must be retained in a Taylor's expansion of the total differential df, i.e. the expectations of S_1^2, S_2^2, $S_1 S_2$, and $S_1 S_3$, and so forth are all replaced by terms in dt and these terms are scaled by the covariances of these original variables (on this interpretation the variance of a variable is its covariance with itself) so that when scaled these terms become $\sigma_1^2 dt$, $\sigma_2^2 dt$, $\rho_{12}\sigma_1\sigma_2$, S_1, S_2, $\rho_{13}\sigma_1\sigma_3 S_1 S_3$, $\rho_{22}\sigma_2\sigma_3 S_2 S_3$.....etc. where p_{ij} is the correlation of S_i and S_j, and $\rho_{12}\sigma_1\sigma_2$ is the covariance of S_i and S_j. The covariance terms have the constant coefficient 2 arising from the binomial expansion of $(dS)^2$. We retain terms of the form $\rho_{ij}\sigma_i\sigma_j dt$ for all i and j.

Various economic models require more than a single random value driver S (multiple 'random factors') so we add variables S_2 onwards. For example, exotic financial options such as 'rainbows' depend on more than one asset value. Likewise the value of a mortgage loan depends on two random factors, house price and interest rate, which are (probably) negatively correlated – see Chapter 10 and Appendix 5. Some real option values are driven by random factors which are not in themselves asset prices (e.g. inflation rates, interest rates, wage rates).

By means of Ito's lemma we have now modelled the change df of a general function f over the time increment dt, where f is a function of the Wiener process (random walk) variable S, and so df is a function of the random change dS in S. We must next specialize the form of function f in order to make it represent the value of a financial asset (i.e. it must be affected by the passage of time). We will then substitute the detail of the Wiener process for dS into the equation that results.

Modifying df to include finance-relevant features

The essential term we need to add to df is in order to reflect the effects of time. For example, when the market gives a return on owning any financial instrument, this often comes at least in part from changes in its value over time (e.g. the present value of the right to receive a payment of $1,000 in two years' time will grow as the payment date approaches; likewise value growth is a major component of share returns). There are alternative types of return, such as interest, rent or dividend, which we can model – see Chapter 4.

We have already modelled the effect of time in equation (1) where we used the risk-free rate of return to value a fixed future payment, but at this stage, before we have eliminated uncertainty, we cannot use the risk-free rate of return r, since our equation is for a stochastic (risky) payoff which is a function of S (see Appendix 2).

We redefine the function of interest as V (modified from f) and we add a term which modifies V only through the passage of time, irrespective of the level of S or of its next change dS. Because V now has two potentially independent influences on its value (namely S and t), we use the partial differential notation $(\partial V/\partial t)$ and $(\partial V/\partial S)$ for these independent effects (recall that the second term in (15) did affect f through the passage of time dt, but the size of this effect depended on the current price S and on the next dS – we also need an effect of time on the current value V that is independent of S). The time-dependent term V incorporates this effect. The component of value change in V from this cause over the time increment dt is $(\partial V/\partial t)dt$.

The extra term changes (15) to

$$dV = (\partial V/\partial S)dS + 0.5\ (\partial^2 V/\partial S^2)\ S^2\sigma^2\ dt + dt(\partial V/\partial t)...... \qquad (16)$$

In this equation V can represent many functions whose value is driven by the random walk of S, including various kinds of options or assets, and even S itself. However, it is not very useful to know dV, since this merely models how V may change randomly over the next time increment dt, due to the next unforecastable dS. We want to know what V itself is now, given the current S. As a first step towards this we must get to a form of (16) that omits the effect of the random term dS. Since this first term on the RHS is $(\partial V/\partial S)dS$, we must somehow take an economic action that will allow us to include a term $-(\partial V/\partial S)\ dS$

Such a negative term will reverse the effect on our wealth of the stochastic change dS in S. If, for illustration only, we consider the example where V is the value of a call option, then $\partial V/\partial S$ is always positive, so we need an economic transaction that will always make us lose value as S increases.

The way to do this is to commit ourselves to selling S at a fixed price at the end of time increment dt (e.g. by making a forward sale, or a short sale, of the underlying asset at a price based on today's price S). The number of units of S we need to sell forward is simply $\partial V/\partial S$. If we make such a sale over a very short time interval dt, then during this interval both S and the slope $\partial V/\partial S$ will change by very little. If we give the name Π to the portfolio containing the option V as in (16) plus the effect of a short sale of $\partial V/\partial S$ units of S, the total value change of this portfolio over the time increment dt is:

$$d\Pi = (\partial V/\partial S)dS - (\partial V/\partial S)dS + 0.5\ (\partial^2 V/\partial S^2)\ S^2\sigma^2\ dt + dt\partial V/\partial t......\qquad (17)$$

The first two terms cancel out as intended, so we are left with a return which lacks the random term dS, and in which the remaining RHS terms are all in the differential of time dt:

$$d\Pi = 0.5\ (\partial^2 V/\partial S^2)\ S^2\sigma^2\ dt + dt\partial V/\partial t......\qquad (18)$$

Hence the value change of this portfolio depends only on time. This makes its return deterministic, or risk free, over the time interval dt. But in a competitive market all assets whose returns are risk free must earn the same rate of return r. So if portfolio Π is indeed risk free, its value is governed by equation (1) which tells us that its return over the time increment dt must be its value Π at the start of the increment, times the rate of return r, times the length of the time increment. This return is rΠdt. Hence we can equate rΠdt to the actual return dΠ given by (18) so that:

$$d\Pi =\ r\Pi dt = 0.5\ (\partial^2 V/\partial S^2)\ S^2\sigma^2\ dt + dt\partial V/\partial t \qquad (19)$$

Making the conventional substitution $\Pi = V - (\partial V/\partial S)\ S$ to remove rΠdt from the LHS we get:

$$rVdt - r(\partial V/\partial S)\ Sdt = 0.5\ (\partial^2 V/\partial S^2)\ S^2\sigma^2\ dt + dt\partial V/\partial t \qquad (20)$$

Dividing throughout by dt and rearranging terms we get:

$$rV = r(\partial V/\partial S)S + \partial V/\partial t + 0.5\ S^2\sigma^2\ (\partial^2 V/\partial S^2) \qquad (21)$$

This is the classic **Black–Scholes (valuation) partial differential equation**. It shows that if an asset's value V is some function of the random walk variable S, the rate of change in its value V with respect to S and t at any instant is not random but is a function (only) of variables that are observable and/or determined at the current moment. These include t, the current price S of the underlying asset, and certain fixed parameters, such as the volatility of the asset price σ and the risk-free rate of return r.

It may be easier to understand the effect of delta hedging in visual terms. In Figure A3.1 a call option at some time t has the value $V(S_t)$ where S_t in this example is 100. Over the next time increment dt the value of S will rise or fall by a random amount. This will move the option's value along the curve XVA. If dt is small enough, the expected change in S is small, and we can approximate[2] the effect on V as a move to right or left along the tangent to the option's value curve at the current value V_t (the tangent is the line YVB). This tangent has the

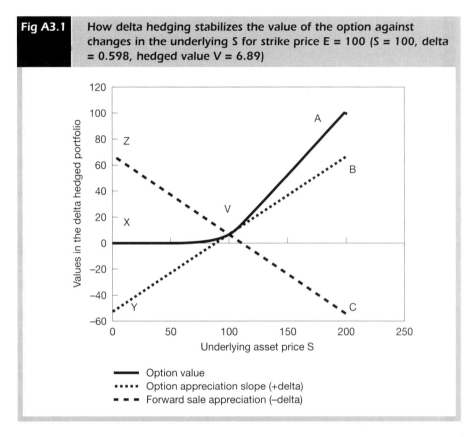

Fig A3.1 How delta hedging stabilizes the value of the option against changes in the underlying S for strike price E = 100 (S = 100, delta = 0.598, hedged value V = 6.89)

Option value
Option appreciation slope (+delta)
Forward sale appreciation (–delta)

slope $\partial V/\partial S$ (called delta = Δ for short). To offset the resulting unknown rise or fall of V along the tangent, we make an uncovered short or forward sale of Δ units of S, and we will buy at the market price after the time increment dt to deliver against this sale.

If we have sold forward one unit of S at price S_τ, then over the time increment dt an increase of $1 in the price of S will give us a loss of $1 on our sale. This means wealth change along a downward slope –1 in S (–45 degrees in S). But if we sell Δ units of S in place of one unit, the value loss will lie along the line ZVC whose slope is $-\Delta$. Hence over the next small time increment dt the rise (fall) of the option's value along XVA is exactly offset by the fall (rise) of the forward sale's value along YVC. Hence the resulting change in the portfolio as S changes is along a horizontal line through V which means the portfolio's value is unaffected by (small) changes in S. The only value change we need allow for over dt is the effect of the passage of time itself, for a risk-free payment we will receive after dt. To value this payment at the start of the interval dt we discount it over the interval dt at the risk-free rate as in (1).

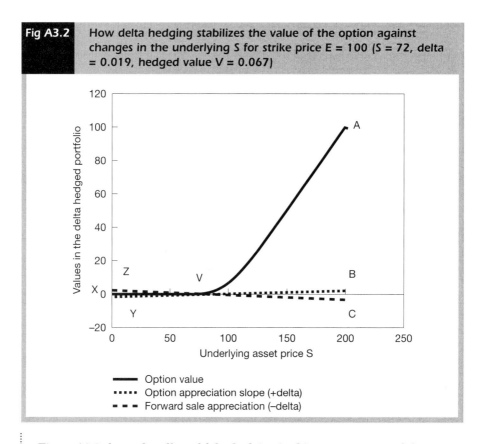

Fig A3.2 How delta hedging stabilizes the value of the option against changes in the underlying S for strike price E = 100 (S = 72, delta = 0.019, hedged value V = 0.067)

———— Option value
••••• Option appreciation slope (+delta)
– – – Forward sale appreciation (–delta)

Figure A3.2 shows the effect of delta hedging in this way on an out-of-the-money option. The option's value is small, and is insensitive to S, so only a small hedging deal is needed to offset the small remaining risk. In the limit of S and V both approach zero, V resembles a risk-free asset, whose delta is zero (unaffected by changes in S) and which therefore needs no hedging deal against changes in S.

Conversely, Figure A3.3 shows delta hedging of a deep-in-the-money call option. Here the option's value rises and falls unpredictably along almost the same slope as S itself (in other words Δ, the slope of the tangent to V, tends towards 1). In this case hedging requires an uncovered sale of one unit of S. Therefore hedging the value of a deep-in-the-money option's value V over the interval dt requires the same action as hedging the present value of S itself over dt (to hedge one unit of S itself we always need to make an uncovered forward sale of one unit of S_t guaranteeing a final payoff of $S_t e^{rdt}$).

These three examples show how delta hedging potentially applies to all possible functions of S (as does the Black–Scholes equation) and the hedging of the option, the hedging of S itself and the (non) hedging of the risk-free asset are all special cases of this.

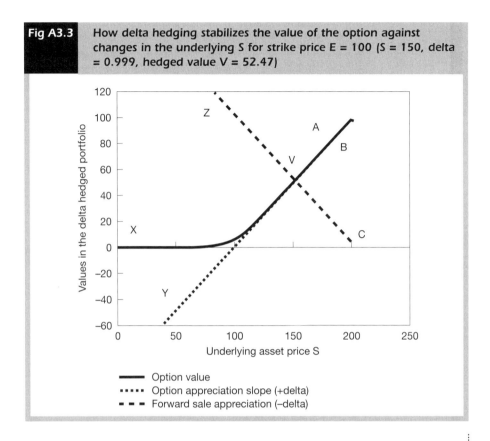

Fig A3.3 How delta hedging stabilizes the value of the option against changes in the underlying S for strike price E = 100 (S = 150, delta = 0.999, hedged value V = 52.47)

The third example also illustrates an argument we made in Chapter 4, namely that when we delta hedge any instrument, the final value of the hedged portfolio after the interval dt is the initial value of the hedged instrument, plus risk-free growth on it. This in turn means that the initial value of the hedged portfolio is simply the value at that instant of the instrument that is being hedged (this value itself is actually derived by discounting the guaranteed payoff at the end of dt using the risk-free rate). This is easier to grasp intuitively in the case of hedging S itself. If we own one unit of S, and if we make an uncovered forward sale of one unit of S, our cash proceeds from the forward sale are $S_t e^{rdt}$, and the price appreciation (or depreciation) of S is exactly offset by the loss (profit) on our uncovered sale. In the special case where S remains unchanged in price, it is obvious that we can make no profit or loss on our forward sale on S itself. Hence the delta hedged

> **The initial value of the hedged portfolio is simply the value at that instant of the instrument that is being hedged.**

portfolio's final value is $S_t e^{rdt}$, but the same final portfolio value is generated for all other nearby values of S.

Returning to the algebra, note that the two terms of the fundamental value differential equation (1) both appear in (21), but the total risk-free return rV is now partitioned on the RHS between straight capital growth $\partial V/\partial t$ and two other terms (both are always positive for a call option). The latter reflect the fact that the absolute value of S will affect the current rate of change in both S and V.

The change in V is a function of various first and second order derivative terms, which are not as yet directly observable (since we do not as yet have an explicit solution for the function V, and such a solution may not exist at all under many boundary conditions). However, we can exploit the first and second order derivative terms in the linearized form of (21) in order to derive analytic or numerical solutions for V.

Notice that there is no term in the Black–Scholes equation which states the exercise price E of a call option, or its expiry date T. Nor does the equation specify whether any specific option (call or put or any other financial instrument) is being modelled.

This is because the Black–Scholes equation applies to every economic function of the random walk variable S. We can particularize this equation to model some specific asset by defining suitable boundary conditions. For any conventional option, for example, the payoff function is the terminal boundary condition, and each different option's economic structure implies its own economically meaningful boundary conditions (for example, when S tends to infinity, at the upper boundary, the value of a European call, which is the right to buy the asset for a fixed price E, tends towards S, but the value of a put, which is the right to sell the asset for a fixed price E, tends to zero).

Basic analytics of the Black–Scholes equation

Intuitively, the Black–Scholes equation controls only the local variations of the valuation surface V, due to small variations in stock price and time.

If we imagine the valuation surface V(S,t) as a piece of fabric (as an intuitive analogy only), the Black–Scholes equation gives only the laws by which that fabric can or cannot flex or stretch. Since the surface is twice differentiable in S, the fabric cannot have discontinuities or tears. In economic terms this feature prevents arbitrage, since similar conditions of S and t do not lead to dissimilar values. However, the Black–Scholes equation leaves the 'fabric' of the value surface free to assume any of an infinity of flexings.

In order to make the valuation surface have a unique shape, therefore, we must 'pin the fabric down' along certain boundaries, by imposing sufficient boundary conditions. Too few boundary conditions will leave the surface unde-fined in position (fabric free to flap) and hence give no unique value V for given S and t. Too many boundary conditions will at best include redundant condi-tions, and at worst some contradictory ones, so which jointly permit no solution at all. In mathematical terms we will have a 'well posed problem' if we impose just enough boundary conditions to ensure a unique solution. See Figure 2.8 for the example of a European option on a non-dividend-paying stock.

Note that for an American option on a dividend-paying stock a free bound-ary exists. For this we can imagine that a part of the curved valuation surface V(S,t) hangs freely onto a flat surface, which is defined by the intrinsic value of the option when exercised, namely the payoff P(S,t) = max(0,S − E) This flat payoff surface is constant for all t up to and including the expiry time T.

The line along which the V surface (value of the unexercised option) meets and rests freely on the payoff surface P (value of the immediately exercised option) is a free boundary, and its projection into the (S,t) plane is the set of val-ues (S*,t) above which it is optimal to exercise the option at any time t. The conditions along this free boundary (value matching and smooth pasting between the option value surface V(S,t) and the payoff surface P(S,t)) are what they would be for a membrane, suitably tensed so that it is free to hang, partly resting on a flat surface (a form of the linear complementarity problem).

In more general valuation problems, it can be difficult or unsafe to use the intuitive analogy between the valuation surface V and any familiar type of physical surface, but the value-matching and smooth pasting conditions con-tinue to apply to free boundaries in all generalizations of the valuation surface, and indeed at all other points on valuation surfaces or hyper-surfaces.

An alternative analogy in terms of heat flow is explored in Appendix 4.

Limitations of the Black–Scholes equation, and transcending them

The standard model (21) models the economic return to (say) an option on the assumption that value change arises only from capital growth (price change) in both the option and the underlying asset. Various generaliza-tions of this basic model are discussed in Chapter 4. Here we will note only that the underlying asset could be paying a dividend. The dividend is an opportunity cost for the holder of a call option on the asset, since it 'drains away' economic return to the stock holder that would otherwise be accessi-ble to the option holder in the form of capital gain.

Dividend-paying assets

The simplest model assumes that dividend will be paid on the stock as a variable, but uninterrupted, flow per unit of time, at a constant fraction δ of the stock's current price S. So the dividend on one unit of stock during the time increment dt is δSdt. This assumption is compatible with the standard valuation model for stocks, which assumes that price S is the net present value of future dividends (which are assumed to be determined by some random walk).

Recall that for a call option the risk-free (delta hedged) portfolio Π has sold short Δ units of stock, where Δ is simply shorthand for $\partial V/\partial S$. Hence in the time interval dt the portfolio must pay out a dividend of $\delta S\Delta dt$ to the purchaser of the stock, assuming the latter has paid for the stock but has not yet received it. The total differential $d\Pi$ of the portfolio's value Π thus becomes:

$$d\Pi = dV - \Delta dS - \delta\, S\Delta dt \qquad (22)$$

To find the RHS of this equation, substitute as before for dV, dS and Δ, where $\Delta = \partial V/\partial S$. Then equate the RHS, which is the value change of the portfolio Π, to the risk-free return $r\Pi dt$. Rearrangement and division by dt, as before, gives the following revised differential equation for V:

$$rV = (r - \delta)(\partial V/\partial S)S + \partial V/\partial t + 0.5\ S^2\sigma^2\ (\partial^2 V/\partial S^2) \qquad (23)$$

The only visible change from (20) is to the first term on the right-hand side.

This also imposes a further arithmetic change on the RHS, since for a given V the LHS is fixed. The intuition for this is that a risk-free economic return per unit of time must be earned on the hedged option's value V at the rate r, as specified on the LHS. However, the fact that the call option holder foregoes the dividend on the stock (which we can also interpret as an opportunity cost of holding the non-dividend paying option instead of holding the dividend-paying stock) is a negative contribution to the RHS, since it reduces the first term.

Therefore to maintain the same overall value on the RHS (without which no one would hold the option) the term $\partial V/\partial t$, which gives the value appreciation of the option over time, must be larger.

But since all call options have identical value functions $\Pi(S,T)$ at the moment of expiry T (when there is no more dividend payable) a faster rate of appreciation for the option on the dividend-paying stock can be achieved only if its starting value at any earlier time (for similar S) is lower.

Hence for a (European) call on a dividend-paying stock, the larger the rate of dividend, and the longer the option still has to run, the lower the option's value V. As seen in Chapter 2, if the stock S reaches a sufficiently high price, sufficiently long before the option's expiry date, the option's value V may fall below its intrinsic value, which is the current payoff P from exercising the option immediately, max $(0, S - E)$, supposing exercise were allowed.

We also need to use changed fixed boundary conditions in order to model a (European) call on a dividend-paying stock. For a European call on a non-dividend paying stock, as already discussed, if the stock price tends to infinity, the value of the option tends towards the stock price itself.

However, for the dividend-paying stock we must allow for the loss of dividend due to holding the option instead of holding the stock. Hence as S tends to infinity, the loss of potential dividend also tends to infinity, except at the expiry date T when no future dividend remains to be lost. Therefore the upper fixed boundary condition for the value V, as S tends to infinity, must vary with the remaining time to expiry (T − t), and it is:

$$V(S,t) \sim Se^{-\delta(T-t)}$$

Clearly this boundary condition for S at infinity converges at the moment of expiry T to the same terminal boundary condition as for a non-dividend paying stock, namely P = max (0,S − E) which converges to S as S tends to infinity.

This completes a simplified model of the problem of valuing a European option on a stock whose dividends are paid continuously in time. The analytical solution to this model is given in every standard finance text. Further refinements to the standard Black–Scholes equation are mentioned in Chapter 4.

It would be more realistic in the financial world to assume that dividends are paid at discrete moments in time, which is discussed in Chapters 7 and 10, but there are many real option situations for which the assumption of continuous dividend at the rate δ is a reasonable model of the continuous, and continuously varying, flow of profit opportunity over time.

We recommend further fundamental reading, starting with Wilmott, Howison and Dewynne (1995), and Dixit and Pindyck (1994). The former is an excellent introduction to financial mathematics, but it does not mention real options explicitly. The latter is about real options, and it covers many important applications, but it assumes greater familiarity with both the economics and the mathematics, and it tends to give more space to analytically tractable problems than to the numerical analysis which industrial applications sometimes need. With these introductions as a basis, you will be able to tackle many other texts and journal articles.

Notes

1. We are keen in this book to introduce readers to the most general forms of problem formulation and solution. In this context certain analytic solutions are themselves incomplete as models of option behaviour (e.g. the analytic solution for a perpetual call is valid only within boundaries, and does not represent the value of the option outside those boundaries, although the latter still exists). Analytic solutions do of course allow qualitative theoretical analysis, but they are too few to make them the main basis for attacking or even expounding the more demanding problems.

2. Notice that if S makes a large movement either way, it is very clear that the resulting option value as predicted by the tangent YVB is below the option's actual curve XVA. This effect is the basis of Ito's lemma (a straight line is always an underestimate of the option's final value, and the underestimate depends on the size of the movement of S in either direction). Intuitively, we need Ito's lemma when we are working out the whole length of the value curve XVA, since the curve is never straight in principle, however small the change in S. But when we are approximating the value curve over very short increments of time and very short increments of S, as we do in delta hedging, it is safe to treat an isolated very short section of the value curve XVA as approximately straight.

APPENDIX **4**

Numerical solution of option valuation problems

by David Newton

S ometimes, the Black–Scholes partial differential equation can be solved with a particular set of boundary conditions to give an 'analytical solution'. This is a formula into which values can be directly substituted to give an option value. Analytical solutions are used in Chapters 5, 6 and 8. 'Numerical solutions' use approximations to the partial differential equation or to a model of the price movements of the asset from which the option is derived. They are 'numerical' in the sense that very many repetitive calculations are needed to obtain an accurate approximation to the option value. At the heart of all methods of solution, analytical and numerical, is the random walk, which is described in detail in Appendix 5.

It is often the case that no analytical formulae are available to solve a particular option valuation problem. Frequently, the problem is simplified to fit a known solution formula rather than finding the solution to the actual problem. There is much to be said for this in terms of both convenience and insight. However, there is no escaping the need for numerical solutions. This can be seen in most situations involving American options (which allow early exercise) and often when the payoff function is complex (as in the two factories problem in Chapter 3) or when there is more than one factor with a random element (such as the two-factor problem in Chapter 10). In Chapter 3, even the superficially straightforward retail mortgage product, a fixed-rate loan with monthly repayments over 20 years, is revealed as a two-factor problem with interacting options (240 European options to default at monthly intervals and an American option to prepay throughout the whole period of the loan).

There are three basic numerical methods for option valuation – Monte Carlo, tree (or lattice) and finite difference – all rooted in the random walk. Of these, the tree and finite difference methods are applicable to common real options valuation problems. It is helpful to understand the link between the numerical pricing methods and the random walk, especially for the 'binomial tree' method, where the link is particularly obvious. We discuss this in Appendix 5.

Tree methods model the possible future prices of an asset upon which there is an option. Starting from a single price today, it is usually assumed that the asset's price can change in a series of equal time steps. At each step, the price can move only to a pre-set number of new prices; commonly this is two (a 'binomial tree') or three (a 'trinomial tree'). We will consider only binomial trees. A tree gives an option value for the single starting price of the underlying asset.

In finite difference methods, the asset's continuous time random walk is set up mathematically using stochastic calculus (see Appendix 3) and the resulting partial differential equation is solved by numerical approximation of its terms to obtain the option value. Finite difference methods calculate option prices for many starting prices of the underlying asset simultaneously. We will illustrate using the most straightforward technique, the 'explicit' finite difference method.

The accuracy of tree and finite difference methods is increased by expanding their sizes but methods are available to considerably improve accuracy without having to use enormous trees (Widdicks, Andricopoulos, Newton and Duck, 2000).

Option valuation using binomial trees

An overview

There is a very clear and direct link between binomial tree modelling and the 'random walk in one dimension' (see Appendix 5). A binomial tree models possible future asset prices in a series of time steps such that, starting from the current price, the next price can only be one of two possibilities. In order to keep the number of possible final outcomes within sensible bounds, the proportional price changes are arranged such that the tree 'recombines' and an upwards price movement followed by a downwards movement results in the same price as downwards followed by upwards. You can see the structure of a binomial tree in Figure A4.1.

Each position on a tree is known as a 'node'. The value of an option at expiry can be calculated for each final node on a binomial tree. For example, a call option with exercise price £10 is worth £5 at a node where the asset price on expiry is £15, whereas a put option with the same exercise price is worthless at that final price. The technique we are about to describe allows us to calculate option values at each node, working backwards in time through the tree, until the initial node is reached and the option price today is found.

Option values at nodes earlier in time can be found by using the ideas of discounting and probability explained in Appendix 1. However, not only are formulae required giving the probabilities of upward and downward movements of the asset's price, but also the discount rate appropriate to the risk borne is needed. As the asset price moves further from or closer to the exercise price, the risk varies, making derivation of a formula for option pricing problematic. The solution lies in the idea of 'hedging', which is explained in Chapter 4 and Appendix 3. Assuming that hedging can be achieved, uncertainty is removed and the valuation problem has effectively been translated into valuation in a 'risk-neutral world' where only the risk-free rate is needed and 'risk-neutral probabilities' apply (see Chapter 4 and Hull, 2000). Practically, as a proxy for the risk-free discount rate, in an economically stable country, we use the rate of return from investment in short-term (three-month) government bonds. It should be noted that the risk-neutral probabilities are not directly observable (even though price movements can be hedged, the price movements themselves do not happen in a risk-neutral world) and are merely convenient quantities which are readily calculated and used for option valuation.

The nodes of a binomial tree at each time step approximate the probability distribution of possible future values of an underlying asset. The number of pathways through a binomial tree grows very rapidly as the number of time steps is increased, and even a modestly sized tree can model an extremely large set of possible future paths for an asset's price (pathways through a binomial tree are discussed further in Appendix 5). As the tree is made larger, the accuracy of the valuation improves (actually, the accuracy fluctuates as the number of time steps is increased, one by one, but the general trend is towards greater accuracy with more steps). Modification for American-style options is easy because as each option value at a node is calculated, it can be compared with the value if the option were to be exercised immediately and the larger of the two values is used at that node.

We now turn to the implementation of binomial models. It is convenient for explanation to use very small trees. Once you know how to use these you can understand much larger trees; it is then just a matter of repetitive calculation on a computer.

Practical option valuation using binomial trees

In Appendix 3, we described a Wiener process, a continuous-time log-normal distribution, with drift, for the underlying asset, S. We need a binomial model of possible movements of S which converges to this distribution as the number of time steps tends to infinity. The model will function in a risk-neutral world where the option value derived will be the same as in the true, risky world.

The model will function in a risk-neutral world where the option value derived will be the same as in the true, risky world.

Mathematically, convergence could be achieved in many ways, but two are often used in practice: either the risk-neutral probabilities of a rise or a fall in price can be taken as equal and formulae derived which give unequal proportional price movements or, alternatively, the prices can be made to move up or down by the same proportion, in which case formulae are derived which give unequal risk-neutral probabilities for those price movements. With a sufficiently large number of time steps, these two models converge on the single, correct option value, though they do not give precisely the same answer when using a small number of time steps. We will use the version with unequal probabilities, which is called 'CRR' after its originators (Cox, Ross and Rubinstein, 1979).

Figure A4.1 shows a tree with six time steps (far too small to give an accurate valuation but good enough to illustrate the method). The tree of possible asset prices starts with the current underlying asset price, S, at the present time. With each time step (towards the right, in Figure A4.1), prices can move upwards by a multiple, u, or downward by a multiple, d. These proportional upward and downward movements are the 'step lengths' in the random walk (see Appendix 5). The multiples u and d are chosen such that the price reached after an upward movement followed by a downward movement, Sud, is the same as that reached after a downward movement followed by an upward movement, Sdu (in the CRR model, $d = 1/u$). The possible prices of the asset one time step into the future are Su and Sd; the possible prices after two steps are Su^2, Sud and Sd^2; the possible prices after three steps are Su^3, Su^2d, Sud^2 and Sd^3, etc.

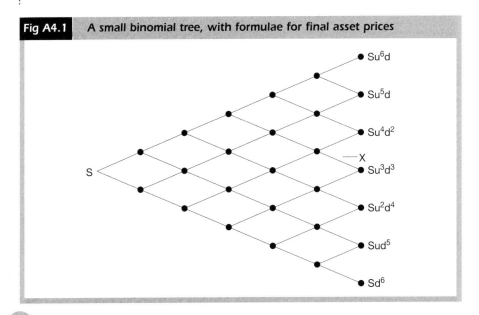

Fig A4.1 **A small binomial tree, with formulae for final asset prices**

Notice that we have drawn the tree as a regular lattice with straight lines connecting nodes on upward or downward paths, just as most textbooks do. Actually, a properly drawn tree to scale in S would curve upwards since, for example, S, Su, Su^2, Su^3, etc. are progressively more widely spaced and also more so than S, Sd, Sd^2, Sd^3, etc. This is purely a matter of display and makes no difference to the calculations, of course. In order not to clutter the diagram, only the asset prices at the start and end have been printed. The 'exercise price' or 'strike price', X, of an option has been included because we will need it later.

Next, we need to know how to calculate u and d. The key number required is the future 'standard deviation' of the underlying asset, commonly known in finance as the 'volatility'. Standard deviation, σ, is a fundamental concept in statistics and its derivation and application are covered in basic statistics textbooks. It is a measure of the dispersion or spread of the random element of asset price movements. For a random walk (Appendix 5) or a binomial tree, it shows up in the size of movement from one time step to the next. Although no one knows exactly how asset prices will change from moment to moment, we often have a reasonably good idea of how volatile they will be. For example, we may have reason to think that the volatility of asset prices will remain the same in the future as it was in the recent past. If we have a history of asset prices we can use those to calculate the asset's price volatility. We will represent prices by A_i for a set of M historical prices, labelled A_1, A_2, A_3, A_4, ... A_M. First, because asset prices move proportionally, we use the ratio of one price to the previous price and take logarithms. Then, the formula for volatility, σ, is applied:

$$y_i = \log_e \left(\frac{A_i}{A_{i-1}} \right) \tag{1}$$

$$\sigma = \sqrt{\frac{1}{M-1} \sum_{i=1}^{i=M} (y_i - \overline{y})^2} \tag{2}$$

Suppose we start at the present time, t = 0, and break the remaining period to the expiry date of the option, t = T, into N steps. Each time step will be T/N. It is conventional to represent a small change in a quantity by inserting Δ (the Greek 'delta') before its symbol and so the time step is commonly represented by Δt. The single entity, Δt, representing a small time step, should not be confused with the quantity called Δ used in 'delta hedging' elsewhere in this book.

$$\Delta t = \frac{T}{N} \tag{3}$$

In Chapter 4, hedging of an asset which can have either of two possible values in the next time step is discussed. This fixes the total overall outcome, regardless of which asset price is reached or their probabilities. It leads to the principle of risk-neutral valuation whereby an option can be valued using only the risk-free rate. In addition, we can derive terms, p and $(1 - p)$, which we can identify with the probabilities of upward and downward asset price movements in the risk-neutral world. It is highly convenient to think of p and $(1 - p)$ in this way although, as shown in Chapter 4, they can equally well be considered simply as weights which define the fixed outcome value of the one-step hedging process. An asset with initial price S would grow to $Se^{r\Delta t}$ at the risk-free rate, r, after time Δt. This must equal the sum of the two possible prices after one time step, weighted by their risk-neutral probabilities:

$$Se^{r\Delta t} = pSu + (1 - p)Sd \qquad (4)$$

where:

$$p = \frac{e^{r\Delta t} - d}{u - d} \qquad (5)$$

We can now give formulae to define u and d to give the required volatility, σ, of future asset prices. There is no single correct pair of formulae and we will simply quote one possibility, the CRR (Cox, Ross and Rubinstein, 1979) approach, in which we choose $d = 1/u$ with u and d as follows:

$$u = e^{\sigma\sqrt{\Delta t}} \qquad (6)$$

$$d = \frac{1}{u} = e^{-\sigma\sqrt{\Delta t}} \qquad (7)$$

We will now show how to use these results with a small tree. Once the calculations have been understood, a larger tree is needed for accurate answers and a computer can be programmed to do the rest. We will first value a European call option on an asset which will neither pay out nor receive cash flows before the option expires (for a stock, a 'cash outflow' would be a dividend payment to stock owners). Actually, tree calculations are not essential for this sort of option because we have available the Black-Scholes analytical solution, but it may be helpful as a familiar example. Later, we will value an American put option, for which there is no exact analytical solution, in order to show how the possibility of early exercise can be easily handled using a binomial tree.

We will use Figure A4.1 to model the possible future underlying asset prices. This splits the time from now until expiry of the option into only six time periods $(N = 6)$. We will suppose that the option will expire one year from now (two months per time step: very rough!). The asset's current price is $100 and its expected volatility is 0.40 p.a. (40 per cent p.a.). Using equations (3), (6) and (7) we obtain:

$$\Delta t = \frac{1}{6} \qquad u = e^{0.4\sqrt{1/6}} \qquad d = e^{-0.4\sqrt{1/6}}$$

This particular binomial model of the future has as its highest asset value $100u^6d^0 = 100u^6 = \$266.39$. Suppose that the option's exercise price is \$110. If, when the option expires after one year, the asset price takes its highest modelled value of \$266.39, the call option to buy the asset for \$110 will be exercised, for a profit of \$156.39 at that time. The other possible outcomes at time, $T = 1$ year, are:

Asset Formula	Asset Value	Option Value
$100u^6d^0$	266.39	156.39
$100u^5d^1$	192.17	82.17
$100u^4d^2$	138.62	28.62
$100u^3d^3$	100.00	0
$100u^2d^4$	72.14	0
$100u^1d^5$	52.04	0
$100u^0d^6$	37.54	0

Each option value in a time period one step, Δt, earlier is related by the risk-neutral probabilities to two of these final option values. For example, for the two nodes \$156.39 and \$82.17, if the probability of an upward movement (to \$156.39) is p and the probability of a downward movement (to \$82.17) is $1 - p$, then the expected value is $(\$159.39)p + (\$82.17)(1 - p)$. The time value of money must be taken into account and so we multiply by $e^{-r\Delta t}$ (see Appendix 1). Notice that this way of thinking, in terms of risk-neutral probabilities, is equivalent to the hedging argument used in Chapter 4 to obtain weights for binomial outcomes.

$$[156.39p + 82.17(1 - p)]e^{-r\Delta t} = 117.17$$

Valuation then becomes a matter of repetition, first for the other nodes at time $T - \Delta t$, then for all the nodes at $T - 2\Delta t$, and so on until the single value 'now' is reached.

The complete tree, showing asset prices with option prices underneath, is given in Figure A4.2. The call option's value 'now' is \$14.39. With such a small tree, the result is not especially accurate, the true value being about \$14.00. Given shorter time steps, in successively bigger trees, the results converge towards the correct answer (though not smoothly). A worksheet on a PC can easily be set up with, say, 30 time steps, which will give modestly accurate results, and these may be good enough if the input data are uncertain estimates. A conventional programming language, such as Fortran 95 (recommended) or C++, can be used for larger trees (hundreds of steps) to give better results.

Fig A4.2 Valuing a European call option using a binomial tree

						266.39
						156.39
					226.26	
					117.17	
				192.17		192.17
				83.99		82.17
			163.21		163.21	
			57.26		54.13	
		138.62		138.62		138.62
		37.38		33.05		28.62
	117.74		117.74		117.74	
	23.53		19.27		13.76	
100.00		100.00		100.00		100.00
14.39		10.89		6.62		0.00
	84.93		84.93		84.93	
	6.02		3.18		0.00	
		72.14		72.14		72.14
		1.53		0.00		0.00
			61.27		61.27	
			0.00		0.00	
				52.04		52.04
				0.00		0.00
					44.20	
					0.00	
						37.54
						0.00

Fig A4.3 Valuing an American put option using a binomial tree

```
                                                        266.39
                                                          0.00
                                              226.26
                                                0.00
                                    192.17               192.17
                                      0.00                 0.00
                          163.21               163.21
                            1.33                 0.00
                138.62               138.62               138.62
                  5.27                 2.61                 0.00
      117.74               117.74               117.74
       11.72                9.05                 5.11
100.00          100.00               100.00               100.00
 19.94           17.99                15.26                10.00
       84.93                84.93                84.93
       27.99                26.68                25.07
                72.14                72.14                72.14
                37.86                37.86                37.86
                          61.27                61.27
                          48.73                48.73
                                    52.04                52.04
                                    57.96                57.96
                                              44.20
                                              65.80
                                                        37.54
                                                        72.46
```

We will next value an American put option (for which there is no analytic solution) with all its parameters equal to those for the European call we have just considered. The tree is shown in Figure A4.3 and has asset prices identical to those in Figure A4.2. For the highest asset price modelled at expiry, $266.39, the put option to sell for $110 will not be exercised. However, were the asset to reach the lowest price, $37.54, the option would be exercised for a profit at that time of $110 − $37.54 = $72.46. The other possible option values at expiry are found in the same fashion.

Calculation of option values at nodes in a tree for an American option includes an extra feature compared with calculations for European options. Look at the option values in Figure A4.3 for the two lowest asset values at expiry, $57.96 and $72.46. First, exactly as for a European put option, we calculate the option value at the connected node one time step earlier, using risk-neutral probabilities and discounting, which gives a value of $64.89. Next, because this is an American option, early exercise could be optimal at the earlier node, so we check for this. The asset price at the node is $44.20 and so exercising early would yield $110 − $44.20 = $65.80. At this node, early exercise is optimal and $65.80 is inserted into the tree at that node in place of $64.89. Similar calculations are repeated at every other node. Again, the option's calculated value is approximate with such a small tree ($19.94 on the tree, which is accurate only to the nearest dollar).

Option valuation using finite difference methods

An overview

In contrast with binomial trees, which are easily visualized models of the process of asset price movements over time, finite difference methods work directly from the Black–Scholes partial differential equation, or some variant of it, plus suitably chosen boundary conditions (see Chapters 2 and 4 and Appendix 3). Without the boundary conditions included, the partial differential equation is applicable to an infinite number of options problems.

In order to appreciate the finite difference method, first imagine a three-dimensional graph. Option values are measured vertically versus asset price measured in a horizontal axis. Time is the other horizontal axis. The option values, which are not yet known, except at the boundaries of the graph (e.g. along the line representing the time of expiry of the option), form a surface above the asset and time axes (see examples in Chapters 2 and 3). This could look rather like a land surface, with high option values on hills and low values in plains. However, unlike hills and plains, the shape of the surface conforms to the partial differential equation, which contains information

> **Unlike hills and plains, the shape of the surface conforms to the partial differential equation.**

about relationships between the slopes of the 'hills' and the rates of change of the slopes.

We start knowing only these relationships plus the values at the boundaries of the graph but from these we can calculate the shape of the surface. Sometimes it is possible to find analytical equations representing the surface down to infinitesimally small detail. If not, then the curved surface can be approximated by a mesh of separate points separated by finite amounts (hence 'finite difference'). The shape of the mesh approximating the surface can then be calculated by working inwards from the boundaries, where values are known, using the relationships between slopes demanded by the partial differential equation. The boundary conditions themselves include some already familiar from binomial tree calculations: the option values at expiry, in this case for each asset value represented on the mesh. The fineness chosen for the mesh determines the accuracy of the option valuation. You will not be surprised to learn that errors in the calculation can rapidly propagate and magnify if the method is not properly applied, but in this appendix we will not spend long on discussion of errors (for this, see Wilmott, Howison and Dewynne, 1995).

The description, so far, of a three-dimensional graph for simple options valuation problems is intended to be helpful as a visual description of the intent of the finite difference method, but it does not provide insights into the shape of the surface and how it develops along the time axis. The Black–Scholes partial differential equation is related to a well-known equation in mathematics and physics, the 'heat equation' (and can be transformed into it, by suitable substitutions of parameters). We can give some intuition into the three-dimensional graph for option values by analogy with what you know from everyday experience about heat flow and temperature changes.

Comparing option pricing with heat conduction

The diffusion of heat from a hot spot on a thin, straight metal bar, is an excellent physical example of the mathematics which underlies option pricing and is comparable with the random walks of the drunken sailor and of the 'underlying asset' in option pricing (see Appendix 5 for more on random walk diffusion). The sailor or the asset start today at a single value and the probabilities of different values in the future develop in essentially the same way as heat spread-

259

Fig A4.4	Temperature changes along a horizontal metal bar after being touched at its centre with a hot needle (time evolving towards you)

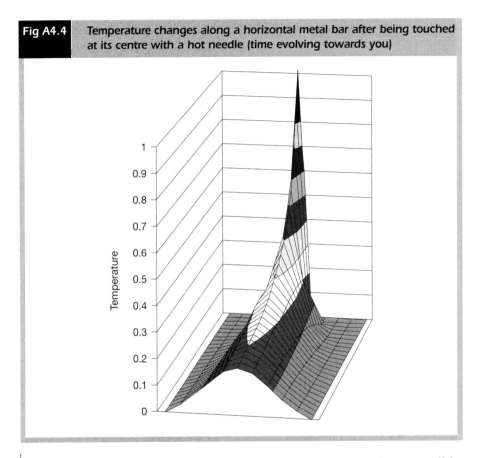

ing out along the bar. However, as you will see, for option values we will be interested in the 'diffusion' of value backwards in time from the known option values at every possible terminal asset price to the unknown option values at each current asset price.

Imagine an experiment in heat conduction. A long, straight, thin metal rod has been fixed to a bench. It is insulated from the bench and its surroundings so that heat cannot flow in or out of the rod through its sides (or, practically, so little that the flows are trivial). The rod is 'thin' so that we need only concern ourselves with heat flow along its length. At each end of the rod, we can set the temperature as we wish and allow heat to flow freely in or out (and, of course, heat flows in the direction 'hot' to 'cold'). Along the rod we have sensors which measure the temperature without significantly affecting the heat flow. Now imagine that we have fixed the temperatures at each end by attaching them to containers of melting ice at 0°C (don't worry about the practical details). We wait a while until the rod is the same temperature, at 0°C, along its whole length.

Then we touch the middle of the rod with the tip of a hot needle point, just briefly, to create a tiny hot spot on the rod. From everyday experience, we know, in general terms, what will happen next: the temperature at the point we touched will fall and the nearby parts of the rod will warm up, before cooling gradually. The heat we added will spread along the rod towards its ends, where it will melt more of the ice. If we show temperature on the vertical axis of a graph and scale the hot spot to a temperature of '1' at the start, the tempera-tures, at points along the rod, would develop through time as in Figure A4.4. The temperature distribution across the rod starts as a spike, then spreads out, over time, into a smooth distribution, centred on the middle of the rod. Eventually, all the excess heat will flow away to the sides and the rod will return to its original uniform temperature of 0°C.

If you are prepared to take the heat equation on trust, we can show you how to calculate the temperature evolution shown in Figure A4.4. It is usual to rep-resent temperature by u, distance along the rod by x and time by t. If the units of measurement for heat, temperature and length are suitably chosen, irritat-ing constant factors disappear (see physics or mathematics books for details) and we are left with the heat equation in 'non-dimensional form':

$$\frac{\partial u}{\partial t} = \frac{\partial^2 u}{\partial x^2} \qquad \text{The 'heat equation' or 'diffusion equation'} \qquad (8)$$

This tells us how temperature changes with distance and time, but it applies to an infinite number of possible situations, whereas we are interested in our spe-cific experiment with a rod. We specify this one particular situation by apply-ing 'initial conditions' and 'boundary conditions'. We know the initial tempera-ture distribution, at the moment when we apply a hot spot to the rod, and we know that the ends of the rod remain at 0°C throughout. Although mathemati-cians have solved this particular problem with an 'analytic solution' (an explic-it equation giving the temperature at any position and at any moment in time), this is not possible for every problem. We will next show how to convert the heat equation into a numerical algorithm which we can use to solve the equation for the particular boundary conditions of our experiment.

In the overview of the finite difference method, we described a three-dimen-sional graph and mentioned that the curved surface would be approximated by a mesh of separate points separated by finite amounts. The left-hand side of the heat equation is a general expression representing the slope of u (heat) versus t (time) at fixed x (distance) over infinitesimally small changes in t. It is a 'deriv-ative' in the mathematician's sense, in calculus, and represents the slope of a graph and it is a 'partial' derivative because it applies at a fixed value of x. In the finite difference method, we approximate this by finite changes and so the

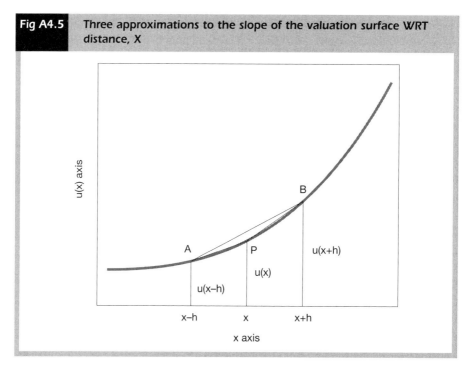

Fig A4.5   Three approximations to the slope of the valuation surface WRT distance, X

smooth curve of u versus t for a given x is approximated by a series of straight lines. The right-hand side is a 'slope of a slope' (a 'second' partial derivative), in other words the rate of change of a slope, but now of u versus x at fixed t.

It is helpful to think about graphs of temperature versus time, at a fixed distance along the rod, and secondly about graphs of temperature versus distance along the rod, at fixed time. On the left side of the heat equation, the partial derivative of temperature versus time is the slope at a point, P, on a graph of u versus t. This is approximately equal to the slope of a straight line drawn between two extra points, A and B, either side of the point at which we are interested in the slope; the further apart the two extra points, the worse the approximation is likely to be. We show this in Figure A4.5, where u(x,t) is plotted versus x at some fixed time. u(x,t) indicates that temperature, u, varies with both distance, x, and time, t. Since t has been fixed, we will represent this on the figure by u(x). Points A and B represent the temperatures at distances a little less (by a small amount, h) and a little more than x, but drawn widely separated, for clarity, in Figure A4.5.

The slopes of the lines AP, PB and AB are all approximations to the slope of the curve (i.e. the first derivative) at point P. Choosing the slope of AB, we have the approximation:

$$\frac{\partial u}{\partial x} \approx \frac{u(x + h) - u(x - h)}{2h} \tag{9}$$

Next, we require the second partial derivative of u versus x. In other words, we need an approximation to the rate at which the first derivative changes, versus x. Pictorially, this is the slope AP, over a length h on the x axis, changing to a slope PB over an equal range and we can immediately write the second derivative by inspection of Figure A4.5 (we are aware that we should have used Taylor's theorem and considered the omitted errors, but we ask mathematicians not to write to complain!).

$$\frac{\partial^2 u}{\partial x^2} \approx \frac{1}{h}\left[\frac{u(x + h) - u(x)}{h} - \frac{u(x) - u(x - h)}{h}\right] = \frac{u(x + h) - 2u(x) + u(x - h)}{h^2} \tag{10}$$

We can repeat this with time as a third dimension, but now holding x fixed and with small changes in t represented by k. Since x is fixed, we represent u(x,t) by u(t) in Figure A4.6.

As before, there are three approximations to the slope of the curve at point P. For convenience later, we will use slope PD (which, for obvious reasons, is said to give a 'forward difference' approximation) rather than CD (a 'central difference' approximation):

Fig A4.6 Three approximations to the slope of the valuation surface WRT time, t

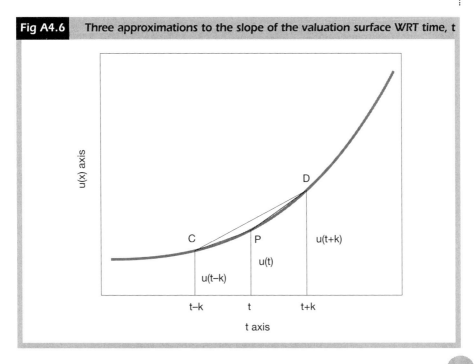

$$\frac{\partial u}{\partial t} \approx \frac{u(t + k) - u(t)}{k} \tag{11}$$

An approximation to the heat equation now appears to be:

$$\frac{u(t + k) - u(t)}{k} \approx \frac{u(x + h) - 2u(x) + u(x - h)}{h^2} \tag{12}$$

Being more careful, we need to show on the left-hand side that u is a function of x as well as a function of t and so the equation is written more fully as:

$$\frac{u(x, t + k) - u(x, t)}{k} \approx \frac{u(x + h, t) - 2u(x, t) + u(x - h, t)}{h^2} \tag{13}$$

Notice that all these temperatures, except the first, are at time t, while the first is at time t+k. We will rearrange the equation, replacing the ratio k/h^2 by ρ, to give an equation which relates u at time t+k to values at the earlier time, t:

$$\rho = \frac{k}{h^2} \tag{14}$$

$$u(x, t + k) \approx \rho u(x + h, t) + [1 - 2\rho u(x, t)] + \rho u(x - h, t) \tag{15}$$

Having found this relationship, it will prove more convenient, when using a finite difference 'grid', to change notation. We will refer to the x axis in terms of the integer i, stepping in units of h (so x, x+h, x+2h, ... are replaced by i, i+1, i+2, ...). Similarly, we calibrate the t axis in steps of length k, using the integer j. In this notation, the equation becomes:

$$u(i, j + 1) \approx \rho u(i + 1, j) + [(1 - 2\rho) u(i, j)] + \rho u(i - 1, j) \tag{16}$$

Here, in very rapid fashion and ignoring mathematical subtleties, we have arrived at an equation which can be used to demonstrate the finite difference method. Using it, we can calculate the results shown in Figure A4.4.

Define the time at the start of the experiment as j = 0, when the rod at 0°C is touched at its centre by a hot needle. Consider any distance along the rod, represented by 'i'. The formula (16) gives its temperature one time step later, at time '1' (j+1 = 0 + 1 = 1), in terms of its starting temperature and those at two points either side (at i+1 and i−1). This is done for all values of i along the rod. The formula is used iteratively, such that values after the next time step are given by replacing j+1 by j+2 and j by j+1. We show this in Figure A4.7, for a rod arbitrarily sectioned into 11 temperature zones. The temperature at i = 5, on the rod at the fifth time step, can be calculated from three values one

> We have arrived at an equation which can be used to demonstrate the finite difference method.

Fig A4.7 Grid of positions on the valuation surface used in the finite difference approximation. Each unknown value is calculated from three known values one time step away.

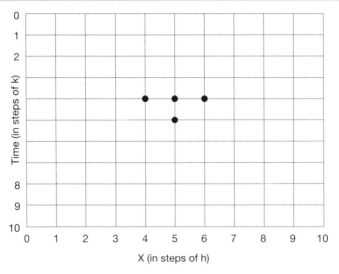

Each unknown value is calculated from three known values one time step before

time period earlier: the temperature at the same point and the temperatures at points either side of it. This grid, extended to more time steps, was used to calculate results for Figure A4.4.

You may have noticed one other element in the calculations: what to do at the extreme left or extreme right of the diagram? The ends of the rod are fixed at 0°C (a 'boundary condition' in the calculations) and so u(0,t), u(0,t+k), u(0,t+2k), etc. and u(10,t), u(10,t+k), u(10,t+2k), etc. are set at zero.

We will demonstrate how to calculate the temperature at the centre of the rod, at position i = 5, one time step after the hot spot is applied. Purely for convenience, we set $\rho = 0.1$ (it is merely a ratio of units of measurement of time and distance). At the second time step, the temperatures are:

$$u(4,1) \approx 0.1u(5,0) + [(1 - 0.2)u(4,0)] + 0.1u(3,0) = 0.1 + 0 + 0 = 0.1$$

$$u(5,1) \approx 0.1u(6,0) + [(1 - 0.2)u(5,0)] + 0.1u(4,0) = 0 + 0.8 + 0 = 0.8$$

$$u(6,1) \approx 0.1u(7,0) + [(1 - 0.2)u(6,0)] + 0.1u(5,0) = 0.1 + 0 + 0 = 0.1$$

Temperatures in the next steps are easily found (we recommend using a spreadsheet rather than trying these with pen and paper). Figure A4.8 shows the first ten steps. By increasing the number of points sampled along the rod and slicing the time steps more finely, the model's accuracy could be improved.

Fig A4.8	A finite difference grid showing results for the heat experiment and including boundary conditions (temperature zero fixed at each end)									
0	1	2	3	4	5	6	7	8	9	10
0	0	0	0	0	1	0	0	0	0	0
0	0	0	0	0.1	0.8	0.1	0	0	0	0
0	0	0	0.01	0.16	0.66	0.16	0.01	0	0	0
0	0	0.001	0.024	0.195	0.560	0.195	0.024	0.001	0	0
0	0.00010	0.0032	0.0388	0.2144	0.4870	0.2144	0.0388	0.0032	0.0001	0
0	0.00040	0.00645	0.05280	0.22410	0.43248	0.22410	0.05280	0.00645	0.00040	0
0	0.00097	0.01048	0.06530	0.22781	0.39080	0.22781	0.06530	0.01048	0.00097	0
0	0.00182	0.01501	0.07606	0.22786	0.35820	0.22786	0.07606	0.01501	0.00182	0
0	0.00296	0.01980	0.08514	0.22571	0.33214	0.22571	0.08514	0.01980	0.00296	0
0	0.00435	0.02465	0.09266	0.22230	0.31085	0.22230	0.09266	0.02465	0.00435	0
0	0.00594	0.02942	0.09882	0.21819	0.29314	0.21819	0.09882	0.02942	0.00594	0

Insights from the heat experiment, applied to option pricing

The diffusion of heat across a metal bar, forward in time, is comparable with the 'diffusion' of option values backwards in time from each final, known option value, in a grid of possible future asset prices. Indeed, the parameters in the Black–Scholes equation can be transformed into the heat equation (which will also transform the boundary conditions) and the heat equation with these boundary conditions can be solved using finite differences, and the results transformed back into financial terms. Next, we have invented a modification of the heat experiment to make it a closer analogy for options calculations. This may be useful as a reminder that solution of the heat equation works forwards in time but solution of the Black–Scholes equation, and its variants, works backwards in time.

For the heat experiment with the metal rod, a spreadsheet set up to perform the calculations for Figure A4.8 can be quickly modified to suit new initial conditions and boundary conditions. Suppose the rod is kept at 0°C by an ice bath along the rod up to the fourth position on the left side and that the extreme right-hand side is kept at a higher temperature ('1.4', in arbitrary units of temperature), with temperatures changing linearly in between. The initial temperature distribution will look like Figure A4.9 (resembling the payoff function for a call option).

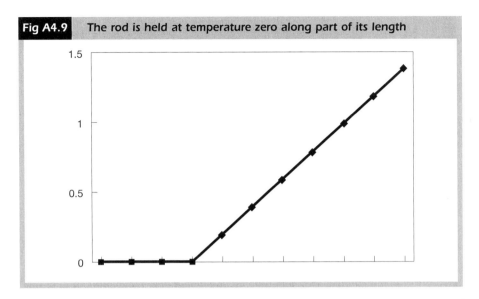

Fig A4.9 The rod is held at temperature zero along part of its length

Previously, we applied a hot spot and 'watched' the temperature changes. Here we will instantly remove the cooling ice from the left part of the rod so that ice is now applied only to the extreme left end. We expect that the sections from the left end to the fourth position will warm up, drawing heat derived from the right-hand end of the rod. The results for the first few time steps are summarized in Figure A4.10.

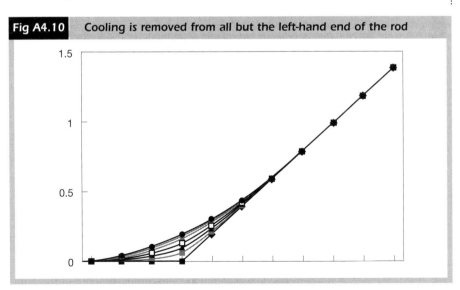

Fig A4.10 Cooling is removed from all but the left-hand end of the rod

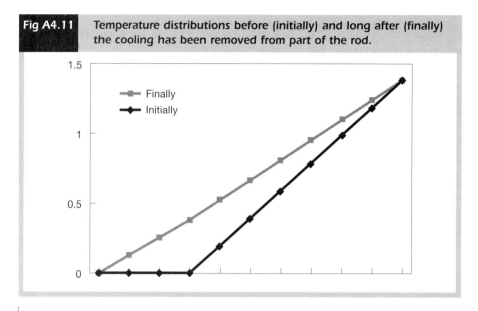

Fig A4.11 Temperature distributions before (initially) and long after (finally) the cooling has been removed from part of the rod.

We expect that eventually, when a new equilibrium has been reached, the temperature will rise linearly from the left end to the right. If the calculations are performed for a sufficiently large number of time steps, the result is as expected (we used 200 steps for the upper line in Figure A4.11).

Figures A4.9, A4.10 and A4.11 already look quite close to the evolution of option value (but with time reversed) that we saw in Chapters 2 and 3, but to enrich the analogy we will add one more detail. Imagine greatly extending the length of the rod beyond its current right-hand limit. As we do so, we also increase the fixed temperature of the rod at its right end, so that, on a graph like Figure A4.11, as we lengthen the rising line for the initial temperature condition the slope of the line is unchanged. The final condition line, completing a triangle, will now rise at a steeper angle. Next, if you can, imagine extending the rod towards the right (and raising the temperature at its right-hand end) for ever, out towards infinity. Ignore the fact that you'd need a rod which could withstand an infinite temperature at its right end. The line for the final condition would rise at the same angle as the line for the initial condition. The first few points for each line would look like Figure A4.12.

In this case, as the cold region on the left warmed up, the curve showing temperature would rise much as before but of course without intersecting the initial line at the eleventh point (which would no longer be at the end of the rod). Eventually, the temperature along the bar would be shown by the left-hand line, rising for ever.

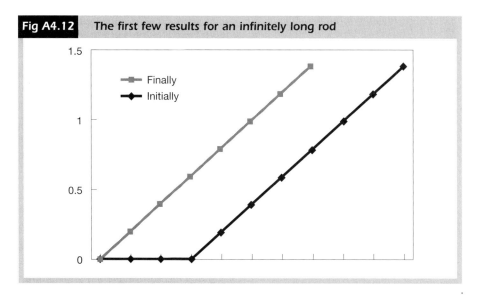

Fig A4.12 **The first few results for an infinitely long rod**

The practicality of creating an infinitely long rod (let alone heating it as required) should make you smile, but the resulting diagram has the same appearance as a standard textbook diagram for a call option. The initial situation looks like the 'payoff diagram' at the expiry of a call option and the final single straight line looks like the 'upper bound' (i.e. maximum possible value) for a call option which has an infinite remaining time before expiry. This value is equal to the current value of the underlying asset.

The evolution of temperature is analogous to the evolution of option prices, reversed in time. The heat experiment is a useful reminder on how to compare heat with option valuation. Heat spreads out, from hot to cold, forwards in time; option values spread out backwards in calendar time, in a way which is related to the probability distribution of all the possible future outcomes at expiry of the option.

The finite difference method applied to option pricing

The results from the finite difference solution of problems in heat conduction are relatively easy to relate to common experience with heat and temperature. We can solve an option pricing problem using finite differences in the same way. We will illustrate by again using a grid only 11 points wide for simplicity and for consistency with our earlier example of a metal rod conducting heat. For practical option valuation, a much finer grid of points would be used to obtain acceptable accuracy.

If you intend to implement a finite difference method there are additional conditions with which you will need to be familiar (stability and convergence; see Wilmott, Howison and Dewynne, 1995). For example, parameter $\rho = k/h^2$ in the difference equation (16) must not exceed 0.5, which means that your choice for the size of the time step k must be related to the size of your chosen asset price step h. If these two are not properly chosen, the valuations become oscillating or explosively large. Conversely, if a graph of valuations looks smooth, you have probably avoided the instability problem and all is well.

We will demonstrate the pricing of options numerically by solving the Black–Scholes partial differential equation for a European-style call option (for which there is actually a known analytical solution). It is possible mathematically to transform the finance problem into one involving the heat equation (e.g. see Wilmott, Howison and Dewynne, 1995) but we will solve it directly. We take as given the Black–Scholes partial differential equation for a stock price, S, and call value C, but with the stock price transformed as its logarithm, lnS.

$$\frac{\partial C}{\partial t} + \frac{1}{2}\sigma^2 \frac{\partial^2 C}{\partial x^2} + r\frac{\partial C}{\partial x} - rC = 0 \quad \text{The Black–Scholes PDE with } x = \ln S \qquad (17)$$

We construct a finite difference grid, just as we did for the heat equation and the metal rod, using steps of lengths h for x and k for t. Be careful when comparing textbooks with similar formulae: here we place the time element second, as j, but you will find books which place it first, as i, as well as those which place them as we do. Additionally, to maintain consistency with our earlier grid for the heat equation, we will define the label j as increasing backwards in calendar time, from the expiry of the option, when option values are known for each stock value on the grid.

$$\frac{C(i, j) - C(i, j + 1)}{k} + \frac{1}{2}\sigma^2 \frac{C(i + 1, j) - 2C(i, j) + C(i - 1, j)}{h^2}$$

$$\qquad (18)$$

$$+ r\frac{C(i + 1, j) - C(i - 1, j)}{2h} - rC(i, j) \approx 0$$

For practical use, this can be simplified by gathering the terms which are calculated only once, when the grid is first set up, and expressing them in three new numbers, p_{up}, p_{mid} and p_{down}. In this form, it is similar to the equation we used to model heat flow in the metal rod:

$$C(i, j + 1) \approx p_{up} C(i + 1, j) + p_{mid} C(i, j) + p_{down} C(i - 1, j) \qquad (19)$$

$$p_{up} = k \left[\frac{\sigma^2}{2h^2} + \frac{r}{2h} \right] \qquad (20)$$

$$p_{mid} = 1 - k \frac{\sigma^2}{h^2} - rk \qquad (21)$$

$$p_{down} = k \left[\frac{\sigma^2}{2h^2} - \frac{r}{2h} \right] \qquad (22)$$

We will now use these equations in a grid, shown in Figure A4.13, to calculate the value of a call option on a stock for a range of current stock prices. The stock will not pay a dividend before the option expires. Suppose the option has half a year to maturity, exercise price £100 per share, an expected share volatility (standard deviation) of 0.2 p.a. (20 per cent p.a.). The risk-free rate is 0.05 p.a. (5 per cent p.a.). We will set up a grid with £100 as the central stock price.

Stock prices across the grid change logarithmically and are shown in the second row, below the grid numbers. These are shown to fewer decimal places than the option values, in order to fit on the page. As with the grid for the evolution of temperature along the rod, calculations proceed downwards, but here this represents calendar time decreasing, the final line giving results for the present. The first row of option values (0.0000 to 49.1825) is found from the payoff function for a call option. For example, one of the 11 final stock values possible using this small grid is £149.1825 (rounded to £149.18). If the stock reaches this value, the option to buy for £100 will be exercised and, consequently, will be worth £49.1825.

The final feature which must be included is a boundary condition at each end. The left-hand stock price is £67.03. At expiry the option would be worth zero at this stock price, as shown in the first row of option values. At earlier calendar times, the option might have positive value at this stock price, and this needs to be taken into account on the grid. However, working down the rows, we require three values from the previous row and, obviously, only two are available at a row end. As an approximation, the values along the left-hand side have been set equal to the adjacent values to the right. At the right-hand boundary, the values after the first (£49.1825) have been set equal to the adjacent value to the left plus the increase in asset price (£149.1825 − £137.7128). These row-end values are chosen to be approximations to the actual effects of the true boundaries at ln S = minus and plus infinity. Actually, we need to use a larger grid, covering stock price values from nearer zero to much larger than the largest shown here, in order to reduce errors.

The estimated option values for each of 11 current stock prices are shown in the final row. With such a small grid these option prices are not very accurate.

	0	1	2	3	4	5	6	7	8	9	10

Fig A4.13 The finite difference grid used to value a call option on a stock

0	1	2	3	4	5	6	7	8	9	10
67.03	72.61	78.66	85.21	92.31	100.00	108.33	117.35	127.12	137.71	149.18
0.0000	0.0000	0.0000	0.0000	0.0000	0.0000	8.3287	17.3511	27.1249	37.7128	49.1825
0.0000	0.0000	0.0000	0.0000	0.0000	1.4055	8.6290	17.6514	27.4253	38.0131	49.4828
0.0000	0.0000	0.0000	0.0000	0.2372	2.4182	9.0873	17.9508	27.7247	38.3126	49.7823
0.0000	0.0000	0.0000	0.0400	0.5704	3.2228	9.5970	18.2722	28.0232	38.6112	50.0809
0.0000	0.0000	0.0068	0.1237	0.9401	3.9075	10.1159	18.6158	28.3242	38.9088	50.3785
0.0011	0.0011	0.0255	0.2442	1.3206	4.5169	10.6274	18.9764	28.6298	39.2061	50.6758
0.0052	0.0052	0.0588	0.3937	1.7013	5.0750	11.1260	19.3483	28.9410	39.5036	50.9733
0.0143	0.0143	0.1075	0.5650	2.0776	5.5959	11.6103	19.7271	29.2576	39.8022	51.2719
0.0300	0.0300	0.1710	0.7528	2.4476	6.0883	12.0806	20.1094	29.5792	40.1026	51.5722
0.0537	0.0537	0.2484	0.9529	2.8110	6.5579	12.5379	20.4930	29.9050	40.4050	51.8747
0.0864	0.0864	0.3385	1.1623	3.1678	7.0087	12.9830	20.8762	30.2342	40.7100	52.1796

The grid gives option values for ten other stock prices, though these become less reliable near the boundaries.

The estimated option value for a stock price of £100 is shown as around £7, whereas an accurate calculation gives an answer about ten pence lower (nevertheless, not bad from such a very small grid!). The grid gives option values for ten other stock prices, though these become less reliable near the boundaries. Using a larger grid, many values can be obtained and those corresponding to stock values intermediate between those on the grid can be found by interpolation. This is a decided advantage over a tree calculation, which gives the option value for only one current stock price.

The final row gives the current price of the option, six months before expiry. In Figure A4.14 we plot this, along with the initial row of option values in the calculation which are, of course, the final calendar values at the expiry of the option.

The initial grid values are the option values at expiry, the final grid values are current option values

We end this introduction to numerical methods with a three-dimensional graph of option prices evolving with time for a range of current stock prices (Figure A.4.15). Remember, the initial condition in the finite difference method here is the *final* (expiry date) outcome of call option price versus stock price. This is important. It is true that heat flow, and the change of temperature along a rod, are both analogous to the probability distribution of future stock prices (i.e. moving forward in time, towards greater uncertainty). However, the diffu-

Fig A4.14 | The finite difference results (third row and last row of Fig A4.13)

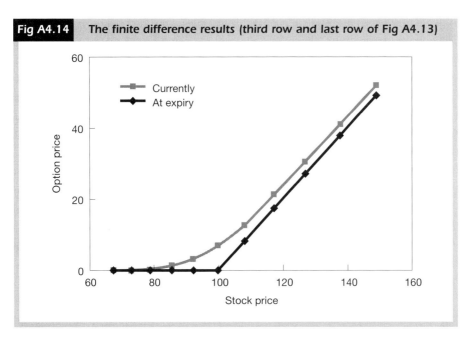

Fig A4.15 | The finite difference results showing option prices evolving with time (away from you) for a range of current stock prices (cf Figure 2.8)

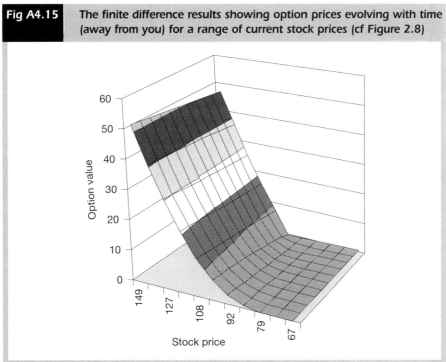

sion equation can equally model the probability distribution moving backwards in time, from each possible final option price, and this is what we need to do for valuing an option.

Therefore in the process of calculating option prices, we switch from diffusion forwards in time (in which uncertainty increases as calendar time passes) to backwards (in which uncertainty decreases as calendar time passes). This is because an option's time value derives from uncertainty about its future value on expiry and, as expiry approaches, uncertainty falls, until the option's value is known with certainty at the instant of expiry (or at whatever earlier instant the option is exercised), after which the option ceases to exist.

Insights into the random walk

by David Newton

Using the random walk to model real-world behaviour

Options derive their value from the future behaviour of something else (the 'underlying' asset), such as the price of a company's stock, the price of a commodity such as oil, or the value of a project (e.g. a drug, as yet undeveloped). The first step in valuing an option is to model the possible future price behaviour of the underlying asset. The number of possible series of asset prices is huge.

A graph of prices versus time will generally be observed as a meandering path, as in Figure A5.1, which illustrates the past path of an asset's price and just four possible future paths. These are modelled by combining an expected future trend – such as constant prices or, more realistically, prices rising at some compound rate – with a random element. Even with a model using rising prices, the random element can be large enough to dominate during some periods, producing downturns as in Figure A5.1.

The way that values spread out in future from the single known value of 'now' has in fact already been shown for the closely related problem of heat. If you look at Figure A4.4, you can see how the complete probability distribution of future temperature 'spreads out' as time advances (down the page, in that figure). In effect, Figure A5.1 is just four realizations from such a probability distribution. Notice how in both figures the probability distribution/future values seem to get more widely scattered as time passes, very quickly at first, but at a decreasing rate afterwards. In fact, the confidence interval grows with the square root of time (because volatility does). You can see a hint of this on the 'floor' of Figure A4.4, where the edge of the raised region meets the flat region outside it along a line (it's a little hard to see where they meet because we have used such a simple grid). This line spreads out on each side, like a parabola down the page. For stock prices, the parabolic confidence interval applies to the logarithm of price, rather than to price itself, and a stock price

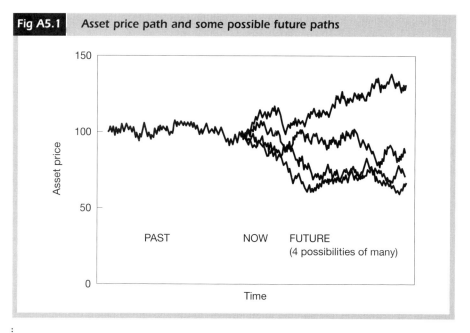

Fig A5.1   Asset price path and some possible future paths

PAST   NOW   FUTURE
(4 possibilities of many)

generally also has some slight upward or downward drift over time, but these details seldom make a detectable difference to the random walk over a short time period.

If we knew now what the future path of an underlying asset's price would be, we would know when to exercise the option, what its value would be at the exercise date and thus its value today. We would also lose the essence of options, which is the value arising from uncertainty. Although we do not know what path the price of the underlying asset will follow, we can imagine (and, more important, model) a large number of possible future outcomes for the asset value, each resulting in a different final option value. If we can appropriately combine the different option values arising from the possible paths, somehow taking into account their probabilities, we can value the option today. The basic model is the random walk, which we introduced in Chapter 1, but it is not restricted to finance and we can discuss it first in physical terms to give a fuller appreciation of the model. From this model we can introduce the different option valuation techniques and show how they work.

A random walk in one dimension

The random walk is fundamental to much of modern finance theory, but usually in finance textbooks its name (why it is called a 'walk') is left unexplained. It has been applied to the financial returns on company stocks, where it is said the 'the market has no memory'. Also, when only one variable (stock return) is concerned, the random walk is described as 'one dimensional'. The essential features of the one-dimensional random walk are contained in the story of a drunken sailor, forced to walk only along a straight line and so drunk that after each step he is unable to recall where he has come from.

A drunken sailor emerges from a pub, near Her Majesty's Royal Naval dockyards in Portsmouth, England. The pub is in the middle of a long, straight row of buildings. Immediately in front of the pub's exit is a wall, running parallel to the buildings. Thus, the sailor, on leaving the pub and trying to walk forward, can only move left or right along the straight line of buildings in front of him. Also (since this is our story) he has string tied between his ankles and takes the same length of step every time he moves (but with no risk of falling over). It makes no difference to him whether he goes left or right. Worse, although he has a strong urge to keep moving, he is so drunk that after each step he cannot remember how he arrived at his new position and there is an equal probability that his next step will be to the left or to the right. This is a random walk. Since the sailor is constrained to move only along a straight line, it is a one-dimensional random walk. (If we invented a story of someone walking randomly over a football field, this would be a two-dimensional random walk.)

Since the sailor is constrained to move only along a straight line, it is a one-dimensional random walk.

As you will see soon, it is possible to calculate the probability that the sailor will end up a certain distance from the door of the pub after he has taken a set number of steps to left or right.

We can demonstrate the sailor's random walk by describing a simple practical apparatus which should be easy to visualize. This will help later in understanding the 'binomial tree' methods, which are widely used to value options.

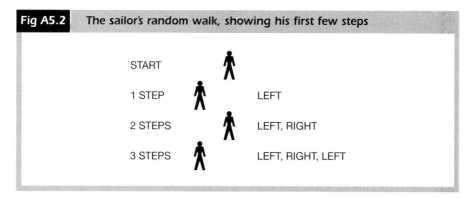

Fig A5.2 The sailor's random walk, showing his first few steps

START

1 STEP   LEFT

2 STEPS   LEFT, RIGHT

3 STEPS   LEFT, RIGHT, LEFT

Here is the physical model (see Figure A5.3): an apparatus is built, through which steel balls will be dropped. A ball is dropped into a hole at the top and hits a narrow bar which directs it randomly left or right, with equal probability since the bar has been carefully placed to ensure this. Depending on which way the ball falls, it encounters one of two holes at the next level down. Falling through either of these two holes, the ball is again deflected left or right as it falls to the next level, and so on until the levels are exhausted and the ball falls through to be collected at the bottom of the apparatus.

Now imagine yourself looking down on a falling ball. Ignore the shrinking view of the ball as it falls away from you and concentrate on its movements left or right. Purely in terms of its progress along a line, left or right, the ball moves in the same way as the stylized drunken sailor. This is the mechanical model of a random walk in one dimension.

A ball may move left twice in succession or right twice in succession and will then be at one of two different positions. However, if it moves first left then right or, alternatively, right then left, it will have dropped into the same position. After a ball has dropped through two holes it can be in one of three positions. There are two ways in which it could have reached the middle position but only one way of reaching either of the other two positions. Suppose we set up three collection tubes under the three possible positions of the ball after it has fallen through the first two levels. A single ball can end up in only one of the three collection tubes, but if many balls are dropped through, approximately half will end up as a vertical column in the centre tube and the others will be split approximately equally between the other two tubes. If the balls are all the same size, the relative heights of the three columns represent the probabil-

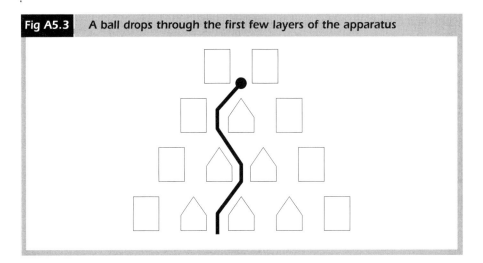

Fig A5.3   A ball drops through the first few layers of the apparatus

ities that a single ball will drop through each of the three final holes. The more balls pass through, the more accurate the representation of probabilities. (You may notice that these are the three possibilities in a game of tossing a coin twice: there is one way of tossing two heads, one way of tossing two tails, but two ways of tossing one of each, so long as you do not distinguish between head followed by tail and tail followed by head.)

If the number of levels is made large and many balls are dropped through the apparatus, we obtain columns of balls with relative heights representing the probabilities that a single ball, dropped into the top, will end up at each final position. For example, if 80 balls were dropped through a simple apparatus with only three levels (and four collection tubes), random chance would cause the distribution of balls to be roughly 10, 30, 30, 10. These correspond to probabilities of 10/80, 30/80, 30/80 and 10/80 or 0.125, 0.375, 0.375, 0.125, giving a total probability of 1 (a certainty; all balls must end up in one of the four tubes). Knowing this, if just one ball were dropped through, you would not know which tube it would fall into but, if asked to select one beforehand, you would choose either of the middle tubes, since there are three ways in which each can be reached out of a total of eight ways; a probability of 0.375.

The important result follows that the distribution of balls in the collection tubes also represents the probabilities in a random walk. Suppose we watch the sailor taking the same number of steps as there are levels in the apparatus. The

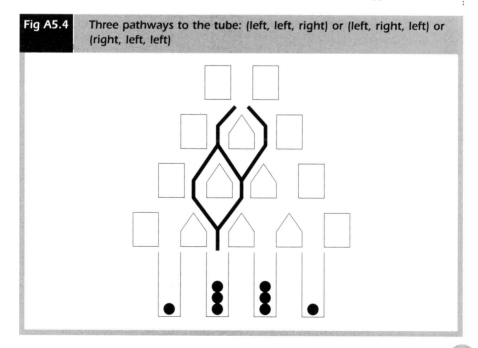

Fig A5.4 Three pathways to the tube: (left, left, right) or (left, right, left) or (right, left, left)

probability that a ball will end up in a particular collection tube is the same as the probability that the sailor will end up in a corresponding position along the line outside the pub. For three steps by the sailor, or three levels in the appartus, the probabilities of the sailor/ball ending at each of the four possible positions are 1/8, 3/8, 3/8 and 1/8. This is illustrated in Figure A5.4, where it is seen that there are three pathways to the position indicated and eight pathways in total.

There is good evidence that proportional changes in stock prices and in the prices of some other assets or commodities do follow a random walk, to the extent that workable, practical financial calculations can be carried out relying on this. The lattice of all possible routes is called a binomial tree. Once on paper, a binomial tree can be turned on its side (no gravity to be considered!), as seen in most textbooks on option pricing, with time increasing from left to right (rather than from top to bottom, as a ball falls). Better than this, now that the nature of model for the random walk has been appreciated, the details of the walk can be modified mathematically, even though construction of a physical model would be more difficult. For example, the probabilities of movements up or down (previously right or left) can swiftly be altered in a model on paper, as can the step lengths.

This is important because underlying asset prices need to be modelled via proportional price changes rather than absolute price changes. Imagine the price of a share of stock in a certain publicly traded company. Fifty years ago, on a particular day, a share could be bought for $1 on Wall Street. The next day, the price was $1.10. Yesterday, a share of stock on the same company could be bought for $100, whereas it is available for $100.10 today. On both occasions the stock rose by $0.10. Fifty years ago that was a 10 per cent rise, but today the rise has been only 0.1 per cent.

A more dramatic modification of the basic random walk is given in Chapter 10, on house mortgage values, where the walk is two-dimensional (house price and interest rate) and for one dimension (interest rate) the walk includes a tendency to revert to a long-term average and the movements in the two dimensions are correlated.

We show, in Appendix 4, how proportional changes are incorporated into option calculations with the binomial tree model. The spread of a binomial tree (the step length in a random walk) can be adjusted to fit practical observations. For stock returns a large step length will correspond to widely fluctuating or highly 'volatile' returns and a small step length to less volatile returns. The future volatility is the key practical number to be estimated for option valuation. When the goal is to value a business expected to arise from a current R&D project, this gives the interesting situation in which the

The future volatility is the key practical number to be estimated for option valuation.

volatility of a business not yet in being must be estimated (Newton and Pearson, 1994; Newton *et al.*, 1996). If past asset values are available, historical volatility can be made the basis of estimates of future volatility (see Appendix 4 for the equations needed to calculate historical volatility).

If options are traded, implied volatility can be extracted from the prices using methods described in all standard financial texts (the result should not differ wildly from an historical estimate, without good reason in the market). These methods are of most use with regularly traded assets, such as stock in public companies. Sometimes, data are available for traded assets considered to be of comparable risk (perhaps a company in the same business area) which can be used as bases for volatility estimates. A particular problem in companies with many research projects can be a failure to document deleted projects (Doctor, Newton and Pearson, 2001).

Alternative ways of using the random walk to value options

There are three broad ways of using the idea of a random walk for option valuation. One (Monte Carlo) is to use a computer to simulate a large number of the possible future asset price paths; rather like following the sailor on a walk, then starting him at the pub again to follow his next walk, and so on. A second uses a tree and calculates option values at each of the positions on the tree, without needing to know the path by which the position was reached. A third sets up the random walk mathematically using stochastic calculus (see Appendix 3), then solves the resulting partial differential equation to obtain the option value.

The two techniques of particular interest in real options analysis, binomial trees and finite differences, are considered in Appendix 4. Here, we will describe the Monte Carlo method in general terms, because it uses the idea of a random walk directly to simulate possible future paths.

'Monte Carlo' option valuation – simulation of a random sample of future asset paths

In order to simulate a large number of the possible future asset price paths, a computer has to be programmed to generate sequences of random numbers as the basis for uncertainty in the calculations. In a reference to gambling casinos, methods using random number generation became known in science as 'Monte Carlo' methods. The option value is determined for each 'walk' by discounting back from the value at expiry and the option value today is estimated as the average of a large number of simulations. For an accurate result, the time until expiry of the option needs to be split into more than just a few time steps. The number of possible 'walks' grows rapidly as the number of time steps is increased. Consequently, only a sample of paths can be used.

The Monte Carlo method has the advantage of directness and clarity. It is useful for valuation of options whose exercise depends on the path that price has followed; for example, an option on oil prices where instead of using the oil price at expiry to determine the option's value, an average of past oil prices, on certain dates, is used. For options dependent simultaneously on the prices of several underlying assets Monte Carlo can be a useful alternative method to those mentioned in Chapter 4.

Monte Carlo calculations may be thought of in terms of paths through a tree, though there is no necessity to set up a tree structure to implement them. For a two-step tree there are only four possible paths (two of which lead to the same finishing position). Adding an extra level doubles the number of possible paths and so even a modest size of tree allows for a large number of future possibilities. For example, a ten-step tree includes 1,024 paths, a 20-step tree 1,048,576 paths, a 30-step tree more than a billion paths, and a 1,000-step tree more than ten to the power 301 paths. Calculations for every possible path are infeasible for all but a small number of steps. However, it is possible to improve the efficiency of the method (for an excellent practical description, see Clewlow and Strickland, 1998).

An essential difference between the main numerical methods is that Monte Carlo methods work forwards in time, observing the individual evolutions of possible paths, whereas the others (tree and finite difference) work backwards in time (see Appendix 4). This presents no problems for options which can be exercised only at expiry (European options), but the Monte Carlo method requires awkward modifications for options which can be exercised early (American options). This is because the decision to exercise early requires an estimate of the option's value if no exercise were to occur, and this requires calculations ahead of the current position in a Monte Carlo path.

For comparison, option valuation via binomial trees involves calculations at each position in the tree working backwards in calendar time (see Appendix 4). The option values at all the final asset values on the tree can be calculated first. One time step earlier, the values at each position are related to two values in the later time step and can be calculated from them. Working backwards time step by time step in calendar time, the (single) option value in the present can be found. Option values for individual paths through the tree need not be calculated, unlike Monte Carlo methods; a computational advantage. In the special circumstance where an option's value depends on asset values earlier in time (for example, outside the field of real options, a financial option whose pay-offs are related to the average of oil prices over several months), this method of working backwards in time fails and a Monte Carlo method is useful (*Editor's note*: Wilmott, Howison and Dewynne (1995) suggest what is effectively a state space method as an alternative general approach to path-dependent options, see Chapter 4).

Glossary

American option Option which gives us the right to invest (or sell out or change state) at any time we choose, usually up to some fixed final expiry date.

analytic solution Formula which can specify in a single calculation step what the option's value V is for any chosen combination of S and t (underlying asset price and remaining time to maturity). Usually only available for simpler problems. If no analytical solution, must use a numerical solution, which involves calculating very many values of V for different combinations of S and t.

arbitrage Riskless profit that arises from noticing that identical items can be bought and sold at different prices simultaneously.

at the money When an option could be exercised at a profit of zero, i.e. underlying asset price is at the exercise price.

barrier diffusion When the underlying asset is free to wander only within one or more fixed boundaries (not at zero or infinity), off which the underlying's price will 'bounce' if it ever reaches the barrier. For example, if there is some upper price barrier, above which new investment in capacity will be triggered, this can prevent market price from ever going above the upper barrier, though it can wander randomly below the barrier.

barrier option Option whose value is drastically changed if the underlying asset reaches some pre-set upper or lower level. For example, a call option which ceases to exist (is 'knocked out') or ('up and out') if the asset rises above a certain price.

binary outcome Only two possible outcomes.

binomial tree Sequence of possible binary outcomes, branching forward from the present, with each branch doubling at each step (and with identical pairs of probabilities for the up and down branches at each step). The most useful binomial trees are 're-entrant' or 'recombining', which means that dissimilar sequences can lead to the same end result, e.g. up-down takes us to the same point as down-up.

Black–Scholes partial differential equation A partial differential equation which relates the rates of change in the value of a derivative to time, and to the values of random variables which are presently observable, without requiring knowledge of the next change in the random variable(s). Can have various forms, depending on the number of independent random factors, and on what inflows or outflows of wealth are occurring other than changes in the capital value of the underlying asset and the derivative.

boundary conditions Conditions which must be imposed in order to constrain the Black–Scholes equation to have a unique solution. They usually include a terminal boundary condition (payoff function) and an upper or lower fixed boundary condition (e.g. that a call option on a worthless option is worthless). If the option includes a right to exercise before expiry, boundary conditions also include free boundary conditions, which are value-matching and smooth pasting conditions. The valuation task is to find a surface such that the boundary conditions are all met, and the Black–Scholes equation holds at all points in between the boundaries. If every point on this surface can be described by the same explicit mathematical expression, we say that we have an analytical solution. The analytical solution is often also mathematically defined outside the boundaries, but its values outside the boundaries are economically meaningless if not even economically perverse (see Chapter 2, Wilmott, Howison and Dewynne 1995, and Dixit and Pindyck, 1994).

bull spread Call option where the payoff rises at 45 degrees to some limit, above which it is flat. This can model a real option situation where there is constrained capacity to produce: at low demand levels we enjoy the better of producing nothing and producing all that the market wants; at high demand levels – near our maximum capacity – we enjoy the worst of producing all that we can produce and all that the market wants. Can also model the financial situation where the writer of a call option can default on us through insolvency: if our option is deep in the money, we receive the lesser of all that he owes us and all that he can afford to pay. Analytic solutions exist in the finance literature.

call option The right to buy something at a known price in the future, however much the market changes between now and then. For example, the right to invest $100 million to build a factory to produce a new hair colourant, whatever the demand for the hair colourant, or the right to spend $2,000 to generate a megawatt-hour of electricity, whatever the selling price of electricity.

compound options Sequences in which the final value of one option consists of the right to acquire the next option. This can justify making (for example) an unprofitable early investment in R&D if it leads to a chain of options in test marketing, further development, production, etc. which have large positive value.

cost of acquiring The cost or price paid to get an option. For a traded financial option this will always be the current market value, but untraded real options may be bought for more or less than their true economic value.

δ Symbol used in this book for the rate of dividend on a continuously dividend-paying asset.

Δ Greek delta, the conventional symbol for $\partial v / \partial S$ in delta hedging.

D_0 Symbol used by Wilmott, Howison and Dewynne for the rate of dividend on a continuously dividend-paying asset (see δ).

decision tree Process for structuring decisions under uncertainty. Possibilities are shown as a branching network, with two kinds of branching: decision nodes are where the decision maker decides which branch of the tree to follow next, and event nodes are where an external random event decides (after each decision node) which branch will happen next, e.g. decision node: decide to carry umbrella or not; event node: it rains or not; total of four possibilities. Decision maker should choose the decision pattern which maximizes expected present value under risk but traditional decision trees are invalid for this.

deep in the money When the underlying asset's price is far above (call) or below (put) the exercise price, so the the option would be highly profitable to exercise immediately (though not necessarily optimal).

delta Derivative of an option's value with respect to changes in the underlying asset price S, which is $\partial V/\partial S$. Such changes can be hedged against. One of the 'greeks'.

delta hedge A method of protecting against fluctuations in the value of an option: a forward deal is struck so that the value of this deal will move in the opposite direction to the value of the option when the underlying asset next changes, thus producing zero effect from the random change of the underlying asset. Delta refers to the slope of the value of the derivative (as a function of the underlying's price) for the current value of the underlying, i.e. $\partial V/\partial S$.

derivative asset Typically a right of some sort, such as an option, whose value is 'derived' from the value of a so-called *underlying asset* over which the option right exists. For example, the value of the rights to a new technology for hair colour is 'derived' from the current profitability and economic value of a factory to produce the colour. In this case the underlying asset is the profitability of the factory (if built) and the derivative asset is the value of the right (call option) to invest in such a factory, a right which may exist for some time into the future.

diffusion process A process in which particles and/or statistical distributions spread on average inexorably outwards from their initial locations over time, e.g. heat, chemical pollutants and stock prices.

dividend paying An asset which pays income over time. Often modelled as a continuous outflow, at some constant percentage δ or D_0 of the underlying asset's current value.

drift Deterministic part of the Wiener process, equivalent to a trend of exponential growth. (Wilmott, Howison and Dewynne)

dynamic hedging Process of changing the hedge transaction after each short time increment dt or δt, because S and $\delta V/\delta S$ have changed.

dynamic programming Optimal way to evaluate a complex decision tree. Start by evaluating the latest possible decisions, then feed the results of optimal decisions at later stages to value the possible outcomes of decisions at earlier stages; also has a version in which the uncertainties and/or decisions are continuous variables.

E Symbol for the exercise price of an option (also used by Dixit and Pindyck for the cost of exit from an activity). Also X is used.

European option Option which gives the right to invest (or to sell out) at a pre-arranged (exercise) price, but on only one fixed future (expiry) date.

exchange option The right to take or buy the better of two or more alternatives, e.g. to be paid $30 or £20, or the right to burn either X units of oil or Y units of gas in order to generate one megawatt of electricity.

exercise price The known price at which we can exercise any option to buy or sell. For example, the investment cost of a factory (call option), or the scrap value of a factory (put option), or the variable cost of producing one more unit of output (call option). Also called **strike price**.

exercised When an option no longer exists because the holder has used up the relevant right to invest or disinvest (can happen on expiry, when the option would cease to exist anyway).

exit General term for departing from an industry. Multiple options usually exist for exit, e.g. scrap, sell as going concern, etc.

exotic option Contrasts with plain vanilla. Includes options on several assets, path-dependent options, etc.

expectation In statistics, the average value expected from an infinite sample of a random process (e.g. 50 per cent for the frequency of heads when tossing a coin). Also used to describe quantitative forecasts, when these are thought to be unbiased.

expiry date The date when an option to invest (call) or to sell (put) expires, e.g. the date when a patent or licence expires; or the date when a pop star or athlete, with whom we have a publicity contract, will become a 'has been' and no longer useful for endorsements; or the expected date when competitors will catch up with our technology.

explicit finite difference A numerical solution method for the Black–Scholes equation. Computes earlier (calendar time) values as linear combinations of later (calendar time) values, using a linearized and discretized form of the equation.

far from the money When the price of an underlying asset is far above or below the exercise price.

fat tails When extreme events have higher probability than implied by the normal distribution. Also called a 'platykurtic' distribution.

financial call option Call option on a traded financial asset, such as a unit of stock in a company.

financial option – An option to buy or sell a financial asset which already exists, and is already actively traded in a financial market in a *standard form* (stocks, shares, bonds, etc.). Buying and selling a financial option on the shares of a business such as IBM is a private deal between two investors, and it has no effect on the physical or economic activities of the business itself.

finite difference Method of getting a numerical solution.

fixed boundary Restriction needed to give the Black–Scholes equation a unique solution: usually reflects certain features of some specific option such as its maximum or minimum possible value.

fixed lower boundary Condition that states what the option's value is when the underlying takes its lowest possible value (usually zero).

forward Contract to deliver an asset on a fixed future date at a fixed agreed price. The forward is a derivative asset, whose price is driven by the price of the underlying asset, namely the commodity to be delivered, and also by the interest rate. At the instant of sale the forward price is fixed by market conditions. An instant later market conditions will have changed, so the existing forward has a new price, and any new forward for the same date will be sold at this price. Forward prices close to expiry are very highly correlated with the price of the underlying asset.

free boundary Set of values of the underlying asset (varying over the remaining time to expiry) at which it becomes optimal to exercise the option before expiry (only possible for American options), e.g. invest, disinvest, activate or inactiate assets, etc.

free boundary conditions Set of c onditions which must apply at a free boundary, without which exercise could not be optimal. They are the value matching and smooth pasting conditions (q.v.).

greeks Partial derivatives of an option's value which show how it responds to changes in specific other variables, such as random walk factors, or parameters such as the interest rate. So called because they are named by Greek letters, e.g. *rho, vega, delta*. Investors can hedge against changes in any of the variables provided they know its relevant greek and can trade in a suitable asset to offset the rate of change produced by the greek as the variable itself changes.

high contact See **smooth pasting**.

in the money Option that could be exercised at a profit (if exercise were permitted) under today's value of the underlying, e.g. for a call option, if the underlying asset's price is above the exercise price, and for a real call, if the potential project has a positive net present value.

intrinsic value The value that would be gained if the option could be exercised immediately at the underlying asset's current price. Usually the same as payoff function and terminal boundary condition, e.g. for a call, max(0, S − E).

Ito's lemma A modification which is needed to Taylor's theorem when one or more independent variables follow a continuous diffusion process.

jump discontinuity Occasion when, at a foreseeable or even at a controllable moment, the value of an option or an underlying asset makes a jump in value. For example, at the instant when a quarterly dividend is paid, the capital value of the stock falls by the amount of the dividend. Boundary conditions must be imposed on each side of the jump to ensure that no opportunities for arbitrage exist, and the Black–Scholes equation continues to rule all points not on these boundaries.

jump process Risk of unforeseeable, discontinuous shift in a random walk, especially one which takes the value permanently to zero. Used to model random failure rates, depreciation, or the chance of total or large loss (e.g. failed trials for a drug; the death, injury or scandal of an athlete who endorses our product). Often modelled as a Poisson process.

killed State after an option has been exercised – any remaining time value has been destroyed by exercising the option, which no longer exists.

lower fixed boundary See **fixed lower boundary**.

market premium In capital market theory, the extra return that investors require to motivate them to hold the market portfolio of risky assets, as opposed to a risk-free asset.

maturity Sometimes used to mean the length of time remaining before option expiry (T − t).

mean reverting Random walk which includes some drift towards a fixed central value, as opposed to completely free diffusion (e.g. Ornstein-Uhlenbeck process). See Dixit and Pindyck.

mispricing When an option is sold for more or less than its economic value: allows one side to make arbitrage profits.

Monte Carlo Method of simulating the behaviour of a stochastic system (e.g. an option's value) by drawing a large number of random trials of the stochastic behaviour in question, and observing the effects on option value.

multiple option Where more than two actions are possible under the variations of a single underlying asset. These actions can be calls, puts or a mixture, e.g. choice of two factory designs or two operating modes. Sometimes also used to refer to options affected by more than one random factor.

multiple random factors When an option's value is driven by more than one random walk variable, e.g. exchange rate and oil price.

net present value The size and direction of the effect that an investment is likely to have on the company's total market value (minimum target for net present value is therefore normally zero, which defends the existing market value).

numerical solution Way to find an option's value when its particular combination of Black–Scholes equation plus boundary conditions does not have an analytic solution. Methods include finite difference (implicit or explicit), finite element and binomial or trinomial tree. All in various ways involve huge amounts of arithmetic, as they construct large areas of the valuation surface, always obeying the Black–Scholes equation and the boundary conditions, until they reach the part of the valuation surface that is of interest (i.e. a specific combination of S and t). See Wilmott, Hewison and Dewynne (1995), Dixit and Pindyck (1994).

oligopoly Market where a few major players effectively control the price and the quantity produced.

optimum early exercise Exercising an American option before expiry in order to maximize economic value for the holder.

option right to choose, at some point in an uncertain future, what will at the time be the best out of two or more actions.

option to defer Option to delay taking a decision, when one or more variable(s) affecting the value of the decision are random. A valuable right enjoyed by an American option.

option to discontinue construction Option to exit from a construction programme before completion, if market conditions prove unattractive. Makes the initial investment less risky/more attractive to undertake.

out of the money Option that could not be exercised at a profit (if exercise were permitted) under today's value of the underlying asset, e.g. for a financial call option, if the underlying asset's price is below the exercise price, and for a real call option, if the potential project has a negative net present value.

partial differential equation Equation that predicts how one variable (e.g. option value) will vary from its present level if at least two other variables (e.g. underlying asset price and time) make small changes from their present values. Must apply under all possible values of the independent variables, except on fixed and terminal boundaries, but while it defines the possible *changes* in the current values, the equation says nothing about what these current values actually are. Hence it has no unique solution until boundary conditions are set.

path-dependent option Option whose payoff or exercise right depends on some past event(s) in addition to the current value of the underlying asset. For example, if payoff depends on the maximum level or on the average level reached by the underlying asset during the life of the option. So called because the 'path' by which S has reached its current value matters, in addition to what that current value of S actually is. Can be valued by **state space** or by **Monte Carlo** methods.

payoff Amount received on exercising an option.

payoff function Rule to explain how payoff will vary under different states of the underlying asset, e.g. for a call option, $\max(0, S - E)$.

perfect competition Situation where all players have equal access to information and resources.

perpetual option Option which remains open for ever, or at least until exercised. Hence it has no set expiry date (seldom available for real options except for decisions on land use, or for exchanges between currencies). Often simpler to solve analytically, since time is no longer a variable, and can be a useful way to set an upper bound on the value of a non-perpetual option.

plain vanilla Simple, basic, well understood option like a European call.

platykurtic See fat tails.

Poisson Statistical process which generates infrequent events (e.g. equipment failures, accidents) used to model the risk of complete or major loss of value, which it does very simply in an option situation by a change to the interest rate (see Dixit and Pindyck).

price takers Players who have no power to set price by their actions, e.g. all players under perfect competition, and minor players in oligopoly.

put-call parity Relationship between the price of a put (P) and a call (C) on the same asset S, having the same exercise price E and same expiry date T.

$$P = C + Ee^{-r(T-t)} - S$$

Hence pricing the call also prices the put, and vice versa.

put option The right to sell something at a known price in the future, however much its market changes between now and then. For example, the right to sell an existing factory for scrap for $20,000 in the future, whatever the profit or loss the factory may be making at that time.

ρ Greek symbol, variously used to denote the correlation between two Wiener processes; also the partial derivative *rho*

of option value with respect to interest rate = $\partial V/\partial r$; and also the ratio of the time step to the square of the asset price step in explicit finite difference methods.

rainbow option Option where payoff depends on the values of several randomly varying quantities.

random factor A variable which drives the value of an option. In simple cases the random factor is the value of the *underlying asset* on which the option exists (e.g. if our option consists of the patent rights to produce a new hair colourant, the underlying asset which this gives us a right to buy is a factory to produce the hair colourant: the random factor is the expected net present value of such an investment). In more complex cases a random factor need not be an asset price (e.g. it could be an interest rate or an exchange rate).

random walk The basic assumption of all real options analysis is that the value of the *underlying asset* is unforecastable, in the sense that it follows a random walk. This means that at any instant an upward movement is as likely as a downward movement (for technical reasons this is actually true of the logarithm of the asset's value). For a random walk the best possible forecast of all possible future values is today's value. A random walk is the behaviour which we expect values to show under perfect competition, so the random walk is a pessimistic or 'bed rock' assumption on which to base our investment strategy when we face very harsh competition.

real call option Option to invest in real assets, where the cost of the investment is fixed but the value of making the investment will vary randomly before the option expires.

real option An option, over time, to change the 'real' physical or intellectual activity of a business (e.g. to create or to bring to market a new technology, a new brand, a new factory or an extra unit of output). In order to create or to exercise a real option, a business usually has to bring together new, non-standard and non-traded combinations of 'real' resources, such as time and effort by a team of people, wear and tear on machinery, use of consumable supplies, etc.

rho Partial derivative of an option's value with respect to changes in the risk-free interest rate r (which the basic Black–Scholes equation assumes to be known and fixed) $\partial V/\partial r$. Such changes can be hedged against. One of the 'greeks'.

risk-adjusted probabilities In a binomial tree, a way of weighting the two possible outcomes at each step, such that the economic value at the end of the step is identical, or risk free. These simulate the effect of having delta hedged away the risks at that step. The way to evaluate a binomial tree is to work forward from the present value of the underlying asset, using actual probabilities, to calculate the distribution of all the possible end states (at expiry date T), then work back from the values of the option under each of these end states towards the present, but using risk-adjusted probabilities rather than actual probabilities to weight the two possible outcomes from every mode. The resulting weighted value of the decision tree is the value of the option at the starting point in time given the underlying asset value at that time.

risk-free rate of interest The rate of interest that the market expects to pay or receive when a future payment has a known and fixed value.

S Symbol for the price of an underlying asset (in financial options this is typically a stock price).

smooth pasting Standard free boundary condition: means that as the underlying asset approaches the 'optimal exercise price', at which the option holder should optimally change states (e.g. invest, disinvest, activate, deactivate, etc.), small changes of the underlying asset have identical effects on the values of the two possible states. This removes the option holder's incentive to wait longer for any further change in the underlying asset once its price has reached the optimum exercise price.

spark spread option Option to produce electricity from fuel, when both prices vary randomly – only profitable if the spead between the two prices exceeds the avoidable fixed costs of operating the generator.

spread option Option whose payoff depends on the difference or spread between two randomly varying quantities, e.g. two interest rates, or two input costs. Resembles an exchange option, but has an exercise price, so is only profitable to exercise if the spread exceeds this price.

state space A method where the option's value depends on more than one variable. Similar to a multiple random factor model, except that at least one of the random variables may measure some current 'state' of the system which is not observable from the current value of S, e.g. the average value, the peak value or the minimum value that S has so far reached.

state variable Variable which measures an aspect of the system's current state, especially if that aspect of the system's state could not be learned simply by looking at the system now (e.g. the system's maximum value ever reached, now or in the past).

stochastic Anything that varies randomly, e.g. stochastic volatility means that volatility itself is varying with time. Tossing a coin is a stochastic process.

stochastic volatility Model which assumes that volatility σ is a random walk variable in its own right, rather than being a fixed and known parameter, as assumed in the basic Black–Scholes model.

strike price See **exercise price**.

T Date of expiry.

t The current actual date.

τ Remaining time to expiry = T − τ.

Taylor's theorem Theorem explaining how small local changes in an independent variable can produce small local changes in another, dependent variable, expressing this effect as an infinite series of ever-higher order derivatives of the dependent variable with respect to the independent variable. Useful for theory and in numerical solutions.

terminal boundary condition Rule which states what value the option can take on its expiry date T, as a function of the then value of the underlying asset S; usually identical to payoff function and to intrinsic value.

time value The expected extra value from being able to defer the exercise of an option. It is always optimal to defer as long as time value is positive. For a European option, deferment until T is compulsory, and time value up to then can be positive or negative, but on the expiry date the option dies anyway, so has no more time value.

tree methods See binominal tree and trinominal tree.

trinominal tree Numerical method in which the underlying asset is constrained to move to one of three possible states

after each time step (up, no change, down). Similar to explicit finite difference.

underlying asset The asset which a real option gives us the right to buy (call option) or to sell (put option), e.g. a factory or a customer base. Its price variations or net present value variations over time drive the changing economic value of the option.

unexercised When an option still exists because the holder has not used the relevant right to invest or disinvest.

upper fixed boundary Fixed boundary condition which says what an option's value must be when the underlying asset takes its largest possible value (usually infinity, except for barrier options).

V Symbol for the value of an option or derivative. If V is driven by S and by time, we write V(S,t).

valuation surface Graph which shows how option value varies as a result of two different causal factors, e.g. underlying asset price S and time t. Interesting in its own right, and it also reflects how the option's values are actually defined, by the Black–Scholes equation and the boundary conditions as a complete surface V(S,t), whether or not a simple analytical function can be found to define every point on the resulting surface.

value matching Standard free boundary condition: means that as the underlying asset approaches the 'optimal exercise price', at which the option holder should optimally exercise the right to change between two states (e.g. invest, disinvest, activate, deactivate, etc.), the option has equal values under the two possible states. This removes the possibility of arbitrage, through holding similar portfolios of very different value. It also removes an incentive to delay the change of states, since if the two states had very different values, a valuable 'option' would exist to wait to see which state would next be most profitable.

value of the option Typically for an unexercised option it is the sum of its intrinsic value and its time value. At the moment of exercise, option value is equal to the intrinsic value (any remaining time value having been killed). After exercise, the option holder simply has the asset which results from exercise, whose value may or may not continue to vary, and which may or may not include subsequent additional options (e.g. to reverse the previous exercise decision, or to exchange for some completely different asset).

variance In statistics, a measure of how widely a variable tends to differ from its expectation, or average value. All deviations from the average are squared (to make them positive) and the variance is simply the average or expectation of these squared deviations. A fixed variable has zero variance. For a diffusion process, variance is linear in time (twice the time horizon, twice the variance). The square root of the variance is called the standard deviation. In option analysis, the standard deviation of the expected price change over a year is used to measure the volatility of the price of the underlying asset.

vega Derivative of an option's value with respect to changes in the volatility σ (which the basic Black–Scholes equation assumes to be known and fixed) $\partial V/\partial \sigma$. Such changes can be hedged against. One of the 'greeks'.

volatility The tendency of the market value of the underlying asset (on which we hold a real or financial option) to diffuse over time away from its present value. The bigger the volatility, the wider the expected variation in value over time, and the more attractive it is to hold any option on the asset. The reason is that a higher volatility means both a larger upside potential and a larger downside potential. If we hold (say) a call option, we can benefit from the larger upside potential, but we lose nothing from the larger downside potential because our option can never be worth less than zero if it expires unexercised, however low the value of the underlying asset may fall. Likewise a put is usually more valuable as volatility rises. Volatility is expressed as a standard deviation per year, and as a fraction of the asset's value. For example, if volatility is 0.2, there is a 33 per cent chance that the asset's value will change by more than 20 per cent in a year, and if volatility is 10 per cent or 0.1, there is a 33 per cent chance that value will change by more than 10 per cent in a year. Symbol: σ

Wiener process Mathematical specification of a diffusion or random walk process which diverges without limit over time, and which may also have a deterministic trend or drift of exponential growth. See Wilmott, Howison and Dewynne (1995), Dixit and Pindyck (1994).

X Symbol for the exercise price of an option.

Bibliography

Chapter 3

Trigeorgis, Lenos (1996) *Real Options*, MIT Press.

Chapter 4

Dixit, Avinash K. and Pindyck, Robert (1994) *Investment under Uncertainty*, Princeton University Press, Princeton.

Howell, Sydney D. (2000) 'A more complete model of the delta hedging transaction, and of the delta hedged portfolio, in the derivation of the Black–Scholes equation', Paper presented at the Portuguese Finance Network Conference, University of Minho, Braga, June.

Wilmott, Paul W. (1998) *Derivatives*, John Wiley.

Wilmott, Paul, Howison, Sam and Dewynne, Geoff (1995) *The Mathematics of Financial Derivatives*, Cambridge University Press.

Chapter 5

Anjos, Tiago Veiga (1999) *Portuguese Football: Watch the Match, Enjoy the Investment*, BPI, Lisbon.

Banks, Robert B. (1994) *Growth and Diffusion Phenomena*, Springer-Verlag, Berlin.

Bateman, Rob, Sutton, Dominic, Taphouse, Gary and Wheat, Tim (1999) *Carling Opta Football Yearbook 1999–2000*, Carlton Books, London.

Cooper, B. and McHattie, A. (1997) *Football*, B.T. Batsford, Fulham.

Cresswell, Peterjon and Evans, Simon (1998) European *Football: A Fans' Handbook*, Rough Guides, London.

Crick, Michael (1999) *Manchester United: The Complete Fact Book*, Profile Books, London.

Davis, Louise, Gontikas, George, Harrison, Katy, Islam, Tariq, Heng Tan, Boon and Vovos, Charalambos (1999) 'Real option theory applied to football clubs', *Real Corporate Finance Report*, Manchester Business School.

Mallios, William S. (2000) *The Analysis of Sports Forecasting: Modelling Parallels between Sports Gambling and Financial Markets*, Kluwer Academic, London.

Malos, Stanley B. and Campion, Michael A. (1995) 'An options-based model of career mobility in professional service firms', *Academy of Management Review*, Vol. 20, No. 3: 611–644.

Manchester City Football Club PLC, *Annual Reports*, 1998–2000 and *Prospectus* 9 November 2000.

Manchester United Illustrated Encyclopedia (1998) Manchester United Books, London.

Manchester United PLC, *Annual Reports*, 1998–2000.

Margrabe, William (1978) 'The value of an option to exchange one asset for another', *Journal of Finance*, 33, 1: 177–186.

Monopolies and Mergers Commission (1999) *British Sky Broadcasting Group Plc and Manchester United Plc*, Cm 4305, Stationery Office, London.

Paxson, Dean A. (1997) 'Exotic options' and 'Real options' in *The Blackwell Encyclopedic Dictionary of Finance*, Blackwell Publishers, Oxford: 66–69, 150–152.

Rich, Don A. (1994) 'The mathematical foundations of barrier option-pricing theory' in *Advances in Futures and Options Research* (D. Chance and R. Trippi, eds), JAI Press Ltd, Hampton Hill, Middx: 267–312.

Rollin, Glenda and Rollin, Jack (1999, 2000) (eds), *Rothmans Football Yearbook, 1998–1999, 2000–2001*, Headline Book Publishing, London.

Scully, Gerald (1994) *The Market Structure of Sports*, University of Chicago Press, Chicago.

Thompson, Andrew C. (1995) 'Valuation of path-dependent contingent claims with multiple exercise decisions over time: the case of take-or-pay', *Journal of Financial and Quantitative Analysis*, Vol. 30, No. 2: 271–293.

Chapter 6

Black, F. and Scholes, M. (1973) 'The pricing of options and other corporate liabilities', *Journal of Political Economy*, Vol. 81, pp. 637–659.

Deng, S., Johnson, B. and Sogomonian, A. (1999) 'Spark spread options and the valuation of electricity generation assets', Proceedings of the 32nd Hawaii International Conference on System Sciences.

Energy Information Administration (1999) 'Why do natural gas prices fluctuate so much?', EIA-XD26, May 1999, downloadable at the web site of the EIA under http://www.eia.doe.gov/oil_gas/natural_gas/nat_frame.html.

Energy Information Administration (1997) 'Electricity prices in a competitive environment: marginal cost pricing of generation services and financial status of electric utilities – a preliminary analysis through 2015, August 1997, downloadable at the web site of the EIA under http://www.eia.doe.gov/oiaf/elepri97/comp.html.

Hamdan, K. (1999) 'Pricing options in the power markets', in *Energy Modelling and the Management of Uncertainty*, Risk Publications, pp. 23–33.

Hull, J.C. (2000) *Options, Futures and Other Derivatives*, Prentice Hall, 4th Edition.

Johnson, B. and Barz, G. (1999) 'Selecting stochastic processes for modelling electricity prices' in *Energy Modelling and the Management of Uncertainty*, Risk Publications, pp. 3–21.

Joy, C. (1999) 'Pricing, modelling and managing physical power derivatives' in *Energy Modelling and the Management of Uncertainty*, Risk Publications, London.

Margrabe, W. (1978) 'The value of an option to exchange one asset for another', *Journal of Finance*, Vol. 33, pp. 177–186.

Putney, J. (1999) 'Modelling energy prices and derivatives using Monte Carlo methods' in *Energy Modelling and the Management of Uncertainty*, Risk Publications, pp. 3–21.

Thierer, A.D. (1997) 'Energizing America: a blueprint for deregulating the electricity market', The Heritage Foundation, downloadable at the web site of the foundation at http://www.heritage.org/library/categories/regulation/bg1100.html.

Tseng, C.-L. and Barz, G. (1999) 'Short-term generation asset valuation', Proceedings of the 32nd Hawaii International Conference on System Sciences.

Chapter 9

Canary Wharf Group PLC, *Listing Particulars*, 1 April 1999.

Capozza, Dennis R. and Sick, Gordon A. (1991) 'Valuing long-term leases: the option to redevelop', *Journal of Real Estate Finance and Economics*, Vol. 4, No. 2, June: 209–224.

Capozza, Dennis R., Sick, Gordon A. and Li, Yuming (1994) 'The intensity and timing of investment: the case of land', *American Economic Review*, September: 889–904.

Dixit, Avinash K. and Pindyck, Robert S. (1994) *Investment under Uncertainty*, Princeton University Press, Princeton.

Grenadier, Stephen R. (1992) 'Real estate and other long-term development projects', Ph.D. Dissertation, Harvard University.

Patel, Kanak and Paxson, Dean (1998) 'Real options-based approach to valuation of property development and investment', *Property Research Digest*, February: 1–11.

Paxson, Dean (1997) 'Real options' in *The Blackwell Encyclopedic Dictionary of Finance* (D. Paxson and D. Woods, eds), Blackwell Publishers, Oxford: 150–153.

Quigg, Laura (1993) 'Empirical testing of real option-pricing models', *Journal of Finance*, June: 621–640.

Sick, Gordon (1989) *Capital Budgeting with Real Options*, Monograph 1989–3, Salomon Brothers Center for the Study of Financial Institutions Monograph Series in Finance and Economics, New York University.

Titman, Sheridan (1985) 'Urban land prices under uncertainty', *American Economic Review*, Vol. 75, No. 3, June: 505–514.

Trigeorgis, Lenos (1993) 'Real options and interactions with financial flexibility', *Financial Management*, Vol. 22, No. 3: 202–224.

Ward, C.W.R. (1982) 'Arbitrage and investment in commercial property', *Journal of Business Finance and Accounting*, Vol. 9, No. 1: 93–108.

Williams, Joseph T. (1991) 'Real estate development as an option', *Journal of Real Estate Finance and Economics*, Vol. 4, No. 2, June 1991:191–208.

Williams, Joseph T. (1997) 'Redevelopment of real assets', *Real Estate Economics*, Vol. 25, No. 3: 387–407.

Chapter 10

Azevedo-Pereira, Jose A. (1997) 'Fixed-rate mortgage valuation using a contingent claims approach', Ph.D. Thesis, Manchester Business School, Victoria University of Manchester, England.

Azevedo-Pereira, Jose A., Newton, David P. and Paxson, Dean A. (1999), 'UK fixed-rate repayment and mortgage indemnity valuation', Working Paper No. 405, p. 56, Manchester Business School.

Azevedo-Pereira, Jose A., Newton, David P. and Paxson, Dean A. (2000a) 'Numerical solution of a two-state variable contingent claims mortgage valuation model', Portuguese Review of Financial Markets, 3(1), 35–65.

Azevedo-Pereira, Jose A., Newton, David P. and Paxson, Dean A. (2000b) 'Fixed-rate endowment mortgage and endowment indemnity valuation', Working Paper No. 418, p. 38, Manchester Business School.

Cox, John C., Ingersoll Junior, Jonathan E. and Ross, Stephen A. (1985a) 'An intertemporal general equilibrium model of asset prices', Econometrica, 53(2), 363–384.

Cox, John C., Ingersoll Junior, Jonathan E. and Ross, Stephen A. (1985b) 'A theory of the term structure of interest rates', Econometrica, 53(2), 385–407.

Epperson, James F., Kau, James B., Keenan, Donald C. and Muller III, Walter J. (1985) 'Pricing default risk in mortgages', Journal of the American Real Estate and Urban Economics Association, 13(3), 152-167.

James, Jessica and Webber, Nick (2000) Interest Rate Modelling, John Wiley & Sons.

Kau, James B., Keenan, Donald C., Muller III, Walter J. and Epperson, James F. (1992) 'A generalized valuation model for fixed-rate residential mortgages', Journal of Money Credit and Banking, 24(3), 279-299.

Kau, James B., Keenan, Donald C., Muller III, Walter J. and Epperson, James F. (1993) 'Option theory and floating-rate securities with a comparison of adjustable- and fixed-rate securities', Journal of Business, 66(4), 595–618.

Merton, Robert C. (1973) 'The theory of rational option pricing', Bell Journal of Economics and Management Science, 4(1), 141–183.

Chapter 11

Newton, David P. and Pearson, Alan W. (1994) 'Application of option pricing to R&D', R&D Management, 24, 83–89.

Newton, David P., Paxson, Dean A. and Pearson, Alan W. (1996) 'Real R&D options' in A. Belcher, J. Hassard and S.J. Procter (eds) R&D Decisions, Policy and Innovations, London: Routledge, 273–282.

Doctor, Ronald N., Newton, David P. and Pearson, Alan W. (2001) 'Managing uncertainty in research and development', Technovation, 21, 79–90.

Appendix 1

Brealey, Richard A. and Myers, Stuart C. (2000) Principles of Corporate Finance, 6th Edition, Irwin McGraw-Hill.

Doctor, Ronald N., Newton, David P. and Pearson, Alan W. (2001) 'Managing uncertainty in research and development', *Technovation*, *21*, 79–90.

Appendix 2

Hull, John (2000) *Options, Futures and Other Derivatives*, 4th Edition, Prentice Hall.

Appendix 4

Clewlow, Les and Strickland, Chris (1998) *Implementing Derivatives Models*, John Wiley & Sons.

Cox, John C., Ross, Stephen and Rubinstein, Mark (1979) 'Option pricing: a simplified approach', *Journal of Financial Economics*, 7, 229–263.

Hull, John (2000) *Options, Futures and Other Derivatives*, 4th Edition, Prentice Hall.

Widdicks, Martin, Andricopoulos, Ari, Newton, David P. and Duck, Peter W. (2000) 'On the enhanced convergence of standard lattice methods for option pricing', Working Paper No. 417, p. 38, Manchester Business School and forthcoming in the *Journal of Futures Markets*.

Wilmott, Paul, Howison, Sam and Dewynne, Jeff (1995) *The Mathematics of Financial Derivatives*, Cambridge University Press.

Appendix 5

Clewlow, Les and Strickland, Chris (1998) *Implementing Derivatives Models*, John Wiley & Sons.

Doctor, Ronald N., Newton, David P. and Pearson, Alan W. (2001) 'Managing uncertainty in research and development', *Technovation*, 21, 79–90.

Newton, David P. and Pearson, Alan W. (1994) 'Application of option pricing to R&D', *R&D Management*, 24, 83–89.

Newton, David P., Paxson, Dean A. and Pearson, Alan W. (1996) 'Real R&D options', in A. Belcher, J. Hassard and S.J. Procter (eds), *R&D Decisions, Policy and Innovations*, London: Routledge, 273-282.

Wilmott, Paul, Howison, Sam and Dewynne, Geoff (1995) *The Mathematics of Financial Derivatives*, Cambridge University Press.

Index

underlying asset 4, 5, 14, 19, 293
  random walk as a Wiener process
    234–6
  underlying real assets 19, 24, 28
unexercised options 20, 293
upper fixed boundary 34, 35, 36, 75,
    293
uptime constraints 127
upwind differencing 185
urban development options 163–76

valuation surface 34–6, 244-5, 293
value, option 9, 19–29, 294
  application of financial option
    valuation to real options 24–6
  investment decisions and real
    option values 26–9
value matching 32–4, 75, 245, 293–4
variance 225, 235, 294

vega 78, 294
volatility 4, 20, 23, 28–9, 253, 280–1,
    294
  decaying term structure of 128,
    134–5
  CAPM 226, 227
  historical 192, 253, 281
  implied 281
  real development options 171–4
  stochastic 293

waiting 18, 29, 47, 160
wasting assets 74
  see also leases; mortgages
weightings on possible outcomes 83,
    87–90
Wiener processes 179–80, 234–6,
    251, 294